PSYCHOSIS UNDER DISCUSSION

Psychosis Under Discussion: How We Talk About Madness examines the ways in which psychosis is discussed by considering the relationship between language and the perception of mental disorder. A wide range of perspectives is discussed – including historical terms, personal accounts, psychiatric terminology, psychoanalysis and later theoretical analyses, advocacy, anti-psychiatry, slang and humour and media coverage – and each way of discussing psychosis is revealing. For example, psychiatric terminology and related research, in its efforts to understand and clarify can seem distancing, dispassionate and too sure of its ground, whereas the language of advocacy, while being supportive and sensitive, can also seem euphemistic and evasive.

In the discourse of mental disorder, both the content of views and the manner in which they are expressed are influential, making it important to take into account both. *Psychosis Under Discussion* puts these and other important issues under the microscope. International in range, the book's analysis draws on psychiatry, psychology, philosophy, linguistics and history. Written in Michael Farrell's well-known clear and direct style, the book is essential reading for all those interested in understanding mental disorder and the role of language.

Michael Farrell managed a UK-wide psychometric project for City University, London and directed a national initial teacher-training project for the UK Government Department of Education; for over a decade, he led teams inspecting mainstream and special schools and units (boarding, day, hospital, psychiatric). Currently, he works as a private consultant with a range of clients and has lectured or provided consultancy services in various countries including China, Japan, the Seychelles, Australia, Peru, Sweden and the United Kingdom. He has broadcast on the BBC World Service and on UK national radio and has written articles in a range of medical, psychological, legal and educational journals. His many books, which are translated into European and Asian languages, include *Debating Special Education* (Routledge, 2010) and *New Perspectives in Special Education: Contemporary Philosophical Debates* (Routledge, 2012).

PSYCHOSIS UNDER DISCUSSION

How We Talk About Madness

Michael Farrell

Routledge
Taylor & Francis Group

LONDON AND NEW YORK

First published 2018
by Routledge
2 Park Square, Milton Park, Abingdon, Oxon OX14 4RN

and by Routledge
711 Third Avenue, New York, NY 10017

Routledge is an imprint of the Taylor & Francis Group, an informa business

© 2018 Michael Farrell

The right of Michael Farrell to be identified as author of this work has been asserted by him in accordance with sections 77 and 78 of the Copyright, Designs and Patents Act 1988.

British Library Cataloguing-in-Publication Data
A catalogue record for this book is available from the British Library

Library of Congress Cataloging-in-Publication Data
Names: Farrell, Michael, 1948- author.
Title: Psychosis under discussion / Michael Farrell.
Description: Abingdon, Oxon ; New York, NY : Routledge, 2018. |
    Includes bibliographical references and index.
Identifiers: LCCN 2017029284 (print) | LCCN 2017030656 (ebook) |
    ISBN 9781315268262 (Master e-book) | ISBN 9781138287457 (hbk) |
    ISBN 9781138287464 (pbk) | ISBN 9781315268262 (ebk)
Subjects: | MESH: Psychotic Disorders | Health Knowledge, Attitudes,
    Practice | Mass Media | Terminology as Topic
Classification: LCC RC454 (ebook) | LCC RC454 (print) |
    NLM WM 200 | DDC 616.89—dc23
LC record available at https://lccn.loc.gov/2017029284

ISBN: 978-1-138-28745-7 (hbk)
ISBN: 978-1-138-28746-4 (pbk)
ISBN: 978-1-315-26826-2 (ebk)

Typeset in Bembo
by Apex CoVantage, LLC

CONTENTS

CHAPTER STRUCTURES

ACKNOWLEDGEMENTS

I would like to warmly thank the following for comments on aspects of the book:

Richard Aird OBE, Special Educator, UK
The Rev. Sue Bull, Chair, Love Me Love My Mind (Mental Health Charity), UK
Dr. Michael Lafferty, UK
Ruth Millington, Clinical Psychologist, UK
Dr. Karen Proner, Child Psychotherapist, New York, USA
Dr. Walid Sarhan, Consultant Psychiatrist, Chief Editor of the *Arab Journal of Psychiatry*, Amman, Jordan

The generous advice and comments of these colleagues does not imply that they agree with everything (or anything) in the book. Any infelicities are of course entirely my own responsibility.

PREFACE

After long periods of being a taboo subject, the importance of mental health is increasingly recognised. But within that broad domain, the subject of psychosis lags behind in public perception and understanding. What psychosis might be and what response it might evoke is strongly debated. How psychosis is discussed, from unadorned everyday slang, to the careful language of advocacy groups, is as disparate as the content of the perspectives. Those holding different views and expressing them in diverse ways seem in many ways uninterested in what others are saying except from time to time to disagree about the content and style of what is said. Consequently, any insights into people's motivations and views in any one perspective are lost on others. In examining these standpoints, I try to give each a fair hearing, while not accepting that all perspectives are equally convincing.

I would welcome any constructive comments and suggestion for any future editions from readers at the e-mail address below.

Michael Farrell
Herefordshire
drmjfarrell@bulldog1870.plus.com

AUTHOR INFORMATION

Michael Farrell was educated in the United Kingdom. After training as a teacher at Bishop Grosseteste College, Lincoln, and obtaining an honours degree from Nottingham University, he gained an M.A. in education and psychology from the Institute of Education, London University. Subsequently, he carried out research for an M.Phil. degree at the Institute of Psychiatry, London, and for a Ph.D. under the auspices of the Medical Research Council Cognitive Development Unit and London University.

Professionally, Michael Farrell held senior posts in schools and units for people with various mental disorders. He managed a UK-wide psychometric project for City University, London, and directed a national initial teacher-training project for the UK government Department of Education. For over a decade, he led teams inspecting mainstream and special schools and units (boarding, day, hospital, psychiatric). Currently, he works as a private consultant with a range of clients and has lectured or provided consultancy services in various countries, including China, Japan, the Seychelles, Australia, Peru, Sweden and the United Kingdom.

He has broadcast on the BBC World Service and on UK national radio and has written articles in a range of medical, psychological, legal and educational journals. Among his many books, which are translated into European and Asian languages, are:

Debating Special Education (Routledge, 2010)
New Perspectives in Special Education: Contemporary Philosophical Debates (Routledge, 2012).
Investigating the Language of Special Education (Palgrave Macmillan, 2014)

1

INTRODUCTION

To begin with

Public awareness of mental disorders, coupled with the willingness of people experiencing such disorders to talk about them, seems to be increasing in recent years. For example, in the UK House of Commons in 2016, several members of Parliament spoke of their own disorders, including depression, general anxiety and obsessive-compulsive disorder. However, none to my knowledge revealed that they had experienced psychotic episodes. Even where the ability of people to speak about mental disorders is increasing, the experience of psychosis (and schizophrenia) still often remains in the shadows, although there are signs that this too is changing (Torrey, 2013, p. 335).

'Psychosis' is a term that can evoke misunderstanding and sometimes fear, making it a difficult subject to broach. Where it is talked about at all, discussion can be one-sided and misinformed. Groups are formed holding views which they are reluctant to change or even to debate openly. If there is anything positive in these rigid positions, it is that they suggest that people care about the issues involved. Against such a background, this book explores some of the ways in which psychosis is discussed and what this might tell us about the phenomena and the people who articulate various views.

At the outset, the title of the book, *Psychosis Under Discussion: How We Talk About Madness*, suggests that certain points require clarification. Among these are:

- interactions between language and mental disorders;
- what is meant by 'psychosis' and its relation to certain other disorders and to the concept of 'madness'.

In addition to these matters, other important preliminaries are the book's aim, its proposed readers and its structure and content.

Language in relation to mental disorders

Some aspects of language

If the book is to concern itself with 'discussion' in relation to psychosis and related issues, it will be as well to consider some relevant aspects of language. By 'language' in the current context, I mean spoken or written communication using words in a structured way according to certain conventions. The book also looks at other forms of discourse in a broader sense, such as movies.

Permeating the book are general questions about language and its use, for example:

- Why does terminology change over time, and what drives this?
- To what extent does language influence how we interpret experience and how we respond?
- What other factors are involved (e.g. experience, knowledge, attitudes and beliefs), and how do these interact with language?
- How might changes in features such as knowledge, attitudes and beliefs influence changes in language, and is this a two-way street?
- What are the motives for and consequences of using language in different ways?
- Is it possible to determine the functions of types of discourse, such as slang and humour?
- Can we identify aspects of 'media language', and do they reflect the views of the public?
- How do groups of people form, and does their language have particular characteristics?

Language and mental disorders

General questions about language and its use can be related to discourse about mental disorders, specifically psychosis and related terms:

- How does language in interaction with factors such as experience, knowledge, attitudes and beliefs affect how we interpret and respond to psychosis?
- How might changes in factors, such as knowledge about psychosis, influence changes in language and vice versa?
- What are the motives for and consequences of discussing psychosis in different ways?
- How are groups, such as psychiatrists, advocacy and support groups, media personnel and anti-psychiatry groups, constituted; does their group language have particular characteristics; and if so, what is its purpose?

In terms of particular chapters, more specific issues arise:

- Why does terminology relating to mental disorders change over time, and what factors influence this?

- What do personal accounts of psychosis contribute to its understanding?
- What are the characteristics of psychiatric discourse, and what are its strengths and weaknesses?
- To what extent do psychoanalysis and subsequent related developments contribute to our understanding of psychosis or schizophrenia?
- What constitutes the language of advocacy and support groups?
- What are the characteristics and motives of anti-psychiatry language?
- How does slang and humour function, and how does it relate to psychosis?
- To what degree does media language about madness reflect the views of members of society?

Psychosis and other disorders

Medical and other perspectives

Psychosis is viewed in different ways. From a medical point of view, psychotic disorders include 'schizophrenia', 'schizotypal personality disorder', 'delusional disorder' and various forms of 'catatonia', and are characterised by features such as delusions, hallucinations, disorganised speech and so-called negative symptoms, such as loss of interest in surroundings (American Psychiatric Association, 2013, p. 99, paraphrased). Psychosis may be seen from the vantage point of personal experience. It can be considered in the context of psychoanalytic frameworks, or as part of emancipatory theories that largely see psychosis as a consequence of oppression and lack of understanding on the part of others. These and other viewpoints are examined in the course of this book.

Psychosis and psychopathy

Members of the public and media professionals sometimes confuse psychosis with psychopathy, which is something quite different. In psychiatric terms, psychopathy is a condition in which the individual shows disregard for the rights of others. In fact, the more commonly used psychiatric expression is 'anti-social personality disorder' (American Psychiatric Association, 2013, pp. 659–663). Among the diagnostic criteria for this disorder is a 'pervasive pattern of disregard for and violation of the rights of others' shown by various features such as 'lack of remorse' (Ibid., p. 659). In addition to 'psychopathy' and 'anti-social personality disorder', the terms 'sociopathy' and 'dyssocial personality disorder' are also used (Ibid.).

Confusion between psychosis and psychopathy may arise partly because sections of the media are not always careful to make the distinction. Indeed, this is not always easy, as terms change over time. Also, in slang and in some parts of the popular media, the expression 'psycho' is used, which does not indicate whether 'psychosis' or the term 'psychopathy' is intended.

Madness

Some books about 'psychosis' also refer to 'madness', perhaps using the two terms interchangeably. A distinction can be made however. 'Psychosis' refers to the condition as it is seen from a medical perspective, in which there are features like hallucinations, disorganised speech or loss of interest in surroundings. 'Madness' tends to refer to the more florid features of psychosis rather than the so-called negative aspects such as lack of interest and motivation. It is this which is reflected in slang expressions, such as 'mad as a March hare', in which what is conveyed is excessive, 'manic' activity rather than passivity.

Aims of the book

This book examines how people depict and discuss psychosis, and a detailed outline of the content is provided in the 'Chapter structures'. Here, the focus is on the broad aims, which are several. The first is to explore the way that language is used in various contexts:

- historical terminology;
- personal accounts of psychosis;
- psychiatry and psychology;
- psychoanalysis and later theorising;
- advocacy groups;
- anti-psychiatry;
- informal settings (slang and humour); and
- media coverage.

Issues arise with each of these contexts. For example, it may be accepted that personal accounts of psychosis can be vivid and powerful, providing unique insights into the phenomena. However, such accounts can be problematic because they tend to be given when the individual is not experiencing a psychotic episode. An individual person is recounting in a 'reasonable' state experiences which are by definition out of touch with typically experienced reality. However vivid and authentic the language may appear, it remains open to question whether someone in a nonpsychotic state can convey the experience of psychosis. In addition to recognising the content of what is said, this book explores the implications of the way that language is used.

Proposed readers

Who might read this book? I hope that among readers will be individuals who have experienced mental disorders, as well as those who try to help them. Among the latter will be relatives, as well as professionals such as psychiatrists, psychologists, therapists and mental health nurses. Other readers I hope will be members of advocacy and self-support groups. Those with an interest in how language might shape perceptions of mental disorders should find the book informative. Indeed, all individuals with an interest in mental disorder and how it is discussed and perceived should find much to engage them.

Structure and content of the book

The book's structure reflects the different ways in which psychosis may be considered. A detailed chapter outline is provided separately, while here, I explain the structure of the book. Following this introductory chapter, the main body of the volume discusses different ways in which people talk about psychosis. A concluding chapter draws together some of the threads that have been explored. A bibliography and index complete the book. Remaining chapters cover the following areas.

Historical terminology

Historical changes as reflected in shifts in terminology illuminate the development of understandings of mental disorder, including psychosis and schizophrenia. Amorphous expressions like 'mad' and 'insane', while still used casually by some, no longer figure in official or clinical debate. 'Lunatic' declined in formal use with the demise of the belief that mental disorder was related to moon phases. 'Maniac' as a label for an individual is rarely used, as the state of 'mania' is presently seen as one aspect of a wider disorder. In the 1800s, the term 'psychosis' was variously used to convey the extent to which organic or mental influences were responsible. Efforts to refine classifications of mental disorders led to the development of various terms, including 'schizophrenia'. Differing views are held about the extent to which 'schizophrenia', 'psychosis' and other terms may act as negative labels.

Personal accounts of psychosis

This chapter looks briefly at historical and literary accounts where it appears that the individual experienced psychosis, then looks more fully at modern day accounts where the assessment of psychosis tends to be more secure. Sources include letters, diaries and verbal reports of what has been experienced later recounted to others. It is argued that personal accounts may have an authenticity of direct experience, and these (and other features) are used to help with assessments of psychosis. However, there may be limitations in individuals recounting experiences (discordant with reality) in later states of rationality. Similar criticisms were made by French philosopher Jacques Derrida ([various dates and 1967]/1968) in discussing the book *History of Madness* by Michel Foucault ([1961, 1972 and 1994]/2006).

Psychiatric terminology

Definitions of psychosis, including schizophrenia, are outlined. Identification, diagnostic criteria, prevalence and incidence, causal factors and treatments are considered as indications of a medical and psychiatric perspective. This is also reflected in scientific terminology, categorising and research. Potential benefits of such terminology include bringing clarity and better reliability and validity to assessments and diagnosis. However, scientific language, Latin- and Greek-derived terms, jargon and acronyms can appear impersonal and distancing, conveying greater sureness of what is known and not known than is sometimes justified, which can be interpreted as arrogance. Some perspectives in psychology may try to avoid medical explanations and approaches to provide an account of the mental experiences of clients and responses to them.

Psychoanalysis and beyond

This chapter considers Sigmund Freud's writings including ideas on psychosis and an interpretation of Judge Schreber's *Memoirs* while accepting that for some commentators understanding psychosis is not the most convincing aspect of his work. I look at the work of Melanie Klein and her followers, who developed Freud's theory and practise, exerting a profound influence on psychoanalysis and the understanding of psychosis. The chapter briefly considers the ideas of psychoanalyst Jacques Lacan, who sought to relate understandings of psychosis to linguistics and other sources. Finally, the chapter touches on the ideas of Giles Deleuze in partnership with psychoanalyst Felix Guattari and their notion of 'schizoanalysis', which is seen less as a clinical concept and more as a social critique.

Advocacy

The language of advocacy and support groups is reviewed by examining the website of a particular group. The site suggests many alternatives to the expression 'mental illness', and these are analysed. From this discussion emerge several themes. One is the view that mental disorder is not an 'illness'. In discussing this, the chapter analyses the concepts of 'illness' and 'treatment'. Another theme is that of negative labelling and potential stigma, leading to awareness of potential difficulties with language generally. It is suggested that language associated with advocacy and support groups can raise sensitivity to the use of language. But it can also overstate the influence of language on perception and behaviour and can be seen counterproductively as euphemistic and evasive.

Anti-psychiatry

The chapter firstly looks at examples of influential anti-psychiatry texts, such as those of Szasz, Laing and Goffman. Next, it examines the language of and the views conveyed in current videos and other sources from the Citizens Commission on Human Rights/Church of Scientology. Among points made by these videos are some of the historical treatments are now considered inappropriate, for example lobotomy, and the potential overuse of drugs. Nevertheless, rhetoric, out-of-date examples, emotive language, broad generalisations and poor logic tend to weaken these points. Such is the position expressed in some videos that they leave little room for engagement with psychiatry, leading some to dismiss the content as propaganda and others to embrace it uncritically.

Slang and humour

I examine the nature of slang and its relationship to specified groups and to taboo areas. Slang and derogatory language for mental illness are considered, including their origins. These include historical derivations; animal and plant analogies; implications of oddness and incapableness; loss, incompleteness and dysfunction; and incorrect ideas of causation or misidentification. Briefly discussed is the nature of humour and it variations. Causes and features of humour are outlined. Jokes making light of delusions and jokes diminishing or ridiculing disorders and other examples are examined. I discuss the possible role of fear and lack of knowledge, relating this to particular instances.

Media coverage

Media coverage of psychosis is briefly reviewed, at first using past examples from movies; television and radio drama; and news, newspapers and magazines. Otto Wahl's well-argued book *Media Madness: Public Images of Mental Illness*, published in 1995, gives a useful comparison point to examine public images in the present day. More recent examples are discussed to demonstrate that while there has been some change, it is still possible to find misleading language which reflects aspects of slang such as fear and lack of knowledge.

Conclusion

In the conclusion to the book, I take an overview of the areas discussed, such as personal accounts of psychosis, psychiatry, advocacy and media coverage. We then look at whether language styles can reflect the motives of people who adopt those styles and, if it can, what might be the consequences. I consider the issue of attempting to change the words used to discuss 'psychosis' and possible implications.

Moving on – looking back

It is now time to look in the next chapter at historical terms, seeing how they change over time.

2

HISTORICAL TERMINOLOGY

Introduction

Here, we look at how terms related to psychiatry and madness may have originated and how they change over time. Firstly, the chapter sets the context by touching on the nature of chronology and outlines a basic timeline relating to mental disorders and psychiatry. After distinguishing between chronology and history, I examine examples of historical interpretation in relation to psychiatry.

Turning specifically to terminology, we review the terms 'mad', 'insane', 'lunatic' and 'maniac', and reflect on how their use has declined in formal language and the possible reasons for this. The chapter then considers how the classifications of psychosis and related conditions, along with their vocabulary, have developed over time. This involves examining the early contribution of the French School of psychiatry and the work of German-speaking psychiatrists in central Europe and looking at the way that terms such as 'schizophrenia' were used by various pioneers of psychiatry. Finally, I look at suggested changes to terminology relating to supposed negative labelling.

Chronology and history regarding mental disorders and psychiatry

Chronology

Chronology concerns events over time and implies placing events in the date order in which they occurred. This activity is comparatively straightforward where there is agreement about the sequence of events. However, such agreement is not always the case, and a preliminary step may be to examine evidence for the ordering of events to make a judgement on the best solution. For example, chronology in the discipline of prehistory was much assisted by the technique of carbon dating of certain materials (Renfrew, 2007). But in historical information too, there may be debate about sequence which chronology has to address with reference to documents and other sources that present a conflicting picture.

A further issue that arises is what constitutes an 'event'. Is it the dates of a person's life, a conflict, the publication of a book, a discovery, the founding of a political movement or something else? Related to how events are defined is the question of how the choice is made about what events are considered important or influential enough to justify including in a chronology.

Psychiatry and chronology

In a general way, one can sketch out chronological aspects concerning mental disorders and related matters. For example Stefanis and Stefanis (2009) present such an outline. They suggest that in Pharaonic Egypt mental disorders were recognised and treated by invoking supernatural forces, including the departed spirits of the dead, to affect a cure. In ancient India, mental disorder was thought to be caused by a combination of bodily passions and spiritual darkness. The Ayurveda and the Charaka Samhita Sutra of around the sixth century BCE mention four types of insanity, which have been compared to modern-day concepts including depression and mania. In ancient China, insanity seems to have been explained in relation to natural and cultural forces, such as loss of face, although treatment was more spiritual and involved a priest taking on a role of appeasing ancestral spirits. Assyrian cuneiform tablets document frequent descriptions of insanity. The Talmud and the Old and New Testaments of the Bible frequently mention madness, providing descriptions that are sometimes compared with modern-day accounts of psychosis (Ibid., pp. 1–2).

In ancient Greece, mental disorders were recognised and discussed. In a quasi-scientific way, Hippocrates (460–377 BCE) had sought to explain mental disorders by reference to the four 'humours' and had made reference to several conditions, including mania and melancholia. By the time of the school of Hippocrates of Cos, natural (rather than supernatural) explanations of insanity were being developed (Lloyd, 1983, e.g. pp. 229–231).

During the Middle Ages in Europe, religious texts tended to attribute insanity to supernatural sources such as witchcraft and demon possession. The Inquisition continued largely along similar lines of thought and superstition. By the sixteenth century, as Renaissance ideas spread, classical texts reemerged and exerted their influence. Paracelsus expressed the view that mental disorder was due to a loss of reason and that it may run in families (e.g. Kales, Kales and Vela-Bueno, 1990). In parts of Europe, institutions began to form during this period (and before) that admitted and attempted to treat 'lunatics'.

Also important, as Majeed (2005) points out, is the contribution in medieval times of Islamic civilisation on many areas, including medicine. For example, Ibn Sina (Avicenna) synthesised Islamic medicine in *The Canon of Medicine*, which remained influential for centuries and included psychological factors regarding treatment. A broader discussion of the influence of Arab Islamic culture on psychiatry and its concepts, theories, practise and treatment, including the work of Ibn Sina and al-Razi (Rhazes), is provided by Kamal and Sarhan (1989).

With the Enlightenment, one begins to move more securely into work that can be related to present-day understandings of psychosis and schizophrenia, and this will be discussed later in the present chapter.

History and interpretation

Having looked at the notion of chronology, we can see that even a process that seems at first glance to be simple and straightforward in fact involves elements of judgement and debate. With history, matters are further complicated. At its heart, history concerns systematically examining evidence of the past. It analyses, interprets and comments upon recorded historical 'facts'. Drawing on primary- and secondary-source material, historians present empirical evidence, shape hypotheses and put forward plausible arguments of events and situations. Some see history as a predominantly scientific pursuit where arguments are formed by an inexorable logic and method derived from clear facts. For others, such as White (1995), history is more a 'craft like discipline' than a scientific one, more likely to be governed by 'convention and custom' than 'methodology and theory' (Ibid., p. 243).

Also, the further that one goes back in time, the less clear it becomes that one is looking at concepts that can be considered similar to categories that are recognised today. In addition to the distance in time potentially distorting comparisons, differences in culture and in frameworks of understanding by which seeming mental disorders were described further complicate matters. Any attempt to try to simply equate descriptions of mental disorders in the past with modern conceptions is fraught with difficulties.

Psychiatry and historical interpretation

When one begins to look at historical interpretation in more detail, it soon becomes apparent that few subjects can have attracted such diverse views as the history of madness and psychiatry. Examples are the debates concerning the recency or persistency of schizophrenia, the extent to which mental disorders are socially constructed and historically situated and the trajectory of developments in psychiatry, including the contribution of psychoanalysis.

French historian of ideas Michel Foucault (1926–1984), in *History of Madness* (Foucault, [1961, 1972 and 1994]/2006), traces historical transformations in conceptions of insanity, considering how madness is made an object of knowledge. As scientific reason developed in the seventeenth and eighteenth centuries, Foucault suggests, 'sanity' and 'madness' became increasingly polarised. Insane individuals came to be seen as beyond the reach of reason. In the nineteenth and twentieth centuries, the influence of psychiatry contributed to shaping madness as an illness that is subject to cure and normalisation. Foucault's theme, as Scruton (1985) summarises it, is that each successive age finds its own version of 'truth' through which the experience of madness is transmuted into sanity seen as 'the condition which is condoned and fostered by prevailing power' (Ibid., p. 36).

There is debate about whether schizophrenia is a condition that has persisted over time or whether, as Foucault would maintain, it is in a sense a new phenomenon, the 'recency-persistency' question. Discussing this, Stefanis and Stefanis (2009) characterise Foucault's position as seeing schizophrenia as 'the ploy of rising capitalism (in tandem with industrialisation and urbanisation) to fill Asylums with deviants who pose a nuisance to society greedy for profit' (Ibid., p. 6).

By contrast, Shorter (1997) sees such suggestions as very wide of the mark. He states that

> to an extent unimaginable for other areas of the history of medicine, zealot researchers have seized the history of psychiatry to illustrate how their pet bugaboos – be they capitalism, patriarchy, or psychiatry itself – have converted protest into illness, locking into asylums those who would otherwise be challenging the established order.
>
> *(Ibid., p. viii)*

Such notions, Shorter believes, are incorrect in suggesting that 'schizophrenia or depression are social constructs'. Nevertheless, 'how patients experience these conditions, and how society makes sense of them, are indeed subject to the influence of culture and convention' (Ibid.).

Shorter (1997) highlights the contributions of biology and physiology to psychiatry. For example, he takes the view that the influence of psychoanalysis in the development of psychiatry was retrogressive and that progress lies in biological understanding. A history of psychiatry proper begins with the therapeutic asylums of the late eighteenth century, when psychiatrists initially believed that the brain was the basis of mental illnesses. There was then a shift when Freudian ideas became prominent and the mind and brain were seen as divorced. In our own times, views establishing the primacy of the brain have been reestablished (Ibid., p. viii, paraphrased).

Considering terms historically

Looking at expressions as they were used in the past has an intrinsic fascination. It can also reveal some of the reasons why words and their meanings may have changed. Part of this approach involves etymology, an account of word derivation. An exploration of word origins can describe the spread of terms from one language to another and how their meanings and forms have changed. Among fertile areas to examine are notions of 'mad', 'insane', 'lunatic' and 'maniac' and possible reasons for the apparent decline in their use in more formal language.

Mad and insane

Meaning 'out of one's mind', the word 'mad' is traceable to the late 1200s as the Old English *'gemaedde'*. A further meaning was stupid or foolish. Relatedly, *'gamaedan'* was to 'make insane or foolish'. In Old Norse, *'meiða'* meant 'to harm'. In comparatively recent historical contexts, the phrase 'stark mad' came into use. 'Stark' in this sense is the equivalent to 'entirely'. English poet John Skelton (1463–1529), in an elegy lamenting the death in 1489 of the earl of Northumberland, poses the question, 'I say, ye commoners, why were ye so stark mad?' (Skelton, circa [1489], line 50). Two centuries later, the expression 'stark staring mad' is found in John Dryden's *Persius Flaccus* (1693), where there is an ironic reference to the Bethlem Asylum: 'Art thou of Bethlem's Noble College free? Stark, staring mad'. An early use of 'stark raving mad' is in Henry Fielding's *The Intriguing Chambermaid* ([1734]/2004), where a character cries, 'I find I am distracted! I am stark, raving mad'. It follows that places in which mad people resided were 'mad houses', while physicians who attended mad individuals were 'mad doctors'. For example, John Perceval ([1838 and 1840]/1961), giving a narrative of his mental disorder, often refers to lunatic asylums but also heads a chapter of his book 'Account of Escape From Mr. C. Newington's Madhouse and Reason &c.' (Ibid., p. 242).

The essential meaning of 'mad' and its earlier origins has remained fairly constant, although the connotations may have changed. For example, in the age of faith in Europe, spiritual and superstitious accounts prevailed, while more recently there have been scientific attempts to explain the phenomenon.

Given that the Latin *'sanus'* meant 'healthy' and 'sound', a past meaning of 'sane' in referring to style was that of 'correctness'. More widely, the expression alluded to being generally healthy, and it is this meaning that has evolved into referring specifically to mental health. To be 'sane' suggests a sound and healthy mind. Reason, judgement and good sense are often part of what is being conveyed. Accordingly, 'insane' derives from the Latin *'insanus'* which combines *'in'* (not) and *'sanus'* to indicate 'of unsound mind' or 'outrageous'.

In the late eighteenth century, William Perfect's *Select Cases of the Different Species of Insanity* was published (Perfect, 1787). In the following century, Dorothea Dix provided reports *On Behalf of the Insane Poor* (Dix, [1843]/1971) for legislators in Massachusetts. William Letchworth, having worked for the New York Board of Charities, later travelled around Europe and the United States and subsequently wrote *The Insane in Foreign Countries* in the late nineteenth century (Letchworth, 1889). Henry Hurd (1843–1927), the original director of the Johns Hopkins Hospital and the first professor of psychiatry at its medical school, edited the four volumes of *The Institutional Care of the Insane in the United States and Canada* in the early 1900s (Hurd, 1916–1917).

The terms 'mad' and 'insane' are still used casually by some but, as official designations, have fallen into disuse. Perhaps this is because, despite the debates about the meaning of the words 'psychosis' and 'schizophrenia' and their slipperiness (as we shall see later), the older expressions are even more amorphous.

Lunatic

'Lunatic' comes from the Latin '*lunaticus*' meaning 'effected by the moon' ('*luna*' meaning 'moon'). As is widely known, the derivation relates to the misconception that madness was influenced by the cycles of the moon. 'Lunacy' therefore applied to the condition of being effected by the moon. In Old English, the word '*monaðseocnes*' referred in a similar way to 'month sickness'.

Institutions in which lunatics were admitted became 'lunatic asylums'. Asylums in general date back to the Middle Ages. Bethlem, which became one of the oldest institutions for mentally disordered individuals in Europe, was founded as the Priory of St. Mary of Bethlehem in London in the thirteenth century. In its early years, it housed mentally disordered people, as well as others, while in later centuries it became an asylum exclusively for the insane. A corrupted form of 'Bethlehem' into 'Bethlem' and then 'Bedlam' gave the world a byword for unruly madness.

PAUSE FOR REFLECTION: BEDLAM

Search the Internet for the video 'A Brief History of Bedlam' (www.youtube.com/watch?v=jda7dyBRlxg).

The short video shows the site of the original thirteenth-century asylum with some impressions of what it was like.

What are the connotations that old terms such as 'asylum' and 'insane' evoke today?

New York Hospital having taken in mentally disordered individuals over a period of time established a separate building for these patients, designating it in 1808 as a 'Lunatic Asylum' (Hurd, 1916–1917, vol. 3, pp. 133–135). In Williamsburg, Virginia, a hospital exclusively for those with mental disorder was founded in 1773 to provide for the 'Support and Maintenance of Ideots, Lunatics, and other Persons of unsound Minds' (Dain, 1971, p. 9). The year 1828 saw the publication of Halliday's *General View of the Present State of Lunatics and Lunatic Asylums in Great Britain and Ireland* (Halliday, 1828). Perceval ([1838 and 1840]/1961) writes in his account of his mental disorder of 'having been under the care of lunatic doctors' and of 'having lived in the company of Lunatics' (Ibid., p. 3).

As it became clearer that mental disorder associated with psychosis was not related to lunar phases, the word 'lunatic' fell into disuse as an official and clinical expression, although slang keeps the expression alive to the present day. The word is also used more widely when clearly not referring to an individual with schizophrenia but whose views or behaviour are irrational or disliked. A parallel is seen in the decline in the use of the phrase 'deaf and dumb'. This was extensively used when it was believed that if an individual was deaf, they inevitably could have no spoken language, either literally or figuratively. With the development of deaf sign languages, it became evident that deaf people could speak in the broad sense. As aids to hearing were improved, including the use of cochlear implants, deaf people were able to speak in the more conventional sense too (Farrell, 2014, p. 13).

Maniac

'Mania' comes from the Greek '*mania*' meaning 'frenzy, fury or wild passion' and a 'maniac' is a person affected by mania. Dr. Willian Perfect (1787) of Kent, England, writes of being summoned in 1776 by the parish officers to see a 'maniacal man' whom they had confined in the workhouse.

The expression 'mania' has been linked to many prefixes to describe the form that the frenzied interest or activity takes. 'Monomania' concerns a driving obsession for one subject, '*mono*' being Greek for 'single'. 'Nymphomania', deriving from the Greek '*nymph*' meaning 'bride', refers to morbid and uncontrollable female sexual desire. From the Greek '*dypsa*', meaning 'thirst', comes the expression 'dypsomaniac', someone craving alcohol. 'Megalomania' refers to delusions of grandeur. 'Erotomania' signifies a morbid feeling of desperate love. In 'micromania' (the Greek '*micros*' means 'small'), the individual is convinced that he or she, or part of him- or herself, is reduced in size. 'Pyromania', from '*pyro*' meaning 'fire', refers to manic fire setting.

Deriving from the Greek '*kleptos*' meaning 'thief', the term 'kleptomania' conveys a supposed fixation on stealing. Since the 1800s the alleged condition has been criticised as providing one law for the rich, who can more easily, it seems, claim to be suffering from kleptomania, and one law for the poor, who tend to be unable to make such an assertion. Humorous adaptations have been made from time to time, such as 'Beatlemania' for the wild enthusiasm that greeted the early concerts of the Liverpudlian music group.

Although the word 'mania' is still used, it is less common to hear the expression 'maniac' except as slang or in certain sections of the popular media. Perhaps this is because the terms 'psychotic' and 'schizophrenic' are considered to include manic behaviour where it is evident. Mania is therefore seen more as an aspect of these conditions rather than a distinctive description of a person and how they behave. As with the expression 'lunatic', increased knowledge appears to have driven the modifications in usage.

Developing classifications of psychosis over time

Earlier in this chapter we looked at a brief chronology of some developments concerning mental disorders, leaving the timeline at about the close of the eighteenth century. Around that time, notions were formed that can be more securely linked to later development in the understanding and classifications of psychosis and schizophrenia. Even so, as Stefanis and Stefanis (2009) acknowledge, the historiography of schizophrenia is 'built on rather shaky ground'. A central problem was (and is) that schizophrenia is encroached upon by 'neighbouring entities' and that it lacks 'identity validation' (Ibid., p. 1). Much of the work in developing ideas and classifications of mental disorder, especially relating to psychosis and schizophrenia, was pioneered by Germans in the late nineteenth and early twentieth centuries. Their forebears were many members of the French School of the early nineteenth century.

The French contribution

As the eighteenth century was coming to a close, Philippe Pinel (1745–1826) was appointed head of two Paris hospitals, the Bicêtre (for men) and the Salpêtrière (for women). Both institutions included a relatively small proportion of individuals with mental disorders, and Pinel with others made early attempts to move towards a more therapeutic regime for their treatment. Pinel proposed a classification of mental disorders into mania, melancholia, imbecility and degeneration (Pinel, [1801/1809]/2008). This basic classification was expanded by Esquirol (1772–1840), who also added the condition of '*folie partielle*', or partial insanity (Esquirol, [1838]/1845).

Generally speaking, both Pinel and Esquirol took a syndrome-like approach to insanity, being interested in signs and symptoms in their classification, rather than the possible origins and causes. Psychiatrist Jean-Pierre Falret (1794–1870), inspired by the work of both Pinel and Esquirol, took a broadly biological view of the aetiology of mental disorders. He is remembered in the history of psychiatry especially for establishing the clinical concept of '*folie circulaire*', in which depression alternates with mania, prefiguring later designations of manic depressive disorder (Falret, 1854).

Stefanis and Stefanis (2009, p. 4) note the shift of focus in clinical research into mental disorder from the French School to the German-speaking countries of central Europe, which highly influenced psychiatric thinking until the mid-twentieth century. They speculate that this may have been due to the 'state-based decentralised administrative governance' that encouraged and supported university departments and clinics to bring together training and research with patient care.

Early uses of the term 'psychosis'

In its origins, 'psychosis' comes from modern Latin meaning 'mental disorder' and derives from the Greek '*psykhe*' (mind) and '*osis*' (a diseased state). As a prefix, the term 'psyche' is well known from expressions such as 'psychiatry', 'psychology' and 'psychoanalysis'. Also, the suffix 'osis' is widely used in physical conditions such as 'cirrhosis', 'thrombosis' and 'tuberculosis' and in the sphere of mental disorders in the terms 'neurosis' and 'alcoholic hallucinosis'.

German physician Karl Friedrich Canstatt (1807–1850), in his *Handbuch der Medizinischen Klinik* (Canstatt, 1841), introduced the concept of 'psychosis' into the literature of psychiatry. He used the term to mean the same as 'psychic neurosis'

(Scharfetter, 1987). At that time, the notion of 'neurosis' referred to all diseases of the nervous system, and Canstatt's point was to indicate the mental expressions of a disease of the brain (Janzarik, 2003). In 1845, Feuchtersleben (1806–1849), the physician and poet, in a German textbook on psychiatry, used the term 'psychosis', highlighting the interactions between physical and mental processes and the change in the whole personality (Feuchtersleben, 1845). Both Canstatt and Feuchtersleben took the view that psychosis originated in a combination of physical brain anomalies and mental vulnerability. German Nikolaus Friedreich (1825–1882) was a pathologist and neurologist who proposed (Friedreich, 1836) that psychosis has a predominantly organic neurological basis. In the second part of the eighteenth century, 'psychosis' was used to refer to broad concepts, including 'insanity' and 'mental illness'. German psychiatrist Carl Friedrich Flemming (1859) used 'psychosis' to mean two things: mental disorders having an *identifiable* organic basis, and disorders of the soul that were *assumed* to be caused organically.

Kraepelin and dementia praecox

German psychiatrist Emil Kraepelin (1856–1926), influenced by the pioneering experimental psychologist Wilhelm Wundt (1832–1920), made significant contributions to early scientific psychiatry. His *Compendium of Psychiatry* was published in 1883, and subsequent editions later called *The Textbook of Psychiatry* developed his ideas and views on the classification of mental disorders. By 1896, he had accumulated a thousand cases to inform his classifications (see, e.g. Kraepelin, [1899]/1991).

In 1907 Kraepelin stated the view that similar disease processes will produce identical symptom pictures, pathological anatomy and aetiology. Each could provide a uniform, standard classification of mental disorders with the classification coinciding for each approach. There were considered to be a definite number of mental disorders, each with its own aetiology (e.g. heredity), pathological anatomy that could be directly observed and symptoms. Some symptoms, such as hallucinations, could occur in more than one disorder, but each disorder was expected to have its own profile of symptoms. It followed that the first step in discovering the causes of mental disorders was to identify the disorders on the basis of certain symptoms. Understanding these was expected to enable researchers and others to work out the biological foundations of madness and the origins of these foundations. Different groups of symptoms appeared to follow different characteristic courses over a period of time.

Taking such considerations into account, Kraepelin grouped illnesses with a poor outcome, namely catatonia, hebephrenia and dementia paranoides. 'Catatonia', formed from the Greek '*cata*' meaning 'badly' and '*tonos*' referring to 'tension', conveys the notion of poor body tone or rigidity. It was first systematically described in 1874 by Karl Kahlbaum, the director of the mental asylum at Görlitz. He saw catatonia as a distinctive disease of motor dysregulation before Kraepelin subsumed it within his notion of dementia praecox.

PAUSE FOR REFLECTION: CATATONIA

Search the Internet for the video 'Catatonia Psychiatry Teacher' (www.youtube.com/watch?v=_s1lzxHRO4U).

(Note that 'patients' are portrayed by role players).

The video shows aspects of catatonia as understood today. These include 'forced grasping', 'waxy flexibility', 'sustained abnormal position', 'opposition' and 'resistance to movement' for example.

What are arguments for and against subsuming catatonia under a broader umbrella that includes hebephrenia and other conditions?

'Hebephrenia' uses the Greek '*hebe*' meaning 'youth' and '*phrene*' meaning 'mind' to convey the idea of adolescent insanity. An expression coined by the German psychiatrist Ewald Hecker (1843–1909), hebephrenia is associated with delusions, hallucinations and odd or silly behaviour (Hecker, 1871)

Dementia paranoides refers to dementia with paranoid features. 'Dementia' derives from the Latin '*demens*' meaning 'out of one's mind', while 'paranoides' comes from the Greek '*para*' meaning 'beside' or 'beyond' and '*noos*' meaning 'mind'. The word conveys the idea of mental derangement. Paranoia is characterised by systematic delusions.

Catatonia, hebephrenia and dementia paranoides were all considered to be manifestations of one condition which Kraepelin called 'dementia praecox'. Dementia we have already mentioned. The expression 'praecox', derived from the Latin meaning 'maturing early', relates to the word 'precocious' and means 'young'. The overall term therefore conveys the idea of a mental disturbance that appeared in young people. Symptoms of dementia praecox were various. Emotions might not be shown or, if they were demonstrated, might be inappropriate. Behaviour might be stereotyped (rigidly patterned) or involve catatonic postures. The individual could be easily distracted or confused. Hallucinations of sounds or touch might be evident. Irrational beliefs might occur, such as delusions of persecution or grandiosity. Throughout all this, the individual's mental powers deteriorated.

Two other broad disorders were identified which Kraepelin thought had better prognosis: 'manic depressive illnesses' and 'paranoia'. Manic depressive illnesses were mood disorders which included cycles of mood changes. Paranoia was a condition in which the individual had delusional beliefs, but unlike the delusions associated with dementia praecox, these were less severe and recovery was possible. Paranoia was later called 'delusional disorder'.

Bleuler and schizophrenia

The German word '*Schizophrenie*' derives from the Greek '*skhizein*' meaning 'to split' and '*phren*' meaning in this context 'mind'. The portmanteau word was coined by Eugen Bleuler (1857–1939), the Swiss psychiatrist, in 1911 (Bleuler, [1911]/1950).

Ashok, Baugh and Yeragani (2012) point out that Bleuler, lecturing at a meeting of the German Psychiatric Association in Berlin in April 1908, expressed reservations about the term 'dementia praecox'. The difficulty with the expression was that the condition that it was meant to denote was associated with neither dementia nor precociousness. Bleuler's proposed term emphasised 'the splitting of psychic functioning' that characterises schizophrenia. Certain interpretations of this word to convey a split mind or split personality have led to misunderstanding as, more accurately, schizophrenia is a separating of the mental functioning of thinking, memory and perception.

Bleuler included catatonia within schizophrenia, a view that has persisted into the modern day. It is debated whether catatonia would be more accurately characterised as a discrete disorder because it is seen rarely in schizophrenia and is identified in individuals with mania and with depression. Fink, Shorter and Taylor (2009) argue that 'it is time to place catatonia into its own home in the psychiatric classification'.

Bleuler proposed that underlying the varied symptoms of schizophrenia was a more fundamental unity reflected in four broad symptoms. These symptoms became known in English-speaking parts of the world as 'the four As': associations, ambivalence, autism and affect. *Associations* that linked thoughts together became loosened, affecting the individual's ability to think coherently and, in severe instances, leading to jumbled speech. *Ambivalence* referred to individuals holding conflicting emotions towards others. *Autism* was intended to convey social withdrawal. *Affect* became inappropriate with an individual's emotions being out of step with circumstances.

Hallucinations and delusions were seen as adjuncts to the four As, being reactions to the disorder rather than direct products of it. Those experiencing 'simple schizophrenia' tended not to experience hallucinations and delusions. Bleuler proposed a subgroup of people with 'latent schizophrenia' who might be excessively punctual, irritable, odd, moody or withdrawn. In addition to widening the concept of dementia praecox and renaming it schizophrenia, Bleuler proposed a relationship between schizophrenia and the already-identified 'manic depression'. However, individuals could still be identified as being predominantly either schizophrenic or manic depressive.

Karl Jaspers

Born in Germany in 1883, philosopher and psychiatrist Karl Jaspers died in 1969 in Switzerland. His *Allgemeine Psychopathologie (General Psychopathology)* was published in 1913. (For an English translation, see Jaspers, [1913]1997.) Jaspers drew a distinction between two kinds of mental symptoms. While the first kind were comprehensible, taking into account the patient's life history and were considered likely to be psychological, the second kind of symptoms were not understandable and were thought likely to be influenced by bodily processes (Häfner, 2013).

Psychoses were *not* understandable and were distinguished from the comparatively less severe disorders that were understandable and that later became known as 'neuroses'. Psychoses could include the presentation of abnormal beliefs, such as ones of persecution or of grandeur. These were held with great conviction, were unresponsive to argument or contradictory evidence, had a strange or impossible content and arose suddenly and without any explanation.

Kurt Schneider

German psychiatrist Kurt Schneider (1887–1967) further differentiated schizophrenia (Schneider, 1959). He proposed several 'first-rank symptoms' which he distinguished from 'second-rank symptoms'. First-rank symptoms were considered particularly characteristic of schizophrenia. They consisted of forms of hallucinations, delusions and experiences of passivity. It was the form rather than the content of the experience that was important for Schneider. For example, if an individual experiences his or her thoughts being withdrawn, it is this, the form of the disorder, that is essential. Less important is who is considered to withdraw the thoughts (a demon, the secret service, etc.), which is seen as relating to the individual's circumstances and life experiences.

Paul Julius Möbius

Looking at aetiology, Paul Julius Möbius (1853–1907), the German neurologist, distinguished 'exogenous' and 'endogenous' psychoses (Möbius, 1892). He, and later Kraepelin and Jaspers (initially), used 'exogenous' to refer to the causes of mental disease, whether somatic or psychic (both being extraneous factors). Since the contributions of Schneider, 'endogenous' has meant that a somatic cause is assumed to exist (even though it is not identifiable) from the psychopathology that can be seen (Beer, 1995). The notion of unitary psychosis indicates the absence of identifiable psychopathological phenomena, instead suggesting that there are many variations of the disease that 'merge in all directions' (Burgy, 2008). This is contrary to the idea of natural nosological entities or many distinguishable psychoses that show individual symptoms, aetiology and course.

Manic depression

We have already touched on the historical development of the words 'mania', 'maniac' and 'maniacal'. More modern expressions using the suffix 'mania', such as 'monomania', were also mentioned. But a related term, 'manic depression', has historical roots too. Bleuler, as we have seen, proposed that individuals could be identified as being predominantly schizophrenic or predominantly manic depressive.

Russian-born American psychiatrist Jacob Kasanin (1897–1946) suggested the notion of 'schizoaffective disorder' (Kasanin, 1933). It had features of both schizophrenia and manic depression but could be distinguished from both. Individuals with schizoaffective disorder experienced disorders of mood and hallucination, but they tended not to show the passivity-type symptoms of schizophrenia, such as delusions that they were being controlled. Symptoms usually appeared suddenly with no previous indications of disorder, and patients often recovered rapidly, although many went on to experience further episodes.

Relatedly, Karl Kleist (1879–1960), the German psychiatrist, proposed the concept of 'cycloid marginal psychosis' (Kleist, 1928). He used this term to describe cases which do not meet the typical presentation of schizophrenia or bipolar affective disorder. As Yadav (2010) notes, these conditions include many cases of psychotic illnesses that are acute and last a short time and where the patient recovers between recurrences. In other words, the acute features are psychotic, as with schizophrenia, but the course is episodic, as is the case with manic depression.

Kliest's former student Karl Leonhard (1904–1988) further developed the notion in describing 'cycloid psychosis' disorders (Leonhard, [1957]/1979). In these disorders, patients appeared schizophrenic at one time and manic depressive at another. This change of symptoms over time distinguished cycloid psychosis from Kasanin's schizoaffective disorder, in which schizophrenic symptoms and manic depressive symptoms appeared at the same time. Leonhard in 1957 described cycloid psychosis and its three forms. The first form is anxiety-blissfulness psychosis (or anxiety-happiness psychosis). On the anxiety pole, there are periodic states of overwhelming anxiety and paranoid ideas of reference and sometimes hallucinations. The blissful pole is associated with expansive behaviour and grandiose ideas. The second form of cycloid psychosis is excited-inhibited confusion psychosis, in which the clinical picture varies between excitement and a state of underactivity with poverty of speech. The third is motility psychosis, in which there are marked changes in psychomotor activity, between 'akinetic' (similar to catatonic stupor), and 'hyperkinetic' (resembling catatonic excitement; see also Yadav, 2010).

Further developments

As we see from the historical sketch presented previously, there have been changes in both terminology and in what the same terms might mean in relation to psychosis and schizophrenia. Among reasons for these changes were efforts to assign organic and mental influences, and attempts to refine classification to try to make the proposed groupings more valid and reliable. Further developments took place leading to an international set of criteria for the diagnosis of mental disorders. A widely used set of criteria is the *Diagnostic and Statistical Manual of Mental Disorders* (American Psychiatric Association, 2013), which is discussed in a later chapter on psychiatric terminology.

Changes relating to perceived negative labelling

Changes can come about in the terms used for mental disorders because of perceptions that the terms have negative connotations. For example, various terms have been used for what is now called 'intellectual disability' in the United States (American Psychiatric Association, 2013, pp. 33–41) and 'learning difficulty' in England (Department of Education and Skills, 2005). In England, under the Mental Deficiency Act (1913), individuals with 'mental deficiency' were categorised as 'idiot', 'imbecile' or 'moron'. The Handicapped Pupils and School Health Service Regulations of 1945 replaced the expression 'mentally defective' with 'educationally subnormal'. Later still, the terms were changed to 'profound learning difficulties', 'severe learning difficulties' and 'moderate learning difficulties', which are still used (Department of Education and Skills, 2005). In the United States, there was a shift from speaking of 'mental retardation' to 'intellectual disability'. Among the reasons for such changes was the wish to discard terms that were deemed negative (Farrell, 2014, pp. 9–12 and 20–22).

In contrast to 'intellectual disability' it is only in comparatively recent times that suggestions have been made to change terms such as 'psychosis' and 'schizophrenia' because they are considered to negatively label individuals. Perhaps this is because for so many years, there was debate about what the expressions 'psychosis' and 'schizophrenia' meant or ought to mean. Once the terms had become widely accepted, then challenges to their appropriateness could be made. For example, regarding 'schizophrenia' Deegan (1993) states, 'I was told I had a disease . . . I was beginning to undergo that radically dehumanising transformation . . . from being Pat Deegan to being "a schizophrenic"'. 'Henry' (in Barham and Hayward, 1995) says, 'I am labelled for the rest of my life . . . I think schizophrenia will always make me a second class citizen . . . I haven't got a future' (Ibid.).

Pembroke (2012) refers to a 'relief response' on learning the name of the 'distress'. But she also argues that 'the label itself does not ease the pain'. Also, 'it does not help the professional or the individual to understand what is happening or what would assist the individual'. For Pembroke, 'the labelled people are seen as inferior or less competent' and 'people become dependent and helpless with the treatments and labels' (Ibid., p. 36). In a report on psychosis and schizophrenia (Cooke, 2014), an anonymous contributor says:

> The name doesn't help. It's psycho . . . that's the only thing people hear . . . and when I got told I just thought I'm a psycho. Psycho, psycho, psycho, and you just think of someone that goes killing people and . . . does crazy things . . . Well I thought they'd got it completely wrong . . . I thought, I'm sicker than I thought I was.
>
> *(Ibid., p. 33)*

Where terms are seen as negative, alternative terms might be suggested. Pembroke (2012) uses the expression 'distress'. The executive summary of a report into psychosis and schizophrenia (Cooke, 2014) states, 'This report describes a psychological approach to experiences that are commonly thought of as psychosis or sometimes schizophrenia' (Ibid., p. 6). Effectively, Cooke's language implies that if there is a condition that is designated as 'schizophrenia', it may or may not be appropriate to call it so and only 'some people' do so. In the present book, in a later chapter on 'Advocacy', labelling is further discussed in the context of labelling theory.

While some find labelling to be a negative matter, others find the act of naming a condition to be beneficial. Falk (2010) (referring to bipolar disorder) asserts:

> I think I prefer my illness having a name because it makes me feel less lonely and I know that there are other people experiencing my kind of misery and that people live through my illness and make a meaningful existence with it.

She adds also, 'But I also have to be careful not to adopt the sick role, since I know I would just give up if I did that' (Ibid., p. 32).

Conclusion

In any chronology of developments relating to mental disorders and to psychiatry, selections have to be made about what constitute important events and how they are sequenced. Regarding history, further judgements are made about how to interpret events and their likely causes. In the history of madness and psychiatry, views are sometimes polarised, for example in debates about the persistency or recency of schizophrenia. Historical changes as reflected in alterations in terminology illuminate the development of understandings of psychosis and schizophrenia. The expressions 'mad' and 'insane', while still used casually by some, are no longer current in official or clinical debate, perhaps because of their amorphousness. 'Lunatic' fell into disuse except as slang with the demise of the belief that mental disorder is related to moon phases. 'Maniac' as a label for an individual survives in slang but is rarely used, as the state of 'mania' is presently seen as one aspect of a wider disorder.

In broader historic terms, the early French School included the contributions of Pinel ([1801/1809]/2008), who proposed a classification of mental disorders into mania, melancholia, imbecility and degeneration. Esquirol ([1838]/1845) added the condition of 'partial insanity'. Falret (1854) established the clinical concept of '*folie circulaire*' in which depression alternates with mania, prefiguring later manic depressive disorder.

Highly influential was the work of German-speaking psychiatrists in central Europe. In introducing the concept of 'psychosis' into psychiatric literature, Canstatt (1841) designated 'psychic neurosis' as a mental manifestation of broader 'neurosis'. For Feuchtersleben (1845), 'psychosis' involved interactions between physical and mental processes. Friedreich (1836) proposed that psychosis has a predominantly organic neurological basis. For Flemming (1859), psychosis referred to both mental disorders having an identifiable organic basis and to disorders of the soul *assumed* to be caused organically. Kraepelin ([1899]/1991) sought a uniform, standard classification of mental disorders, each with its own aetiology, pathological anatomy and symptom profile. Illnesses considered to have a poor prognosis were catatonia, hebephrenia and dementia paranoides (all manifestations of what Kraepelin called 'dementia praecox'). Disorders with better prognosis were manic depressive illnesses and paranoia. Bleuler ([1911]/1950) proposed replacing 'dementia praecox' with the wider term '*schizophrenie*', which included catatonia. He saw underlying the varied symptoms of schizophrenia a unity reflected in broad symptoms concerning associations, ambivalence, autism and affect. Bleuler suggested a relationship between schizophrenia and the already-identified 'manic depression'. Jaspers ([1913]1997) distinguished between 'psychoses', which were comprehensible in terms of the patient's life history and were likely psychological, and symptoms (later known as the neuroses), which were not understandable and likely influenced by bodily processes. Schneider (1959) suggested several 'first-rank symptoms' of schizophrenia. Möbius (1892) aetiologically distinguished 'exogenous' and 'endogenous' psychoses. Kasanin (1933) proposed 'schizoaffective disorder', which had features of both schizophrenia and manic depression. Kleist (1928) nominated 'cycloid marginal psychosis' for cases differing from schizophrenia or bipolar affective disorder. Leonhard ([1957]/1979) described 'cycloid psychosis' disorders in which patients appeared alternately schizophrenic and manic depressive. The contribution of these pioneers has been variously adopted in current understandings of psychosis, as will be discussed in a later chapter, 'Psychiatric terminology'.

Changes can evolve in terms used for mental disorders because of perceptions that the expressions have negative connotations. Only comparatively recently has it been suggested that 'psychosis' and 'schizophrenia' might be negative labels, perhaps because for so many years there was debate about what they meant and only when the terms were established could their appropriateness be challenged. Others find the act of naming the conditions to be beneficial. Having already heard some views of individuals who experienced these disorders, in the next chapter we look further at personal accounts of psychosis.

Thinking points

Readers may wish to consider:

- any terms other than the ones already discussed that are connected with psychosis, schizophrenia and madness that have changed over time and possible reasons for the changes;
- the extent to which past attempts to refine classifications have paved the way for a clearer picture of psychosis and schizophrenia in the present day; and
- possible reasons for differing views about which terms do and do not constitute negative labelling.

Key texts

Eghigian, G. (Ed.) (2010) *From Madness to Mental Health: Psychiatric Disorder and its Treatment in Western Civilization* New Brunswick, Rutgers University Press.
   This book includes sections on the contributions of thinkers of the ancient world and of medieval times.

Farrell, M. (2014) *Investigating the Language of Special Education: Listening to Many Voices* New York and Basingstoke, England, Palgrave Macmillan.

The first chapter outlines historical changes in terms associated with a wide range of disabilities and disorders and examines the possible reasons for such changes.

Foucault, M. ([1961, 1972 and 1994]/2006) *History of Madness* London and New York, Routledge (Translated from the French by J. Murphy and J. Khalfa).

An engaging account of what Foucault sees as the influences of power and social ostracism in the story of madness.

Lieberman, J. A. and Ogas, O. (2015) *Shrinks: The Untold Story of Psychiatry* London, Weidenfeld and Nicholson.

Lieberman, a former president of the American Psychiatric Association, traces the field of psychiatry from pseudoscience to a more evidence-based discipline.

Internet resources

The National Coalition for Health Professional Education in Genetics and the Jackson Laboratory provide a glossary of psychiatric terms courtesy of the National Society of Genetic Counselors at the following web address: www.nchpeg.org/index.

3

PERSONAL ACCOUNTS OF PSYCHOSIS

Introduction

Psychosis exists worldwide and it is estimated that about one individual in a hundred will at some point in their lives personally experience schizophrenia. If one wants to develop an understanding of psychosis, including schizophrenia, it is clearly important to consider descriptions of psychosis made by people that are experiencing it or have experienced it. Personal accounts may take the form of a narrative, a diary, notes or letters and come from various sources. Some reports written by physicians, while being second-hand, may directly quote a patient's speech. There are also many examples of first-hand accounts by people who have directly experienced psychosis. Testimonies may be written in retrospect or may be contemporaneous. Each form has its own qualities and restrictions. All other things being equal, a contemporaneous representation might be expected to be more authentic but not well considered, while a retrospective account might be less spontaneous but more coherent.

Second-hand sources directly quoting a patient's speech

Frith and Johnson (2003) provide examples from case material in the Northwick Park study of first episodes of schizophrenia (e.g. Johnstone, Crow, Johnson and MacMillan, 1986). This study was conducted with the cooperation of a large number of hospitals and medical centres all over north London and some surrounding counties (private communication, Eve Johnstone, January 2016). Many examples are general observations of behaviour and speech. Sometimes, what seem to be direct quotations of what a patient said can help to convey something of the patient's experience.

For example, the authors state that a 20-year-old woman at the initial interviews had 'very disorganised behaviour'. She would 'sit for only moments in a chair and then wander around the room, picking up articles and occasionally sitting on the floor'. She 'repeatedly removed her dressing gown and made inappropriate sexual advances to the male staff, then tore bits off a picture of a swan'. She said, 'the thoughts go back to the swan, I want the cross to keep it for ever and ever. It depends on the soldier, Marcus the nurse' (Frith and Johnson, 2003, p. 22).

Such reports may give a glimpse of what may be done and said by people experiencing psychosis. We have to assume that the accounts are accurate and that sufficient orientating context has been provided by the observers. In addition to second-hand reports, there are also many first-hand accounts and it is to such examples that we now turn.

First-hand accounts

The Reverend Mr. George Trosse

A memoir written by the Reverend Mr. George Trosse (1631–1713) and published in 1714 soon after his death recounts a period of illness which the Reverend experienced as a young man and from which he appears to have recovered. Describing three episodes of disorder during the years 1656 and 1657, Trosse reports that these included seeing frightening visions and hearing voices, which he later recognised were unreal but which at the time seemed real to him. Voices commanded him to perform tasks such as removing his clothing which he felt compelled to carry out (Trosse, [1714]/1974).

While such historical accounts are interesting, it is not always clear whether the symptoms to which they refer are those which we would now describe as schizophrenia (Petersen, 1982). Indeed, Hare (1988) suggests that, in Trosse's instance, a 'more plausible' diagnosis of his symptoms would be alcoholic psychosis and affective disorder.

John Perceval

John Perceval (1803–1876) was the fifth son of Spencer Perceval, a British prime minister who had been assassinated in the House of Commons in 1812 when John was only 9 years old. In early life, John became a cavalry officer and later was influenced by an 'extreme evangelical cult' (Bateson, 1961, p. vi). In 1830, while visiting Dublin, he began behaving in a disordered manner, necessitating his being placed under restraint in the inn at which he was staying. His oldest brother fetched him from Dublin and in January 1831 placed him in an asylum run by a certain Dr. Fox at Brisslington near Bristol, where John remained until May 1832. Perceval was then moved to an asylum run by a Mr. Newington at Ticehurst in Sussex, where he stayed until 1834 (Ibid.).

After his recovery John Perceval wrote a 'narrative' originally published in two volumes (Perceval, [1838 and 1840]/1961).[1] Its full title was *A Narrative of the Treatment Experiences by a Gentleman During a State of Mental Derangement Designed to Explain the Causes and the Nature of Insanity and to Expose the Injudicious Conduct Pursued Towards Many Unfortunate Sufferers Under That Calamity.* While today the title seems absurdly long, it does have the advantage of indicating the author's intentions. These are not only to describe his experiences but also to discuss 'insanity' more widely and to complain of the way 'unfortunate sufferers' might be treated. In fact, since its republication by anthropologist Gregory Bateson, the book has been acclaimed as an early work of mental health advocacy. It describes the contemporary treatments which Perceval received, including being strapped to his bed, being constrained in a straightjacket and being made to undergo cold baths.

Stark words open the book: 'In the year 1830, I was unfortunately deprived of the use of reason' (Perceval, [1838 and 1840]/1961, p. 3). Speaking of his delusions and given his religious status, Perceval is at pains to point out that despite appearances he did not contemplate taking his own life. He states,

> During the whole period of my confinement I was never tempted to commit suicide; under my delusions I often was commanded to commit acts endangering my life and safety, but always with a view to my salvation, or that of others, and so far from any intention of self-destruction, that I expected to be raised again immediately if any evil happened to me.
>
> *(Ibid., p. 115)*

Elsewhere, he recounts, 'Then new delusions succeeded those that were dissipated . . . I was still a disobedient angel whom the Lord had made pass for a lunatic in order to preserve me. But I was watched with jealousy' (Ibid., p. 146).

Yet at other times his 'voices' gave him directions and twisted them so that it was impossible to know how to respond. Speaking of a 'spiritual body' (Herminet Herbert), Perceval recounts,

> I was ordered to wrestle with Herminet Herbert, or to kiss Herminet Herbert, the voices explained to me that I was to take each of these directions in a contrary sense – ironically. That is, when I was desired to kiss him, I was to wrestle with him or strike him, – when to wrestle with him, to kiss him; but I disobeyed, and then I was told I disobeyed through cowardice, – that I was affecting not to understand and, in consequence, losing all patience: at last I knew not which was which; and then the voice said, that my understanding became confounded through my hypocrisy.
>
> *(Ibid., p. 280)*

In other delusions, 'the stature of persons appeared to change' (Ibid., p. 285). Of the voices he heard, Perceval says that they 'were mostly heard in my head, though I often heard them in the air, or in different parts of the room' (Ibid., p. 286). Of the voices in his head, 'there were upwards of fourteen'.

PAUSE FOR REFLECTION: JOHN PERCEVAL'S ACCOUNT

John Perceval's account is an example of a narrative composed some time after his experience of psychosis and of his treatment in two asylums and written after his recovery. What are the likely advantages and disadvantages of such a retrospective account?

The 'madness letters' of Friedrich Nietzsche

On 3 January 1889, at the age of 44, German philosopher Friedrich Nietzsche (1844–1900) suffered a mental collapse. It was thought to have been brought about by syphilis, although subsequently other diagnoses have been suggested. In the days around the time of the collapse, Nietzsche sent letters that became known as the 'Wahnzettel' (madness letters) to various friends, including Cosima Wagner (widow of the composer) and his former colleague Jacob Burkhart. Some were signed 'Dionysus', others 'der Gekreuzigte' ('the crucified one').

For example, on 4 January Nietzsche wrote in a marginal postscript to a letter to Burkhart, 'I have had Caiaphas put in chains. I also was crucified last year in a prolonged way by German doctors. Wilhelm Bismarck and all anti-Semites, abolished' (Nietzsche, [various dates 1861–1869]/1997). The letters (sometimes only very brief notes) suggest identification with Christ and with pagan gods and an accompanying idea of unlimited power. As the concern of his friends grew, Nietzsche was taken from Turin where he was residing and admitted to asylums in Switzerland and Germany, later living in a villa in Weimar where he died in 1900.

Schreber's Memoirs of My Nervous Illness

German judge Daniel Paul Schreber (1842–1911) described his mental disorder in *Memoirs of My Nervous Illness* (Schreber, [1903]/1955 and 2000). Like Perceval, Schreber wished to draw attention to the harshness of some of his treatment. In the German original, a subtitle was included, to consider 'under what circumstances a person declared insane can be detained in an asylum against his expressed will'. Today, the judge's disorder would probably be seen as a type of schizophrenia involving paranoid delusions. The disorders which he described occurred during 1884–1885 (and were only briefly referenced) and in 1893–1902. Schreber also experienced a third period of illness, from 1907 until his death in an asylum in 1911. No one else, it has been suggested, has been 'as mad, as vividly hallucinated' and has at the same time described his experiences with 'such detail and lucidity' (Dinnage, 2000).

Broadly, the memoir sets out a system of a mythic universe that Schreber created involving upper and lower gods, rays, miracles, nerve language, souls and soul murder and a certain 'Order of the World'.

Among his delusions, he believed that other humans had been turned into phantasms. He had been chosen in order to redeem the world, but had to be first transformed into a woman. Schreber, in an open letter to Professor Flechsig, stated his belief that 'the first impetus to what my doctors always considered mere "hallucinations" but which to me signified communication with supernatural powers, consisted of influences on my nervous system emanating from your nervous system' (Ibid., p. 8).

In the introduction to the memoir, Schreber expresses his conviction that 'owing to my illness, I entered into peculiar relations with God – which I hasten to add were in themselves contrary to the Order of the World' (Ibid., pp. 17–18).

Schreber ([1903]/1955 and 2000) refers to a period leading up to his second illness. He was in bed one morning, 'whether still half asleep or already awake, I cannot remember', and had the idea that 'it really must be rather pleasant to be a woman succumbing to intercourse'. The idea, says Schreber, was 'foreign to my whole nature' and 'I would have rejected it with indignation if fully awake' (Ibid., p. 46). Various 'miracles' are referred to throughout the body of the memoir. These were responsible for 'various changes in my sex organ', 'an actual retraction of the male organ' and 'particularly when mainly impure rays were involved, a softening approaching almost complete dissolution' (Ibid., p. 142).

Miracles on his body were performed by 'little men' – for example pulling his eyelids up and down. If he resisted, 'the little men became annoyed and expressed this by calling me "wretch"' (Ibid., p. 149). If he wiped the little men away, others 'were assembled almost continually on my head in great number'. These 'little devils' as he called them 'even partook of my meals, helping themselves to a part, although naturally only a tiny part, of the food I ate' (Ibid., p. 150).

Schreber's account has generated numerous books and articles. Sigmund Freud (1911) interpreted Schreber's psychotic conviction that he was being turned into a woman as repressed homosexual wishes (see the later chapter in this volume, 'Psychoanalysis and beyond'). Much later, the memoir was discussed in the context of the possible oppressive influence of Schreber's father, an authority on child rearing (e.g. Schatzman, 1973). A further account was provided by Lothane (1992). The impact on Schreber's mental state of the isolation of the asylum has been perhaps only belatedly recognised (Dinnage, 2000, p. xiv).

Nijinsky's diaries

Ukrainian ballet dancer and choreographer Vaslav Nijinsky (about 1889–1950) made his name with Diaghilev's Ballets Russes. After leaving this company and towards the end of the Great War, he moved to a villa in neutral Switzerland with his wife and daughter in 1917. Before the War ended Nijinsky was diagnosed with schizophrenia. For the rest of his life he was in and out of asylums, never dancing publicly again. His diary, written between 19 January and 4 March 1919, records his experience and is a rare example of an account of madness written contemporaneously by a consummate artist. First published in an English translation in 1936, the diary was greatly expurgated and rearranged by his wife and others. It was only in 1999 that the full unexpurgated version was published in a new English version (Nijinsky, [1919]/1999, 2000).

Around January 1919, as Acocella (2000) puts it, 'Nijinsky began to fall apart' and he started shutting himself in his studio all night, producing drawings at, 'furious speed'. He also began to write in notebooks (Nijinsky, [1919]/1999, 2000, p. xviii). One theme of the diary indicated that Nijinsky hoped that it would help to combat what he regarded as the world's materialism. Eating, digestion and elimination are other themes. He suspected that his servants were having sex with animals. He ruminated on building a bridge from Europe to America. He believed he was God: 'Lynching is a beast. Lynching is not God. I am God' (Nijinsky, [1919]/2000, p. 22); 'I am not the anti-Christ. I am Christ' (Ibid., p. 53). He planned to invent a new type of fountain pen which he would call 'God': 'The pen will be called God. I want to be called God' (Ibid., pp. 31–33). Nijinsky believed that blood was draining from his head and that the hairs in his nose were moving around.

Broadly, the diary indicates delusions of grandeur, of persecution, of certain events in his surroundings being directed at himself and of his actions being controlled by outside forces. Trains of thought are erratic and idiosyncratic. Words might be linked through sounds rather than meaning and there is considerable repetition. The diary reflects disorganised language and behaviour. Yet parts of the diary reflect Nijinsky's accurate awareness that the people around him, including his wife and a visiting physician, are increasingly alarmed about his behaviour and mental health. He is acutely aware that they are making arrangements to have him taken for assessment and treatment. Oswald's (1991) book *Nijinsky: A Leap Into Madness* provides further context.

PAUSE FOR REFLECTION: NIETZSCHE'S LETTERS AND NIJINSKY'S DIARIES

Nietzsche's notes and letters appear to have been written during a period when he was entering a psychotic period. The same applies to Nijinsky's diary. What are the advantages and disadvantages of such accounts in providing insight into psychosis?

'Renee'

An autobiographical account by a girl known as 'Renee' (Séchehaye ([1951]/1970) describes her experiences from the age of 5 to adolescence. She lived with her mother, brothers and sisters (Ibid., p. 58). From childhood, Renee experienced distortions to reality. While skipping with friends, she related seeing one of her companions as 'an enlarged image' (Ibid., p. 20). When she was in the school principal's office, 'suddenly, the room became enormous'. She later reported to her teacher that everyone she saw had 'a tiny crow's head on his head' (Ibid., p. 22). Stress seemed to produce 'an atmosphere of unreality' (Ibid., p. 24). She states that feelings of great fear that were at first episodic 'now never left me' (Ibid., p. 26). Another friend suddenly appeared unreal, 'like a statue' and 'a manikin moved by a mechanism, talking like an automaton' (Ibid., pp. 28–29).

Meeting her analyst, whom she referred to as 'mama', Renee felt more secure. She had feelings of being punished and of guilt (Ibid., p. 35). There seemed to be a 'System' that was punishing her. Her experiences of unreality she referred to as 'the land of enlightenment' (p. 44). She received 'orders from the System' not as voices yet still 'imperious'. These orders included 'to burn my right hand or the building in which I was' (p. 41).

Renee was admitted to a private voluntary hospital and later to a psychiatric hospital, 'an institution with locked wards' (pp. 46–47). She wrote letters to 'Mama' but did not eat because the 'system' forbids her (pp. 52–53). On leaving the psychiatric hospital, Renee stayed in her analyst's home (p. 56). Absorbed with tiny things, such as 'a drop of coffee', she lacked energy and interest, experiencing a state of 'torpor' (pp. 56–57). On a holiday with her analyst, Renee gained some weight, which she associated with 'impurity'. The 'orders' became more pressing: 'I was to throw myself into the sea; I was to open a vein' (p. 61). Admitted to a hospital in Geneva, she talked to the head of the 'system' who is called 'Antipol' (the name of a skin salve used in the facility). She harmed herself: 'I bit my hands, my arms, cruelly; I beat my head against the wall' (p. 63). Renee was then transferred to a private psychiatric hospital and later stayed at the home of a nurse. She recalled her analyst bringing her a toy monkey to try to help her reduce her self-harming and believed that her hands turn into 'cat's paws' (pp. 65 and 67).

Eventually, after further such experiences, changes of hospital and more analytic interventions, Renee reported that she gradually gains contact with her own body (pp. 73–74) and 'becomes firmly established within wonderful reality' (pp. 85–89). Questions raised by this account include the unconventional aspects of the relationship between the girl and her analyst, which extended beyond the usual therapeutic one. (Her analyst Margarite Séchehaye eventually adopted the girl.)

David C. Boyles's My Punished Mind

In *My Punished Mind*, Boyles (2004) describes himself as a 'mental health consumer' and provides a memoir of his experience of being psychotic. The account goes through a period of several weeks when he experienced psychosis before being admitted to hospital, the stay in hospital and events afterwards. Living in St. Augustine, Florida, David Boyles had intense feelings of euphoria, began to avidly read the Bible and started watching religious channels on television. He was laid off from his work. With 'psychosis setting in' (Ibid., p. 11), he goes to visit his brother at Virginia

Beach, Virginia. Songs that he hears on the radio start to take on a special significance. He felt guilty for reading the Bible and questioning God, cried increasingly and was 'very emotional' (p. 16). His thoughts often race. In his bedroom, he saw 'white figure formations' and 'colourful patterns' (p. 18).

Visiting his parents at their house in New York, David was 'compelled to bless the house' (p. 24). He said, 'God was punishing me' (p. 27). His family was concerned and eventually took him to the local emergency room. He was admitted to hospital and later, while his mother was visiting him, he heard voices: 'something said' not to scare her (p. 31). After a few weeks on regular medication, he was discharged and returned to Florida and then to his brother's place in Virginia Beach. There, he had intrusive thoughts ('It was non-stop thinking') (p. 41). He experienced hallucinations, such as 'a small face looking at me slowly moving round the edge of the pillows of the couch' (p. 50).

Back at his work, David attended a support group and continued taking medication, though sometimes intermittently (p. 51). When he gets 'shivery sensations' in his head, this indicated to him not to 'test' his medication and to resume taking it (p. 52). Zoloft worked for him 'on the obsessive thinking and the depression'; Depakote was the mood stabiliser keeping him from 'becoming hyper-manic'; and Risperdal helped prevent his delusions and hallucinations (p. 56). Later David started a new job and attended the community mental health clinic 'for medication management' (pp. 59–60). Over Christmas 2002, David experienced 'paranoia', thinking he was being punished by God for being involved in a prank involving cigarettes (p. 59).

Listing some early warning signs of schizophrenia, Boyle identifies the ones that he experienced. These were 'hearing and seeing things that aren't there', irrational statements', 'inability to sleep', 'shift in basic personality', 'hyperactivity', 'inability to concentrate', 'extreme preoccupation with religion', 'indifference', 'inability to express joy', 'excessive crying' and 'unusual sensitivity to stimuli (noise, light, colour, textures)'. Looking back, he states that he has come to accept his condition (p. 75). He feels fortunate for having 'medications that work for me' and can only imagine 'how I would have been treated just five hundred years ago' (p. 76). Explaining that when he was in psychosis, he was no longer himself, he says, 'For reasons not yet understood, my brain's chemistry malfunctioned causing thoughts that weren't mine and were not valid'. He also felt compelled to do things that he would not normally do. He states, 'I perceived sights and sounds that were not there' and 'my emotions . . . were amplified to the point of inappropriateness'. The theme of his psychosis was 'persecution from God, for having questioned the Bible' (p. 79). Therapy and medication seemed to work together. For example, therapy made him recognise that he was 'not on the proper dosage of Risperdal'. Also, therapy helped him realise that 'when I have thoughts (about anything) to think about them and not be afraid' (p. 80).

David states, 'This condition is a biological-chemical imbalance in the brain. *I felt it so I know* (p. 81, emphasis in the original). His medication helped him to realise 'the differences between reality and delusions' (p. 81). He was thankful to science and medicine for 'the help they are giving to the people who are experiencing this problem', enabling most of those affected to 'live normal and healthy lives' (p. 82). At the time of completing the book, David was living independently and had gained a new job as an electrical installer (Ibid.).

Elyn Saks

Elyn Saks is a professor of law and psychiatry at the University of California. Saks (2008) provides an account of her living with schizophrenia in *The Center Cannot Hold: My Journey Through Madness*. Her experiences as a young student and her later life are recounted, as well as the thoughts, feelings and behaviours associated with her schizophrenia. At Oxford University, she harboured thoughts of suicide: 'I'll douse myself with gasoline and light a match. A fitting end for a person as evil as I' (Ibid., p. 61). In the hospital, meeting with a group of doctors, she is asked why she is not eating and replies that 'food is evil . . . and anyway, I don't deserve to have any. I am evil too, and food would only nourish me. Does it make any sense to you to nourish evil? No it does not' (p. 74).

Elyn began to feel that she was receiving commands to do things. These were issued by 'shapeless, powerful beings' that controlled not with voices but with thoughts that 'had been placed in my head' (p. 79). Commands included 'Now lie down and don't move'; she was also told 'you are evil' and told to hurt herself, leading her to burn herself with cigarettes, lighters, boiling water and electric heaters. She states that with psychosis, 'the wall that separates fantasies from reality dissolves . . . The images I saw, the actions I took were all real, and it made me frantic' (p. 104). One of the worst aspects of schizophrenia was 'the profound isolation'. There is constant awareness that you are 'some sort of alien, not really human' (p. 179).

Treatments were not always benign. Elyn states,

> I write then because I know what it is like to be psychotic. And I know, better than most, how the law treats mental patients, the degradation of being tied to a bed against your will and force fed medicine you didn't ask for.

She desires to see change and wants to bring 'hope to those who suffer from schizophrenia and understanding to those who do not' (p. 306).

An 18-year-old man

Lewis (1967) quotes an account written by a young man, aged 18 years, who had had a condition (apparently schizophrenia) for a year or more:

> I am more and more losing contact with my environment and with myself. Instead of taking an interest in what goes on and caring about what happens with my illness, I am all the time losing my emotional contact with everything including myself . . . Even this illness which pierces to the centre of my

whole life, I can regard only objectively. But, on rare occasions, I am over-whelmed by the sudden realisation of the ghastly destruction that is caused by this creeping uncanny disease . . . My despair sometimes floods over me. But after each such outburst I become more indifferent. I lose myself more in the disease. I sink into an almost oblivious existence.

The account conveys vividly an impression of the so-called negative aspects of schizo-phrenia: withdrawal from the world and oneself and indifference to what happens.

Dominic

Dominic, a 'former service user of the Early Intervention in Psychosis Service', describes his experience of psychosis as follows:

It was more like slipping gradually – my thoughts and feelings changed significantly – but it was more – it was like a natural – and it's a complete change of outlook and all of life – all your world, the people around, your job, your relationships – everything suddenly becomes different. Your perception has changed.

(Sussex Partnership, 2014)

Andrew, a 17-year-old student

When he was a 17-year-old student, Andrew spoke of his experiences of having psychosis. He was interviewed by a physician in the presence of his mother, who also responded. Andrew mentions features such as feelings of losing touch with reality:

Me, personally, I had no idea what was going on. It was not like I became angry at something or that something had really happened to me that was emotionally devastating. It was just like I lost touch with reality . . . The reality that I had known was distant and I couldn't communicate . . . At that point I was hearing voices . . . mainly in music. I don't know how to explain it but the song lyrics would change and they would say hateful things, racist things, homophobic things. They would talk about harming people. They would tell me to harm people.

(PBS NewsHour, 2011)

Discussion of personal accounts

The chronological range of the accounts considered

We have now looked at various accounts from sources going back to the seventeenth century. The Reverend Mr. George Trosse ([1714]/1974) describes experiences that occurred in the years 1656 and 1657. John Perceval's memoir (Perceval, [1838 and 1840]/1961) refers to his incarceration in asylums between 1831 and 1834. Nietzsche's 'madness letters' (Nietzsche, [various dates 1861–1869]/1997) were written in 1869. Judge Daniel Schreber's memoir (Schreber, [1903]/1955 and 2000) refers to disorders occurring during 1884–1885 and 1893–1902. Nijinsky's ([1919]/2000) diary was written in early 1919. The experiences of 'Renee' (Séchehaye ([1951]/1970) and the 18-year-old man quoted by Lewis (1967) come from the mid-twentieth century. Twenty-first-century accounts include those by Elyn Saks (2008), the memoir by David Boyles (2004) and, from Internet sources, the experiences of Andrew and Dominic. In summary then, these accounts span a period from the seventeenth century to the present day.

Strengths of first-hand accounts

First-hand accounts of people who have experienced or who are experiencing psychosis have an immediate authority of personal experience. Reports of those who have closely observed them (e.g. relatives or medical personnel) are further removed from the personal experience, and even if we can be confident about their accuracy, they do not seem to carry the same authenticity.

Where the material is generated during a psychotic episode or episodes, as appears to be the case with Nijinsky's diary and with Nietzsche's letters and notes, it seems as close as one is likely to get to the experience of psychosis. Indeed, the material is the very product of psychosis and is assumed to be revealing. Such accounts, however, tend to be written by individuals experiencing active psychosis as opposed to the negative symptoms of schizophrenia. These negative aspects tend to debilitate the individual, diminishing activities, including the possibility of recording one's thoughts and experiences. Memoirs prepared after the psychosis either from contemporary jottings as with Schreber or from memory as with Elyn Saks and others draw on the previous experience and are presented after reflection so as to give a considered and perhaps more rounded picture.

Initially, it might appear that the only sources necessary to begin to understand psychosis are the first-hand accounts of people who have experienced it. On reflection, it becomes clear that individual accounts, like any other source, have, in addition to their obvious strengths, some limitations. It is some of these that we now consider.

Can psychotic states be conveyed 'from the inside'?

A general issue was raised by the French philosopher Jacques Derrida ([various dates and 1967]/1968) in reviewing Michel Foucault's *History of Madness* (Foucault, [1961]/2006). This is the question of whether it is possible to write about madness as it were from the 'inside'. Derrida challenged Foucault's claim to be writing a history of madness in such a way. His point was that if madness is a state in which one cannot distinguish fantasy from reality, how is it possible for a historian of ideas like Foucault (or anyone else) to write about it from within the experience? By extension, if memoirs of madness are produced when the individual not in that state, how is it possible to communicate the psychotic state? Foucault 'wanted to write a history of madness *itself*' (Derrida, [various dates and 1967]/1968, emphasis in the original). He aimed to do this 'by letting madness speak for itself'. He aimed for 'madness speaking on the basis of its own experience' and not 'a history of madness described from within the language of reason'. Yet, for Derrida, this attempt constitutes the 'very infeasibility of his book' (Ibid.).

There may be a parallel (although imperfect) with the task of recounting a dream. Dreaming takes place in a state of semiconsciousness, and attempts are made to recount it in a state of consciousness. We are aware sometimes that we have had a dream but have a feeling that we are merely able to recount it imperfectly or hardly at all.

The shaping of accounts

Any type of personal account and autobiography when recounted has to be shaped and presented in a narrative. Questions arise as to accuracy of memory, perceptiveness of insight, evaluation of experiences and honesty. Issues emerge about the choice of phrases and figures of speech. There are differences according to which form is used, for example letters, a diary or narrative memoir. Autobiographical reflections may vary in the degree to which they coincide with testimonies of the same incidents given by others, making the task of the biographer or anyone else trying to evaluate accounts a subtle one. All these issues apply to narratives written about the experience of psychosis.

In *The Quiet Room*, Lori Schiller (1996) intersperses her personal narrative of psychosis with accounts provided by others: her college roommate, her psychiatrist, her parents and her two brothers. Schiller states, 'In many ways too these people serve as my memory' (Ibid., author's note and acknowledgements, and passim). Extracts from the medical records of the clinic in New York where she was admitted are included (pp. 51–52). Rubin-Rabson ([1951]/1970) expresses reservations about 'personal retrospections of mental illness during periods of remission or recovery'. She finds that their value can be reduced by 'the rampant over dramatisation, the search for appealing literary devices, the defects in recall, and the confusion in sequence' (Ibid., p. v). There is no negative criticism in this of course. It is simply to note that any account, whether first-, second- or third-hand, is likely to be structured and shaped to convey views, feelings and ideas in the most effective way.

Schreber's memoir was written while he was in Sonnenstein Asylum and seems to have been based on jottings made at the peak of his illness (Dinnage, 2000, p. xi). Indeed, Schreber ([1903]/1955 and 2000) states that he started the memoir 'without having publication in mind', the idea of publication only occurring as he 'progressed with it' (Ibid., p. 3). Schreber's memoir, he states, was 'largely unrevised' (p. 4), although the contents of his original chapter 3 concerning other members of his family were subsequently omitted as 'unfit' for publication. The memoir was later translated into English from the original German.

Conveying a personal recollection of schizophrenia may involve consulting others to get the right metaphor or taking account of lessons learned from a 'memoir teacher', as Elyn Saks does with her friend Stephen Behnke (Saks, 2008, p. 311).

The autobiographical account by 'Renee' (Séchehaye ([1951]/1970) is also accompanied by a description by her analyst Marguerite Séchehaye and is further discussed in the later chapter 'Psychoanalysis and beyond'. Rubin-Rabson ([1951]/1970), after voicing reservations about 'personal retrospections of mental illness during periods of remission or recovery', in general finds Renee's account more convincing. This is because the 'retrospections were under control' and the analyst was able to 'verify the manifest behaviour' (Ibid., p. v). Conroy ([1968]/1970), in the foreword, suggests that the book 'proved that a writer could successfully re-create states of consciousness despite his failure to understand those states when they had originally occurred' (Ibid., p. ix). Renee 'attempted to recreate through metaphor and in the simplest possible language, sensations in the mind of the presumably sane reader that were in her mind while she was insane'. She 'writes of scenes and sensations she could not clothe in language even at the time she experienced them' (Ibid.).

Yet there are constraints to the narrative. Séchehaye ([1951]/1970) points out that Renee's 'introspections' represent 'only certain periods of her illness' and that there were 'long periods of hebephrenic catatonia when her confusion made it impossible to register what went on either round or within her' (Ibid., p. xv). The account is 'Renee's intimate story as she recounted it shortly after her recovery' (Ibid., p. 19), but it sometimes appears to be filtered through medical and analytic language which one suspects could come as much from Séchehaye as from Renee. While in the hospital, Renee states, 'The doctor came in and administered two effective hypodermics' (Ibid., p. 76). She elsewhere states that 'a severe attack of pyelonephritis accompanied by agonising renal pain contrived to stimulate the crisis markedly' (p. 82). Visited by 'Mama', Renee makes an arrangement of shoes and a pair of scissors and describes them analytically or symbolically: 'The shoes were to signify departure; their disarray, anger; the string, the tension of unreality; the scissors represented the aggression' (p. 76). Later, she states, 'Through Mama, I have learned to like myself, to achieve the integrity of my ego' (p. 84).

Common threads in personal accounts

If one listens to only one account, it is limiting. One cannot establish what is idiosyncratic to that account and what might be typical of psychosis in general. Schreber reports the experience of 'little devils' on his face. Renee states that she saw others in distorted or gigantic form. Student Andrew speaks of hearing voices in the form of music. John Perceval recounts how his voices issued commands seemingly designed so that he could not know how to correctly fulfil them. Nietzsche wrote notes signed as a Christ figure or a pagan god. Dominic and David Boyles speak of changes in perception. In one respect, these accounts are rich in differences. Yet in another sense, looking at various experiences begins to reveal what is often common to psychosis. The personal accounts that have been looked at suggest that there are some common (although not necessarily universal) experiences of psychosis.

Hearing voices is often mentioned. These voices may be recognised later to have been unreal but at the time are taken as real. They may be thought to come from different parts of the person's own body or may be of dead or living people. The voices may issue commands to do certain things, and the individual may feel compelled to comply, or a cacophony may debate and argue with one another. They may make remarks of a sexual nature or mention other matters that the individual finds distressing. Sometimes it seems possible to distinguish that the voices are not external but exist in the person's head, so to speak, and then there may be a change so that the voices are experienced as clearly external (as seems to be the case in Renee's account).

Visual hallucinations may occur. These may be frightening. The appearance of one's body and face may seem to change or become like something else, perhaps an animal. Other people or one's surroundings may become distorted or change in scale.

Belief of *being controlled by others* may be evident; for example, an individual may be convinced that others (perhaps aliens) are inserting thoughts into his or her mind or are controlling his or her body. Others, it may be believed, can read one's thoughts.

Language may be disjointed, jumping from one topic to another with no apparent connection. This appears to be reflected in the disconnected nature of Nijinsky's diary. He seems to be wrestling to keep some form of control over his account. He attempts this by maintaining brevity and trying to return to a point when he has followed a phonetic link rather than a semantic one.

Odd beliefs may be apparent. These might include the belief that the individual has stayed the same age for many years, can fly or has been contacted by God.

Feelings of persecution may occur. Individuals may believe that others are out to harm them.

Movements may be repetitive or *meaningless* to others. The person may take up the same position (standing or sitting) for hours on end or may assume odd limb postures.

Apathy and self-neglect may be reported. The individual may say very little or be silent for long periods. Loss of interest in activities and neglect of one's appearance may be evident. The person may feel that they are losing contact, including emotional contact, with themselves and their surroundings.

Feelings of being lost in body and mind may be very strong.

Conclusion

Second-hand sources directly quoting patient's speech include Frith and Johnson's (2003) examples, drawing on case material drawn from the Northwick Park study of first episodes of schizophrenia (e.g. Johnstone, Crow, Johnson and MacMillan, 1986).

A memoir written by the Reverend Mr. George Trosse published soon after his death recounts a period of illness which he experienced as a young man (Trosse, [1714]/1974). John Perceval experienced mental disorder and wrote his 'narrative' following his recovery (Perceval, [1838 and 1840]/1961). Nietzsche suffered a mental collapse during which he sent his 'madness letters' to various friends (Nietzsche, [various dates 1861–1869]/1997). Schreber described his mental disorder in great detail in his 'memoir' (Schreber, [1903]/1955 and 2000). Nijinsky, diagnosed with schizophrenia, wrote his diary recording his views of what was happening (Nijinsky, [1919]/1999, 2000).

An autobiographical account by a girl known as 'Renee' (Séchehaye ([1951]/1970) describes her experiences from the age of 5 to adolescence when she experienced mental disorder. Boyles (2004) provides a memoir of his experience of being psychotic. Elyn Saks (2008), a professor of law and psychiatry at the University of California, provides a record of her life with schizophrenia. Lewis (1967) quotes an account written by a young man aged 18 years who had had a condition (apparently schizophrenia) for a year or more. Examples on Internet sites include Dominic, a 'former service user of the Early Intervention in Psychosis Service', describing his experience of psychosis, and Andrew, who, when a 17-year-old student, was interviewed by a physician and spoke of his experiences of having psychosis.

We have considered a range of accounts spanning a period from the seventeenth century to the present day. Among the strengths of first-hand accounts is their authority based on experience. However, there are questions about the extent to which it is possible to convey madness from the 'inside'. Accounts (of any kind) are also shaped, and elements of artifice are unavoidable. Yet from the personal accounts can be seen several common features that begin to add to our understanding of psychosis and schizophrenia.

Thinking points

Readers may wish to consider:

- possible differences between recorded verbal personal accounts, such as video interviews, and written accounts;
- whether a verbal or a written account is likely to be the more authentic.

Note

1 https://archive.org/stream/percevalsnarrati007726mbp#page/n7/mode/2up

Key texts

Boyles, D. C. (2004) *My Punished Mind: A Memoir of Psychosis* Lincoln, NE., iUniverse.
Perceval, J. ([1838 and 1840]/1961) *Perceval's Narrative: A Patient's Account of His Psychosis 1830–1832* Stanford University Press (Edited by G. Bateson), https://archive.org/stream/percevalsnarrati007726mbp#page/n7/mode/2up

Perceval's narrative was originally published in two volumes in 1838 and 1840. Bateson's edited version contains all of the first volume and most of the second.

Saks, E. (2008) *The Center Cannot Hold: My Journey Through Madness* New York, Virago.

Both of these books offer a more modern-day account of psychosis than the historical texts, and both are examples of individuals speaking plainly about their experiences and trying to make sense of them.

Schreber, D. P. ([1903]/1988) *Memoirs of My Nervous Illness* Cambridge MA, Harvard University Press (Edited and Translated from the German by I. Macalpine and R. A. Hunter).

Schreber's detailed narrative has intrinsic interest and was also used by Freud and other writers to interpret the possible underpinnings of psychosis.

4

PSYCHIATRIC TERMINOLOGY

Introduction

A psychiatric view can be gleaned from various sources, including published guidance on the diagnosis of psychoses and related criteria. Psychosis appears in a range of disorders where it may be integral (as with schizophrenia) or associated (as with bipolar I disorder). Terminology linked with psychiatry and psychosis includes medical and scientific language; psychiatric terms in general; psychiatric expressions associated with psychosis; the use of Greek and Latin terminology; and the language of categorisation and classification. Alternative views to those conveyed by psychiatry include ones which represent psychiatry as solely using a 'medical model'; propose continua and similarities between psychosis and everyday experiences; and which take a relativist view of psychosis.

Psychiatry and a psychiatric view

Until the twentieth century, practitioners of the new discipline that would become psychiatry were known as 'alienists' because they treated 'mental alienation' (Shorter, 1997, p. 17). It was only in 1808 that the word 'psychiatry' was first coined (as '*psychiatrie*' in German) by the physician Johan Christian Reil (1759–1813). Derived from the Greek, the new word combined '*psukhē*', meaning 'soul or mind', and '*iatreia*', indicating 'healing' (the Greek for 'healer' being '*iatros*'). In the middle of the nineteenth century, the expression 'psychiatry' became increasingly used as the discipline developed. For example, German psychiatrist Emil Kraepelin (1856–1926) called the first edition of his influential overview of the area published in 1883 a *Compendium of Psychiatry*.

In contemporary thinking, disorders in general are 'a complex interaction of biological, psychological, cultural and socio-political factors' (Shakespeare, 2006,

p. 38). Similarly, in understanding mental disorders, a psychiatric view is likely to take account of biological factors, including genetic evidence, brain functioning and brain chemistry, as well as the influence of social and psychological factors. The relative importance of all these is judged from evidence available. From a psychiatric perspective, administering medication is not the inevitable response to mental disorder, including psychosis.

For example, referring to schizophrenia, the *Diagnostic and Statistical Manual of Mental Disorders, Fifth Edition* (hereafter, *DSM-5*) (American Psychiatric Association, 2013) includes among its discussion of 'risk and prognostic factors' the season of birth and growing up in an urban environment (Ibid., p. 103). Diagnostic issues include 'culture and socio-economic factors' (Ibid.). It is recognised that ideas that appear delusional, such as witchcraft, in one culture may be 'commonly held' in another, and phenomena such as hearing God's voice, which may be considered odd in certain circles, are in some societies a 'normal part of religious experience' (Ibid.).

In *DSM-5*, evidence of a high degree of impairment is part of the assessment criteria for schizophrenia. For a 'significant time' from the start of the disturbance, in one or more areas such as work, self-care or interpersonal relations, the 'level of functioning is . . . markedly below the level achieved prior to the onset'. If the disorder started in childhood or adolescence, assessment includes evidence that there is a 'failure to achieve expected levels of interpersonal, academic or occupational functioning' (American Psychiatric Association, 2013, p. 103). Regarding the development or 'course' of schizophrenia, there is no presumption that the condition is static or that symptoms will not diminish. For example, it is recognised that 'the predictors of course and outcome are largely unexplained, and course and outcome may not be reliably predicted' (American Psychiatric Association, 2013, p. 102).

Generally, *DSM-5* uses the expression 'disorder' to refer to various conditions. For instance, there is reference to 'delusional disorder', 'brief psychotic disorder', 'schizophreniform disorder', 'schizoaffective disorder', 'substance/medication-induced psychotic disorder', 'psychotic disorder due to another medical condition' and 'schizotypal personality disorder' (American Psychiatric Association, 2013, pp. 97–118). Schizophrenia is discussed in terms of 'disturbance' and 'disorder' (Ibid., p. 99). Sometimes a condition is referred to as an 'illness'. For example, schizoaffective disorder (pp. 105–110), although described at one point as a 'disturbance' (criterion D), is also discussed as an 'uninterrupted period of illness' (criterion A), and mention is made of 'the active and residual portions of the illness' (criterion C) (pp. 105–106).

Some sources view schizophrenia unequivocally as an illness or a disease. Kasper and Papadimitriou (2009) state, 'Schizophrenia, as a disease, and as a field of study, is shrouded with a large number of misunderstandings', and 'in general, patients with schizophrenia are overwhelmed by the complexity of the problems emerging with the disease'. They add, 'Schizophrenia is a disease of the brain, and it is worthwhile to emphasise that it is a real (physical) disease like diabetes, epilepsy and high blood pressure'. Their concern where schizophrenia is not treated as a disease is clear. They argue that 'in the medical community, schizophrenia is sometimes not viewed with the same methodological rigour like the latter diseases'. The authors contrast views about schizophrenia to those towards diabetes, epilepsy and high blood pressure, stating that there is 'less tolerance and understanding in the society when someone suffers from schizophrenia'. Citing community studies, Kasper and Papadimitriou (2009) point out that these reveal that 'a number of people think that schizophrenia is not a real disease'. Instead, it is incorrectly seen as 'more related to an irritable personality as a result of trauma in early life or the result of an unfavourable social environment' (Ibid., p. xiii).

However, in *DSM-5* psychoses are not described as 'diseases' either of the brain or anything else. There is no mention of the conditions being 'cured' or of them being 'incurable'. Views about whether psychosis and related conditions should be considered as an 'illness' or a 'disease' are further discussed in a later chapter on 'Anti-psychiatry'. Further discussion of the *DSM-5* definition may be found elsewhere (e.g. Torrey, 2013, pp. 58–74).

Psychiatric definition of psychoses

Key features that define psychotic disorders are:

1   Delusions;
2   Hallucinations;
3   Disorganised speech;
4   Grossly disorganised or catatonic behaviour;
5   Negative symptoms (American Psychiatric Association, 2013, p. 99).

Delusions are rigid beliefs that are 'not amenable to change in the light of conflicting evidence' (Ibid., p. 87). Delusions of persecution are most common. Other typical delusions are 'referential' ones in which a person believes that certain comments or environmental cues are directed at them. With grandiose delusions, the individual may incorrectly believe that they are famous, fabulously wealthy or possess exceptional ability. 'Bizarre' delusions might include that of 'thought withdrawal', in which an outside force is believed to have removed the person's thoughts. Other examples are 'thought insertion', in which the individual believes that alien thoughts have been inserted into his or her mind, and 'delusions of control', in which it is held that one's body or actions are being operated by an outside force (Ibid.).

Hallucinations are involuntary 'perception-like experiences' but they occur without an external stimulus (Ibid.). While they may be in any sensory mode, the most common in schizophrenia are auditory hallucinations. These are usually voices which may be familiar or unfamiliar and which are perceived as 'distinct from' the individuals' own thoughts (Ibid.).

Disorganised speech is taken as an indication of disorganised thinking. The individual may switch from one topic to another or respond to questions in an only partially related or unrelated way. Disorganisation is generally so severe as to substantially impair communication (Ibid., p. 88).

Grossly disorganised or abnormal motor behaviour can include 'unpredictable agitation' and problems in carrying out goal-directed actions. Catatonic behaviour refers to a significant decrease in reactions to one's surroundings. For example, the person may retain a rigid posture for long periods. By contrast, 'catatonic excitement', which can also occur, refers to excessive motor activity without any apparent cause (Ibid., p. 88).

'Negative symptoms' include reduced emotional expression, such as that reflected in facial expression, eye contact and flat speech. Other negative symptoms are 'avolition', a decline in 'motivated self-initiated purposeful activities'; 'alogia', or diminished speech output; and 'anhedonia', which is a reduced ability to experience pleasure from positive experiences (Ibid., p. 88).

For several psychotic disorders including schizoaffective disorder, assessments are made of cognition, depression and mania in order to make distinctions between them (American Psychiatric Association, 2013, p. 107).

Psychosis in disorders

Disorders with which psychosis is fundamental or associated

Having outlined characteristics of psychosis, we can now look at a range of conditions in which psychotic disorder is fundamental or with which it is associated. *DSM-5* (American Psychiatric Association, 2013) provides diagnostic criteria for several psychotic disorders grouped as 'schizophrenia spectrum and other psychotic disorders' in which psychosis is integral (Ibid., pp. 87–122). These include 'schizophrenia', 'delusional disorder', 'brief psychotic disorder', 'schizophreniform disorder', 'schizoaffective disorder', 'substance/medication-induced psychotic disorder', 'psychotic disorder due to another medical condition' and 'catatonia'. 'Schizotypal personality disorder' is listed with these other psychotic disorders and is fully described in the *DSM-5* chapter on 'personality disorders'.

Other disorders too can be associated with psychotic episodes. Psychotic features can be found in 'major depressive disorder' and 'persistent depressive disorder' (American Psychiatric Association, 2013, pp. 155–188). 'Bipolar I disorder' and 'bipolar II disorder' can also include psychotic features (Ibid., pp. 123–154).

Schizophrenia

Criteria for schizophrenia are categorised A through F. Criterion A will serve as an example to indicate some key aspects. It specifies that two or more of five possible features must be present for a 'significant period of time' during a period of one month. This period may be less if the condition is successfully treated. The five features are those of psychosis generally: delusions, hallucinations, disorganised speech, grossly disorganised or catatonic behaviour and negative symptoms (American Psychiatric Association, 2013, p. 99). At least one of the features must be delusions, hallucinations or disorganised speech.

PAUSE FOR REFLECTION: *DSM-5* CHANGES

Search the Internet for the video 'APA 2013 Psychosis Chapter in DSM-5' (www.md-fm.com/apa-2013-psychosis-chapter-in-dsm-5_vn_63.html).

What changes were made to the criteria for schizophrenia in *DSM-5* compared with previous versions?

What reasons are given for why these changes were made?

Delusional disorder

In delusional disorder, one or more delusions are present and persist for a month or more (American Psychiatric Association, 2013, p. 90). Delusions may be of different types. In 'erotomanic' ones, the person may falsely believe that someone else is in love with him or her. Grandiose types involve being convinced that one has a great but unrecognised talent. There may be jealous or persecutory delusions or somatic ones involving sensations or functions of the body, such as insect infestation (Ibid., pp. 90–92, paraphrased). However, in delusional disorder, a key criterion for schizophrenia is not evident (i.e. that any hallucinations are not prominent, and they relate to the theme of the delusion).

Brief psychotic disorder

Brief psychotic disorder (American Psychiatric Association, 2013, pp. 94–96) involves the presence of one or more of four symptoms. The first three are delusions, hallucinations and disorganised speech, and the individual must experience at least one of these. Behaviour that is 'grossly disorganised or catatonic' is the fourth criterion (Ibid., p. 94). It is specified that episodes last at least a day but less than a month before the person resumes his or her previous levels of functioning.

Schizophreniform disorder

For schizophreniform disorder (American Psychiatric Association, 2013, pp. 96–99), the criteria involve the presence of two or more of five symptoms. As with brief psychotic disorder, the first three are delusions, hallucinations and disorganised speech, and the individual must experience at least one of these. The fourth criterion is behaviour that is 'grossly disorganised or catatonic' (Ibid., p. 96). The fifth criterion is 'negative symptoms', or a reduction in emotional expression or 'avolition' (a diminution in the power of using one's will, deciding, choosing or resolving on a certain course of action). An episode lasts at least a month but less than six months (Ibid., p. 97).

In fact, the characteristics of schizophreniform disorder (criterion A) are the same as those for schizophrenia. Duration is a key difference, being intermediate between that for brief psychosis (more than a day and less than a month) and schizophrenia (at least six months). While social or occupational functioning may be impaired, this is not a necessary requirement for the diagnosis (Ibid., p. 98).

Schizoaffective disorder

In schizoaffective disorder (American Psychiatric Association, 2013, pp. 105–110), there is an 'uninterrupted period of illness' in which there is a 'major mood episode'. This mood episode may be 'major depressive' or 'manic'. At some time during this period, criterion A for schizophrenia is present. There are also 'delusion or hallucinations for 2 or more weeks in the absence of a major episode (depressive or manic) during the lifetime duration of the illness'. The symptoms that meet the criteria for a 'major mood episode' are present for most of the whole duration of the 'active and residual portions of the illness' (Ibid., pp. 105–106).

It is recognised that evidence increasingly indicates that schizoaffective disorder is not 'a distinctive nosological category' (Ibid., p. 90). Accordingly, it is considered important that clinicians consider 'dimensional assessments' of depression and mania with regard to all psychotic disorders and that these will alert them to 'mood pathology' and the need to treat it 'where appropriate' (Ibid.).

Substance/medication-induced psychotic disorder

With regard to substance/medication-induced psychotic disorder (American Psychiatric Association, 2013, pp. 110–115), either delusions or hallucinations (or both) are present. Additionally, there is evidence that these symptoms developed 'during or soon after' intoxication with a substance or withdrawal from it or after 'exposure to' a medication that is capable of producing delusions or hallucinations. The disturbance causes 'clinically significant distress or impairment' in important areas of functioning, such as social or occupational ones (Ibid., p. 110). Importantly, hallucinations that the person realises are substance or medication induced are not included (pp. 112–113).

Psychotic disorder due to another medical condition

Psychotic disorder may be due to another medical condition (American Psychiatric Association, 2013, pp. 115–118). These include Huntington's disease (an inherited condition involving the loss of brain cells), epilepsy, nerve injury (auditory or visual) and hypoxia (oxygen deprivation). Other implicated medical conditions concern the thyroid gland, which produces the thyroxine hormones: hyperthyroidism refers to an overactive thyroid, while hypothyroidism designates an underactive thyroid gland (Ibid., p. 117). In such instances, hallucinations or delusions are prominent, and there is evidence that the disturbance is a direct consequence of another medical condition (p. 115).

Catatonia

Catatonia (American Psychiatric Association, 2013, pp. 119–121) involves the occurrence of three or more of a range of twelve symptoms. These include stupor, catalepsy (in which a posture is rigidly held), opposition (or no response) to instructions, stereotyped behaviour, echolalia (where another person's speech is copied) and echopraxia (in which another person's movements are mimicked) (Ibid., p. 119). Catatonia can occur within the context of another mental disorder (e.g. schizophrenia, major depressive disorder or bipolar disorder) or can be due to another medical condition (Ibid.).

In addition to the conditions and manifestations of psychosis already described, other disorders may have associated psychotic features, as discussed next.

Personality disorders: schizotypal personality disorder

In *DSM-5* (American Psychiatric Association, 2013) 'schizotypal personality disorder' is listed in the chapter concerning 'Schizophrenia Spectrum and Other Psychotic Disorders' and described more fully in a chapter on 'Personality Disorders'. An essential feature is a 'pervasive pattern of social and interpersonal deficits' (Ibid., p. 656). This affects close relationships because the individual's capacity for these is reduced and he or she feels considerable discomfort about them. Perceptions and thinking may be distorted and behaviour may have eccentricities. Appearing in early adulthood, this set of behaviours is shown in different contexts (Ibid., paraphrased).

Among the diagnostic criteria for this disorder are that individuals may incorrectly interpret events as having a particular meaning for them. However, these ideas are not held with delusional certainty. The person may be overoccupied with paranormal phenomena or hold superstitious beliefs that are at odds with their subculture, for example believing that they have magical power over others. Furthermore, the individual may have 'unusual perceptual experiences', such as hearing a voice say their name (Ibid.). (Other personality disorders include 'schizoid personality disorder' and 'paranoid personality disorder', neither of which occurs exclusively during schizophrenia.)

Depressive disorders: major depression and persistent depressive disorder

Major depressive disorder (American Psychiatric Association, 2013, pp. 160–168) occurs with psychotic features that are 'mood congruent' or 'mood incongruent' and catatonia may also be present (Ibid., p. 162). Persistent depressive disorder (pp. 168–171) can also be accompanied by mood-congruent or mood-incongruent psychotic features (p. 169).

The psychotic features involve delusions and/or hallucinations. Regarding mood-congruent psychotic features, the content of all the hallucinations and delusions are 'consistent with' the usual depressive themes. These are 'personal inadequacy, guilt, disease, death, nihilism, or deserved punishment'. In the case of mood-incongruent psychotic features, the content of delusions and hallucinations either lacks such content or is a mixture of mood-congruent and mood-incongruent themes (p. 186).

Bipolar disorders I and II

Bipolar I disorder (American Psychiatric Association, 2013, pp. 123–132) represents a contemporary comprehension of 'the classic manic depressive disorder or affective psychosis described in the nineteenth century' (Ibid., p. 133). However, neither psychosis nor the 'lifetime experience of a major depressive episode' is a requirement (p. 123). There is provision though for physicians and others to record when bipolar I disorder occurs with 'mood-congruent' or 'mood-incongruent' psychotic features and with catatonia (p. 127).

Bipolar II disorder (American Psychiatric Association, 2013, pp. 132–139) involves 'the lifetime experience of at least one episode of major depression and at least one hypomanic episode' (Ibid., p. 123). It can be associated with 'mood-congruent' or 'mood-incongruent' psychotic features and with catatonia (p. 135).

PAUSE FOR REFLECTION: RESEARCH AND *DSM-5*

Search the Internet for the video 'DSM-5: An Overview from APA's New President' (www.youtube.com/watch?v=m7RCgCkrXXo).

What reference is made to scientific research?

What is the relevance of such research to the development of *DSM* in its various iterations?

Terminology associated with psychiatry and psychosis

Medical and scientific terminology

Medicine combines the use of scientifically based evidence with a physician's social and personal skills to elicit information from a patient, enabling judgements to be formed about diagnosis and possible treatment. Psychiatry as a branch of medicine takes a similar approach. Given the scientific element of medicine and psychiatry, it is to be expected that the language of psychiatry has a scientific basis. Definitions of mental disorders, the notions of diagnosis, causal factors, prevalence and incidence and treatment all reflect such a scientific stance.

Indeed, medical terminology is typical of psychiatric discussions of psychosis and schizophrenia. Expressions such as 'prevalence and incidence', 'development and course', 'risk factors' or 'aetiology' and 'treatment' are synonymous with terms used to refer to physical illnesses. This may be resisted by those who consider that psychosis and schizophrenia are not illnesses, because illness is usually taken to refer to physical problems with known physical causes.

Psychiatric terms in general

Some broad psychiatric terms convey clearly what the disorder is in plain language. Examples are 'hoarding disorder', 'acute stress disorder' and 'illness anxiety disorder'. These terms may require elaborating, and the severity level at which they are considered problematic might need to be specified. But essentially the nature of the disorder is apparent from the language used. Sometimes medical-sounding words are employed where there is a simple equivalent, as with 'trichotillomania' (hair-pulling disorder) and 'excoriation disorder' (skin picking).

In yet other instances, while unusual expressions are used, they differ from apparent equivalents in everyday language. For example, at first sight is seems difficult to justify speaking of 'bulimia nervosa' when there is an alternative plain-language phrase: 'binge eating disorder'. But unlike binge eating disorder, with bulimia nervosa the individual adopts inappropriate compensatory behaviour to prevent weight gain, for example self-induced vomiting and the misuse of laxatives. This has implications for treatments and prognosis so that the use of a technical term to indicate this is considered justified.

Psychiatric terms associated with psychosis

When we turn to examples of expressions relating to psychosis, a similar picture emerges to that of psychiatric terms in general. Plain language may be used. Knowing what delusions are tends to make it clear what 'delusional disorder' is. Similarly, what 'major depressive disorder' is likely to mean is fairly apparent. Regarding 'bipolar disorder', the idea of there being two poles or extremes of experience is clearly conveyed. Once the meaning of 'psychosis' is understood, it becomes evident what 'brief psychotic disorder' or 'substance/medication-induced psychotic disorder' probably means. Certainly, the more exact nature of the conditions may need to be more fully explored, but the terms themselves give a fair orientation.

Sometimes it seems that medical-sounding words are used where there is a simple equivalent. It can be argued that terms such as 'schizophrenia' could be replaced by something like 'fragmented personality' or that a substitute for 'psychosis' might be 'being out of touch with reality'. Such expressions as initial alternatives might give the gist of the psychiatric alternative. However, at some point the detail that is conveyed by the psychiatric terms is necessary. Generally, then, where unusual psychiatric expressions are used, they differ in meaning from apparent plain-language equivalents.

Greek and Latin origins

As discussed in the chapter on historical terms, 'schizophrenia' was coined by Bleuler ([1911]/1950) as the German word '*Schizophrenie*' and was derived from the Greek '*skhizein*', meaning 'to split', and '*phren*', meaning in this context 'mind'. This has led to similar naming of various disorders using the Greek '*skhizein*'. Examples are 'schizotypal personality disorder', which combines the notion of 'split' with 'type' but conveys little of what the disorder might be. With 'schizophreniform disorder', the combination is of Greek '*skhizein*' with the Greek '*phren*', conveying 'mind', and the Latin '*forma*', meaning 'form'. 'Schizoaffective disorder' includes the idea of affect or emotion being involved. The Greek '*cata*', meaning 'down', and '*tonos*', referring to 'tone', led to the use of the term '*katatoia*' and later the medical Latin 'catatonia'.

Although it is difficult to envisage good alternatives to terms associated with psychosis, it is important to recognise their origins in Greek and Latin terms associated with medicine, which can give an exaggerated impression of their exactitude. In fact, great care is needed to clinically distinguish different disorders. For example, delusional disorder has to be identified as different from 'psychotic disorder due to another medical condition' and 'substance/medication-induced psychotic disorder' by gathering evidence that the delusions are brought about by the other medical condition or by the medicine or substance in question (American Psychiatric Association, 2013, p. 93).

Categorisation and classification

The notion that categories can be useful (a neo-Kraepelian perspective) is represented in the past, for example, by American psychiatrist Gerald Klerman (1978) and it is carried forward in guidance such as *DSM-5* (American Psychiatric Association, 2013, passim). Essentially, the view is that there is a boundary between wellness and illness, that discrete mental disorders can be identified and that research effort should be put into improving the validity and reliability of classification and of diagnoses.

Certainly, categorising and naming is a staple of a scientific approach. In psychiatry, classification involves taking from a large group – say, of the general population – smaller groups differentiated according to defined qualities or attributes. Identification is typified by allocating individuals to the subgroups that make up the classification, thus 'operationalising' the definitions that arise from the classification. The process of diagnosis applies the operational definitions to individuals to decide membership in one or several groupings. Critical is the validity and reliability of these groupings. If the grouping is valid, it covers that which it is expected to and is supposed to. If the grouping is reliable, it consistently comprises the defining qualities. Furthermore, good classifications help communication, for example between parents and various professionals. Suitable classification has practical implications, such as when the identification of a condition affects provision and outcomes. (For a discussion concerning intellectual disabilities, please also see Richards, Brady and Taylor, 2014, pp. 38–62.)

Some maintain that there is no boundary between mental wellness and mental disorder, proposing a continuum of mental states rather than a categorical difference. It may be pointed out that certain individuals have hallucinations even though they do not have mental disorder. Others have weird beliefs, such as aliens abducting earthlings, but are not necessarily considered psychotic. Such considerations lead some commentators to prefer a non-Kraepelinian approach. This approach eschews boundaries between mental health and mental illness, claims that there are no discrete mental illnesses and maintains that categorical diagnoses insufficiently define the nature of psychological complaints (e.g. Bentall, 2003, p. 143, Table 6.1). Some observers maintain that the divisions between 'madness' and 'sanity' are blurred, again suggesting a continuum. Scull (2011) argues that boundaries between 'madness and malingering' and between 'insanity and eccentricity' are unclear. He suggests that modern psychiatry attempts to 'obfuscate and obscure the existence of continuing profound uncertainties about how to establish the boundaries between the mad and the sane' (Ibid., p. 2).

Various criticisms of *DSM-5* (American Psychiatric Association, 2013) classifications are made by Nemeroff, Weinberger, Rutter and colleagues (2013). In his contribution, Rutter maintains that there are far too many categories 'for any clinician to remember the criteria for each', while the co-occurrence of diagnoses is 'unacceptably high'. He argues that 'growing evidence' of a lack of distinctiveness between some diagnoses is ignored. While future research findings pertinent to classifications might lead to 'modifications in the classification', Rutter suggests that it is unclear who will decide when and how this is necessary.

Relatedly, criticisms have been made that the category of schizophrenia is not reliable or stable enough to ensure secure identification (Bentall, 2003, pp. 44–47). In response to such criticisms, a judgement has to be made as to whether they justify abandoning the category or whether it requires modification as further research and information is gathered. The view of psychiatry in general is the latter one, while recognising that categorisation has limitations and is a 'best-fit' approach. Also when evidence indicates problems, this needs to be recognised, as with schizoaffective disorder, for which *DSM-5* notes growing evidence that it is not 'a distinctive nosological category' (American Psychiatric Association, 2013, p. 90).

Challenges relating to apparently straightforward terms

Despite the apparent precision of some terms, there are still challenges in the approaches that they might suggest. An example is the concepts of 'prevalence' and 'incidence' and how these are determined. At face value, it appears that these terms and the findings relating to them will directly help to establish how common psychosis or schizophrenia is. It soon becomes clear however that matters are not straightforward.

Regarding disorders, 'prevalence' refers to the number of people experiencing the condition present in a defined population at a specified time or over a specified period of time. 'Point prevalence' is the number of people who were experiencing the symptoms (who were ill) on a particular day. 'One year prevalence' concerns the number of people ill at any time during a specified year. 'Lifetime prevalence' refers to all those people who have experienced the disorder during their lifetime (Tsuang and Tohen, 2002). Importantly, prevalence rates can give planners of services and those allocating finances a cross-sectional picture of the impact of diseases and disorders on a population at a specific time (Goldner, Hsu, Waraich and colleagues, 2002). But clearly, the type of prevalence has to be specified and understood, as they each show different aspects of the impact of the conditions.

But further challenges arise. Where reviews involving prevalence are comprehensive, they are likely to reach back to earlier studies. However, definitions (e.g. of schizophrenia) have been modified over time. Also in different pieces of research, the method of population sampling has differed. One finds such complications in a comprehensive review published by the World Health Organization (Warner and de Girolamo, 1995). It examined 130 studies from all parts of the world conducted after 1931 and found almost differences of almost twenty-fold between studies. Surveys reporting point prevalence and prevalence up to one year varied from 0.09% to 1.74% (Ibid.). More recent reviews have defined their criteria for inclusion in (and exclusion from) the review more tightly in order to draw on more consistent methodologies allowing the different studies to be compared (Bromet, Drew and Eaton, 2002).

Wancata, Freidl and Unger (2009) give the best estimates for one-year prevalence for schizophrenia disorders as 0.60 (range 0.36–0.91) and for schizophrenia as 0.34 (range 0.22–0.50). Best estimates for lifetime prevalence for schizophrenia disorders is 1.45 (range 0.8–2.37) and for schizophrenia as 0.55 (range 0.37–0.80). They explore this topic further regarding both prevalence and incidence. The main point to be made here is that where figures for prevalence for a disorder or group of disorders is provided it can appear more exact and settled than in fact it is. Subtleties of the different types of prevalence and the differences and similarities of the studies that fall under the remit of the review all need to be taken into account.

Alternative views

Representations of a 'medical model'

Discussions about disorders have sometimes been polarised between a largely individual 'within person' view and a predominantly social (and socially constructed) view of disability (Farrell, 2010, 2012). Critics of the scientific leanings of psychiatry sometimes use the term 'medical model' to convey a perceived overemphasis on individual 'within person' factors. Sometimes the term 'illness' model is used (e.g.

Read and Dillon, 2013). By contrast, a 'social model' focuses more on environmental factors in relation to mental disorders. (In the present text, a social approach is discussed further in the chapter on 'Advocacy'.) Some representations depict a medical model as unbendingly biological, simplistic and outdated. Indeed, commentators sometimes refer to what they are describing as the 'medical model' in just these terms.

Campbell (2010) speaks of his gradual disillusionment with a 'medical model' which placed 'an emphasis on distress' and encouraged 'a resort to exclusively physical treatments'. For him, it encouraged a view that 'having a chronic and *incurable illness*' took away 'power of agency' and confined him 'within an essentially negative category'. He states that the model lacked the 'capacity to encompass the complexity of my interior or exterior life and give it positive value' (Ibid., emphasis added).

Sally Edwards (quoted in Cooke, 2014, p. 69) speaks of joining a self-help group where she was introduced to others. She states that these people 'accepted my experiences as part of who I am and not part of a *medical illness*'. Edwards adds, 'I didn't believe I was a psychiatric patient with a *lifelong brain disease* any more, but an overcomer of childhood sexual abuse, an activist for change in the current system that is based on an *outdated medical model*' (Ibid., emphasis added).

A report *Understanding Psychosis and Schizophrenia* describes the 'medical model' as 'the assumption that experiences such as hearing voices indicate illness and result from some sort of problem with the brain' (Cooke, 2014, p. 103, 13.1). The report suggests that when difficult decisions have to be made, it is 'tempting to rely on a *simplistic medical model*: "this person has no insight into their illness so they need to be detained and *administered medication*, by force if necessary"' (Ibid., emphasis added). An alternative is for professionals to 'support people in whatever way they personally find most helpful' (Ibid). Relatedly, the pros and cons of drugs might be represented differently from those of psychological approaches. The report states that 'service users and their supporters have the right to information about the pros, cons, possible adverse effects ('side-effects') and evidence base for any medication that is offered' (Ibid., p. 108, section 13.3.3). However, it adds that psychological help 'should be available to all, as should help for family members who support people experiencing psychosis' (Ibid., p. 108, section 13.3.2).

Continua and similarities between psychosis and everyday experiences

As already touched on earlier, some commentators maintain that experiences of all kinds lie on a continuum, making it difficult or even impossible to distinguish between them. The *Understanding Psychosis and Schizophrenia* report takes such a view, stating that 'there is no clear dividing line between "psychosis" and other thoughts, feelings and beliefs' (Cooke, 2014, p. 6, Executive Summary). It continues, 'there is no dividing line between "psychosis" and "normality". There is no "us" and "them" – we're all in this together' (Ibid., p. 113, section 14.1). The report argues that 'there appears to be a continuum (a continuous line) between good and poor mental health that we all move up and down along at different points in our lives' (p. 18, section 3.1). Discussing 'hearing voices', it suggests that, 'as with other psychological problems, it makes sense to think of experiences like hearing voices in terms of a continuum' (p. 17, section 3, key points).

Those considering categories of disorders to be useful might question the continuum view. It might be argued that black and white are on a continuum and when dealing with shades of grey it may be difficult to distinguish them. But this does not lead to a conclusion that black and white cannot be usefully distinguished. A central question is not whether phenomena might be arranged on a continuum, but whether distinctions are possible, and if so, whether they are justifiable.

In addition to commentators proposing a continuum of experience, it can also be suggested that psychosis and everyday experience are similar. Discussing 'thought disorder', the *Understanding Psychosis and Schizophrenia* report states, 'Many of us become somewhat "thought disordered" and say confused or confusing things when we are emotionally stressed' (Cooke, 2014, pp. 10–11, 1.1). Regarding 'hearing voices', it adds, 'Many people experience them occasionally or to a minor degree, for example at times of stress, whereas for others they are more intense, enduring and/or distressing' (Ibid., p. 17, section 3, key points). The report goes on:

> Many of us hear voices occasionally, or have fears or beliefs that those around us do not share. Given enough stress, for any of us these experiences might shade into psychosis. Sometimes what constitutes 'psychosis' is in the eye of the beholder.
>
> *(Ibid., p. 113, section 14.1)*

It describes delusions as 'unusual beliefs' that are 'very similar to other beliefs or prejudices' (Ibid., p. 47). The report maintains that delusions involve 'holding strong beliefs that others around you do not share', for example 'a belief that there is a conspiracy against you by the CIA, or that someone else is controlling your thoughts' (Ibid., p. 10, 1.1).

Arising from such comments is the question, 'are symptoms of psychosis similar to what most people experience or are they different in degree'? It may be suggested that the thought disorder associated with psychosis is like getting mixed up when we are 'emotionally stressed' (Cooke, 2014, pp. 10–11, 1.1). Yet those taking a categorical view would argue that thought disorder (inferred from disorganised speech) involves a level of disorganisation that is generally 'so severe as to substantially impair communication' (American Psychiatric Association, 2013, p. 107). Delusions might be equated with 'holding strong beliefs that others around you do not share' (Ibid., p. 10, 1.1). Yet it can be argued that delusions as defined in psychiatry are not just unusual beliefs but 'fixed beliefs that are not amenable to change in the light of conflicting evidence' (American Psychiatric Association, 2013, p. 87). Unusual beliefs may sometimes overlap with delusional ones, but central differences are still apparent. Holding strongly held conservative or Republican views when in a group of socialists or Democrats is an example of 'holding strong beliefs that others around you do not share'. Believing 'that there is a conspiracy against you by the CIA' is something rather different. Other indications of psychosis are even harder to present as very similar to ordinary experience and behaviour. Examples are where catatonia involves staying in a 'rigid posture for long periods' or where 'negative symptoms' involve a decline in 'motivated self-initiated purposeful activities' (American Psychiatric Association, 2013, p. 88).

Presenting a relativist view of psychosis

In seeking to challenge a 'traditional' view of psychosis (and schizophrenia) as an 'illness' that might be 'treated primarily by medication' (Cooke, 2014, p. 5, Foreword), a relativist view of psychosis might be taken. In the *Understanding Psychosis and Schizophrenia* report, the words 'psychosis' and 'schizophrenia' are often put in quotation marks perhaps to show that the reference is not to something real that is called psychosis but that it is only a term (Ibid.). The report suggests that, regarding hearing voices, calling them, 'symptoms of mental illness, psychosis, or schizophrenia is only one way of thinking about them' (Cooke, 2014, p. 6, Executive Summary). It states that

> people often assume that mental illnesses 'exist' in the same way that broken bones exist and can be revealed by medical tests in the same way. However, there are many different theories as to what causes experiences such as hearing voices. The idea that they are symptoms of illness, perhaps caused by some sort of chemical imbalance or other problem in the brain, is just one of the theories.
> *(Cooke, 2014, p. 17, section 3, Introduction)*

Yet such a perspective seems to suggest that if there are different views of psychosis, one should not consider if there is evidence from observation or research that one view is more accurate (or more in line with the evidence) than another. Instead, one should accept that everyone might have a different view and no one person's view is any better than another's. To say that 'some people' say this or that avoids judgement and evaluation about what is said. Regarding psychosis a key issue is the question, 'what evidence is there that one view or the other is correct?' A scientific approach is interested in such matters, while a relativist view can appear to simply accept the range of opinions. The explanation that psychosis relates to some 'problem in the brain' so long as that problem is specified can be tested and found to be correct or incorrect. It is not 'just another theory' in that sense. Attempted explanations can be judged to be correct or accurate or at least plausible to different degrees. They are not solely based pragmatically on just what 'some people' find a helpful way to think about things.

Conclusion

Contemporary psychiatry sees mental disorders as influenced by biological, environmental and other factors. It is not inevitably assumed that administering medication is the sole response to mental disorders. Also, assessment criteria for schizophrenia specify that level of functioning is 'markedly impaired' (American Psychiatric Association, 2013). There is no presumption that schizophrenia is static over time or that symptoms will remain. Generally, *DSM-5* uses the expression 'disorder' and occasionally 'illness'. It does not describe psychoses as 'diseases' nor mention the conditions being 'cured' or being 'incurable' (Ibid.).

In *DSM-5*, psychotic disorders are characterised by delusions, hallucinations, disorganised speech, grossly disorganised or catatonic behaviour and negative symptoms (American Psychiatric Association, 2013). For several psychotic disorders, including schizoaffective disorder, assessments are made of cognition, depression and mania to make distinctions between them. *DSM-5* provides diagnostic criteria for several psychotic disorders grouped as 'schizophrenia spectrum and other psychotic disorders'. These include 'schizophrenia', 'delusional disorder', 'brief psychotic disorder', 'schizophreniform disorder', 'schizoaffective disorder', 'substance/medication-induced psychotic disorder', 'psychotic disorder due to another medical condition', 'catatonia' and 'schizotypal personality disorder'. Other disorders can be associated with psychotic episodes. Psychotic features can be found in 'major depressive disorder' and 'persistent depressive disorder'. 'Bipolar disorder I and II' can include psychotic features (Ibid).

Definitions of mental disorders, the notions of diagnosis, causal factors, prevalence and incidence and treatment all reflect a scientific stance. Expressions relating to psychosis may be in plain language, and where medical-sounding words are used there may be no exact everyday-language equivalent. Expressions relating to psychosis are founded in Greek and Latin terms associated with medicine, which can give an exaggerated impression of the exactitude of terms and their application.

The neo-Kraepelian use of categories implies a boundary between wellness and illness, that there are several discrete mental disorders and that research should help to improve the validity and reliability of diagnoses and classification. An alternative view is of a continuum with no discrete mental illnesses. However, suitable classifications can help communication, for example between individuals affected by mental disorder and various professionals, while identifying conditions has implications for provision and outcomes. *DSM-5* has been criticised for having too many categories. But psychiatry tends to value categorisation, while recognising its limitations as a 'best-fit' approach. Despite the apparent precision of some terms, there are still challenges. Figures for prevalence for disorders can appear more precise and settled than they in fact are, obscuring the different types of prevalence and the variations in the studies in any review.

Views of disorders are sometimes polarised between a largely individual 'within person' perspective and a predominantly social and socially constructed view (Farrell, 2010, 2012). Critics of the scientific leanings of psychiatry see a 'medical model' as overemphasising individual, 'within person' factors and as unbendingly biological, simplistic and outdated (Campbell, 2010; Cooke, 2014). By contrast, a 'social model' focuses more on environmental factors.

It may be maintained that 'there is no clear dividing line between "psychosis" and other thoughts, feelings and beliefs' (Cooke, 2014). For those taking a categorical view of disorders, the question is whether, even if there is a continuum, distinctions are possible and justifiable. Similarities can be suggested between psychosis and everyday experience, for example that the thought disorder associated with psychosis is like getting mixed up when 'emotionally stressed' (Ibid). In a categorical view, thought disorder involves a level of disorganisation that 'substantially' impairs communication (American Psychiatric Association, 2013). A relativist view of psychosis may take insufficient account of evidence from observation or research in accepting that no one person's view is better than another's.

Thinking points

Readers may wish to consider:

- why scientific terms tend to be used in psychiatry and the associated benefits and disadvantages;
- the extent to which psychiatric terminology can distance people with mental disorders from others;
- arguments for and against a category view of psychotic disorders.

Key texts

American Psychiatric Association (2013) *Diagnostic and Statistical Manual of Mental Disorders Fifth Edition* Washington, DC, APA.

   As the most widely used psychiatric diagnostic guide, this text can sometimes excite resistance from those who consider psychosis and other mental disorders as predominantly environmentally influenced.

Kasper, S. and Papadimitriou, G. N. (Eds.) (2009) (2nd. Edition) *Schizophrenia: Biopsychosocial Approaches and Current Challenges* (Medical Psychiatry Series) New York and London, Informa Healthcare.

   This edited international text has contributions from the United States, United Kingdom, Europe (Austria, Italy, Germany, Spain, the Netherlands, Greece, Denmark, France), Africa (Egypt, South Africa), Australia and Korea. Its main parts deal with 'Diagnosis and Psychopathology', 'Neurobiology', 'Pharmacological Treatment Strategies' and 'Schizophrenia and Society'.

Read, J. and Dillon, J. (Eds.) (2013) (2nd. Edition) *Models of Madness: Psychological, Social and Biological Approaches to Psychosis* (International Society for Psychological and Social Approaches to Psychosis Series) London and New York, Routledge.

   This book criticises what it depicts as an 'illness' model of psychosis and supports more social and psychological approaches to understanding and treating 'madness'.

5

PSYCHOANALYSIS AND BEYOND

Introduction

Sigmund Freud's writings include ideas on psychosis and an interpretation of Judge Schreber's memoirs, although understanding psychosis is not the most central nor the most convincing aspect of Freud's work. An interpersonal understanding of psychosis was proposed by American psychiatrist Harry Stack Sullivan. Melanie Klein and her followers developed Freud's theory and practise, exerting a profound influence over psychoanalysis and the understanding of psychosis. Jacques Lacan, the French psychoanalyst, sought to relate conceptions of psychosis to linguistics and other sources. Philosopher Giles Deleuze, in partnership with psychoanalyst Felix Guattari, formed the notion of 'schizoanalysis' less as a clinical concept and more as a social critique.

Freudian psychoanalysis

Freud, psychoanalysis and psychosis

Sigmund Freud (1856–1939) is renowned as the founder of psychoanalysis, which can refer variously to a 'theory of personality and psychopathology', a 'method of investigating the mind' and 'a theory of treatment' (Wolitzky, 2003, p. 24). Here, we look firstly at some of the key conceptions of psychoanalysis: the id, ego and super ego; drives; developmental sexual stages, including the Oedipal phases; and unconscious, preconscious or conscious psychical processes. These form the backdrop of subsequent developments and discussions, including contributions by Melanie Klein and her followers, Jacques Lacan and more tangentially Deleuze and Guattari, as we shall see later. Harry Stack Sullivan, who is also briefly mentioned, formed his ideas more in response to the formulations of Emil Kraepelin.

Following a broad look at some of the mainstays of classical Freudian psycho-analysis, we examine particularly Freud's notion of psychosis. This involves noting distinctions between Freud's view of neurosis and psychosis and looking at the importance of loss of reality in his conception of psychosis. We look at Freud's interpretation of Judge Schreber's memoirs. Finally, we consider the language that is associated with Freudian psychoanalysis. While Freud's foundational work is important, it is probably fair to observe that his understanding of psychosis was not the strongest aspect of his theorising (or his clinical work). For example, his observations of the case of Judge Schreber were not based on direct personal analysis but on Freud's reading of Schreber's memoir.

Id, ego and super ego

Among key concepts in Freud's psychic picture are the id, ego and super ego. The 'id' is the oldest of the forces containing 'everything that is inherited, everything present at birth, everything constitutionally determined' (Freud, [1940]/2003, p. 176). It consists of drives having their origins in bodily organisation, which in the id find a 'first psychical expression in forms unknown to us' (Ibid.).

Striving for pleasure and avoiding nonpleasure, the ego mediates between the id and the external world. Among the ways in which it deals with the external world is by adapting to moderate stimuli while it mediates the id's internal panorama, for example by deciding whether drives should be gratified or their excitations suppressed (Ibid., p. 177). During a child's long period of dependence on parents, the super ego develops, reflecting parental influence. The super ego forms as the child emerges from the 'Oedipus complex', casts off incestuous desires for the parent of the opposite sex and internalises the father's prohibitions that make these desires taboo.

At its most effective, the action of the ego reconciles the demands of the id, the super ego and reality. As the seat of rational perception, the ego mediates between demands of the id and super ego. The ego is in part produced by the differentiation of the id as the psyche responds to outside reality, and because part of the ego remains unconscious, it can communicate with the id. The ego functions to 'test' reality and impose external norms on unconscious impulses and drives.

Drives

Drives are the forces behind tensions brought about by the needs of the id and represent the 'physical demands on the psyche' (Freud, [1940]/2003, p. 178). While there are numerous drives, they can be traced to two: the Eros ('libido') and Thanatos ('destruction drive'). Libido, seeking to 'establish and maintain ever greater unities', and the destruction drive, aiming to 'dissolve connections', work with and against each other to produce a multitude of life phenomena (Ibid., p. 179). The entire amount of the libido is initially stored in the ego in a state termed 'primary narcissism', which continues until the ego begins to 'invest its notions of objects with libido, to transform narcissistic libido into object-libido' (p. 180).

Developmental sexual stages

Sexual life starts to manifest itself soon after birth. Sexual phenomena emerge in early childhood and increase, peaking around the age of 5 years when they enter the 'latency period'. After this, towards puberty, the process resumes. Events in the early period of sexuality become the subject of infantile amnesia (Freud, [1940]/2003, p. 182).

Sexual phenomena are envisaged in stages. In the initial oral stage, erotic activity centres on the mouth. 'Sadistic impulses' begin at this stage with the cutting of the infant's teeth (Ibid., p. 183). In the second, 'sadistic-anal' phase, gratification is sought in 'aggression and in the excretory function' (Ibid.). The third, 'phallic' (Oedipal) phase is associated with the Oedipus complex. A boy, sexually attracted to his mother, may fear castration by his jealous father. As he comes to recognise the threat and identify with his father, the boy's Oedipus complex fades. A girl may, in recognising a lack of a penis or seeing the 'inferiority' of her clitoris, experience her first disappointment in rivalry, influencing future character development (pp. 183–184). At puberty occurs the complete organisation of the fourth, genital phase. Any inhibitions in the development of this phase express themselves as 'disruptions to sexual life' (p. 184).

Psychical processes and psychoanalysis

Psychical processes may be unconscious, preconscious or conscious (Ibid., p. 188). Psychoanalysis offers treatment that allows the client to participate in uncensored self-observations. This enables the analyst to deduce the client's 'repressed unconscious material' and share it with him or her (p. 202). In this process, the patient sees the analyst as the reincarnation of an important person from his or her past. The patient transfers feelings originally associated with the past figure to the analyst, who uses and reveals these feelings to help the client to recognise and resolve conflicted wishes.

Freud and psychosis

Neurosis and psychosis

In a paper 'Neurosis and Psychosis', Freud ([1923 and 1924]/2001) proposes that whereas neurosis originates in a conflict between the ego and the id, psychosis is the outcome of a disturbance in the 'relations between the ego and the external world' (Ibid., p. 149).

In Meynert's amentia, a psychosis in which there is 'acute hallucinatory confusion', the external world is either not perceived at all or the perception of it has no effect (Ibid., p. 150). Normally, the external world governs the ego in two ways: by 'current perceptions which are always renewable', and by the memories of earlier perceptions (Ibid.). These memories in the form of an 'internal world' are a constituent part of, and are 'possessed' by, the ego. Importantly, the internal world is a copy of the external world and represents it. In amentia, new perceptions are not accepted, and the internal world loses its significance (its 'cathexis') (Ibid., p. 151). 'Autocratically', the ego creates a new internal and external world which is made in accordance with the id's 'wishful impulses'. It appears that the motive for the dissociation from the external world is an intolerable frustration of a wish by reality.

In other forms of psychosis, 'the schizophrenias' tend to end in a loss of participation in the external world. A delusion is thought to originate as a 'patch' that has been placed over a tear in ego's relation to the external world.

Psychosis then originates in the frustration of a childhood wish (or its nonfulfilment). Such wishes are 'forever undefeated' and are 'deeply rooted in our phylogenetically determined organisation' (Ibid., p. 151). The frustration is ultimately external. However, in individual instances, the frustration may emerge from an internal agency in the super ego that 'has taken over the representation of the demands of reality' (Ibid.). Psychosis occurs if, in such a conflict, the ego allows itself to be overtaken by the id and detached from reality. The super ego also has a role in potential reconciliation in that it unites itself with both influences from the id and those from the outside world (Ibid., pp. 151–152).

Loss of reality

In a further paper, 'The Loss of Reality in Neurosis and Psychosis', Freud ([1924]/2001) suggests that when a psychosis originates, there is first a step which 'drags the ego away . . . from reality' (Ibid., p. 184). A second step attempts to rectify the loss of reality by creating a 'new reality' which 'no longer raises the same objections as the old one that has been given up' (p. 185). In neurosis, a 'piece of reality is avoided by a sort of flight'. In psychosis, however, the reality is 'remodelled'. The transforming of reality is carried out on the 'psychological precipitates' of former relations to reality. These are 'memory traces, ideas and judgements' previously derived from reality and by which reality was 'represented to the mind' (Ibid.). The relation was continuously being changed by new perceptions. Accordingly, the psychosis is faced with the task of 'procuring for itself' perceptions corresponding to the new reality achieved, for example, through hallucinations (p. 186). Indeed, hallucinations, delusions and paramnesias (memory distortions confusing fantasy and objective reality) are, Freud argues, associated with anxiety because the process of 'remodelling' is carried out against forces strongly opposing it (p. 186).

Freud's interpretation of Schreber's Memoirs

From a reading of Schreber's *Memoirs* (Schreber, [1903]/1955 and 2000), Freud wrote a psychoanalytical interpretation (Freud, [1911]/2001). In his memoirs, Schreber ([1903]/1955 and 2000) refers to having the idea in an apparently half-awake state that 'it really must be rather pleasant to be a woman succumbing to intercourse'. The idea, says Schreber, was 'foreign to my whole nature' (Ibid., p. 46).

Freud ([1911]/2001) suggests that such ideas, and other experiences reported by Schreber relating to 'feminine fantasy' (Ibid., p. 42), may have become connected to 'a feeling of affectionate dependence' on his physician, Dr. Flechsig. This unaccountably may have become 'intensified to the pitch of an erotic desire'. When Schreber entered a period of psychosis, the feminine fantasy overpowered everything and Schreber feared 'sexual abuse at the hands of the doctor himself' (p. 42). The cause precipitating Schreber's illness was, therefore, 'an outburst of homosexual libido', the object of which was Flechsig. It was Schreber's struggles against the libidinal impulse that produced his symptoms (p. 43). The 'ensuing defensive struggle' took the shape of 'a delusion of persecution' (p. 47).

Later, in Schreber's delusions, he replaced the figure of Flechsig with that of God, and the intention to sexually abuse him became part of the 'Order of Things' so that emasculation was no longer disgraceful but became 'consonant with the Order of Things' (Freud, [1911]/2001, p. 48). The sun, which figured largely in Schreber's vision of a heaven and Gods, was a 'sublimated symbol of the father' (Ibid., p. 54). In the final stages of Schreber's delusion, Freud suggests, sexual desires ('voluptuousness') became God fearing. Also, 'God Himself (his father) never tired of demanding it from him'. Indeed, 'His father's most dreaded threat, castration, actually provided the material for his wishful fantasy . . . of being transformed into a woman' (p. 56). Ultimately, Freud suggests that the causes of the conflict that broke out in relation to the 'feminine wishful fantasy' were related to a 'frustration' or privation in real life, namely the frustrated desire of Schreber and his wife to have children (p. 55). Schreber may have formed a fantasy that, were he a woman, 'he would manage the business of having children more successfully' (p. 56).

Language and Freudian psychoanalysis

Freud writes with conviction and clarity, presenting arguments followed by possible objections to build a convincing case. He can judiciously and effectively use homely metaphors to make concrete his proposals. Among the strengths of a psychoanalytic approach is the dynamic nature of the psychoanalytic model, which has a flexibility and subtlety seemingly necessary to depict the enormously complicated nature of mental life and behaviour. The notion of unconscious forces of which we are normally unaware is an attractive concept that seems to reflect the common experience of doing things that we find difficult to explain. Such is the power of Freud's explanations and concepts that many of his terms have become part of common parlance, even though not always with a full understanding of the related Freudian ideas. Notions of ego, super ego, the power of infantile experiences and the recognition of strong unconscious forces are widely if loosely accepted in Western society. Aspects of Freud's theories, such as the exact development of the Oedipus complex, have been extensively debated.

Yet criticisms of psychoanalysis stem from the very permeating nature of the concepts, which seem at first glance to have an explanation for everything. Scepticism towards psychoanalytic perspectives has been expressed, for example, regarding the difficulty of testing meaningful hypotheses relating to outcomes. Still, there is some evidence of the effectiveness of specific psychodynamic approaches, with brief dynamic psychotherapy for children with emotional disorders being an example (Muratori, Picchi, Casella, Tancredi, Milone and Patarnello, 2002).

However, Webster (2005) suggests that Freud himself (and by implication, his findings) were influenced by his proneness to being star-struck by charismatic healers such as Charcot. Afterwards, Webster argues, Freud insufficiently interrogated the ideas that emerged from these encounters. Criticisms of Freud's theories include that from the beginning they were based on likely misdiagnoses of hysteria. Anna O., the woman who Freud's colleague Breuer had treated, was viewed as suffering a psychological condition. But evidence indicates that Anna was not suffering from hysteria and neither was she cured (Ibid., pp. 103–135). Similar doubts are raised about the nature of the illness of another early patient, Frau Emmy von N.

The mechanisms that Freud uses to describe the apparent functioning of the psyche are considered by Webster (2005) to be little more than pseudoscience, unknowingly immersed in the traditions of Judeo-Christian religious culture (Ibid., pp. 168–181 and passim). Freud is fluent in 'mystical exegesis', which helps to create the illusion of explanatory power (p. 295). The development of psychoanalysis as a movement is presented in terms of religious dogma, rather than a scientific enterprise, with Freud its messianic figure. Borch-Jacobsen and Shamdasani (2011), in their book *The Freud Files: An Inquiry Into the History of Psychoanalysis*, also challenge Freudian orthodoxy, questioning the idea that psychoanalysis is a form of scientific enquiry.

Freud's language as it relates to psychosis reflects his language more widely. It speaks of relationships between the ego (itself part of a structuring of the psyche envisaged by Freud) and the external world. Hallucination (in Meynert's amentia) was explained regarding the ego creating a new internal and external world according to the wishful impulses of the id. In schizophrenia, there tends to be a loss of participation in the external world, and delusions seem to originate as a 'patch' that has been placed over a tear in the ego's relation to the external world. Childhood conflictual frustration (ultimately external but also potentially emerging from internal agency in the super ego) can lead to psychosis if the ego is taken over by the id and detached from reality. Hallucinations, delusions and paramnesias involve a process of 'remodelling' carried out against forces strongly opposing it. Conflict between competing elements of the psyche, powerful 'forces', tearing and patching all convey the damaged yet originally structured nature of Freud's vision of the psyche. Freud's interpretations of Schreber's *Memoirs* reflect his understanding of psychosis.

Interpersonal psychoanalysis and psychosis

Freudian influences did not directly appear to influence the ideas of early practitioners taking a more interpersonal view of psychopathology. In the United States, for example, the influence of the German pioneer Kraepelin was still felt, and an interpersonal approach was in some sense a reaction to his individualistic view of mental disorders, including psychosis. An important figure here is American psychiatrist Harry Stack Sullivan (1892–1949), who, working with patients with schizophrenia, developed an interpersonal emphasis. (This subsequently helped shape the ideas of psychiatrist R. D. Laing, whom we consider in a later chapter on 'Anti-psychiatry'.) Sullivan took the view that if one is to understand psychopathology, the unit of study should be not only the individual who is experiencing a disorder but also the wider context of other people. Pathology is not helpfully seen as exclusively existing within an individual person but rather consists of interactions with others in that person's environment. Indeed, human personality is formed by such personal interactions (Sullivan, 1938, 1940).

Kleinian analysis

Melanie Klein

In considering the contribution of Melanie Klein and her followers to an understanding of psychosis, we first briefly look at how her ideas differed from those of Freudian psychoanalysis as it was continued by Freud's daughter Anna. This leads to a discussion of Klein's conception of the 'paranoid-schizoid position' and the 'depressive position'. Next, Klein's influence is illustrated, mainly referring to the work of Wilfred Bion. Finally, the nature of Kleinian language is examined.

Klein's work

Melanie Klein (1882–1960) had a profound influence on psychoanalysis. Within British psychoanalysis, wide differences formed between the views of Anna Freud (Freud's daughter) and those of Klein. Melanie Klein took the view that children were analysable in a similar way to adults through interpreting their play just as an adult's free associations might be interpreted. For Anna Freud, children were not analysable because their undeveloped ego cannot deal with deep interpretations of instinctual conflicts. These approaches separated into (Anna) Freudian analysis, or the Vienna School, and Kleinian analysis, or the London School.

PAUSE FOR REFLECTION: MELANIE KLEIN

Begin to gain some impressions of Melanie Klein's life and work by exploring the website of the Melanie Klein Trust at www.melanie-klein-trust.org.uk.

Klein considered that she had evidence that Sigmund Freud's theory of child psycho-sexual development could be applied to much younger children and infants

(Klein, [1932 and 1975]/1998). Klein believed that fantasies of incestuous union (in the Oedipus complex) and frightening self-punishment (super ego) were present in more primal and terrifying form from a very early age. In the 1950s and 1960s, Klein and her followers applied the understanding they had gained from work with young children to adult psychotic patients. As Mitchell and Black ([1995]/2016) summarise it, Klein understood the withdrawal and bizarre behaviour of psychotic adults as 'desperate efforts to ward off the terrors she had witnessed in the play of children' (Ibid., p. 87). Klein put forward a psychic vision different from Sigmund Freud's portrayal of the mind that was a 'stream of primitive, phantasmagoric images, fantasies and terrors' (Ibid.). Among important concepts in Kleinian psychoanalysis are the 'paranoid-schizoid position' and the 'depressive position'. (Please also see Klein, [1935]/1964, [1940]/1964, [1957]/1975.)

Klein and the 'paranoid-schizoid position'

The 'paranoid-schizoid position' refers to an organisation of experience which occurs in all people in the early months and years of life and which is maintained (episodically at least) throughout life. Differing from Freud's, Klein's notion of instinctual libidinal and aggressive impulses was as broad ways of experiencing one's self as good (loved and loving) or as bad (hated and destructive). Libido and aggression are expressed as 'body parts and substances' but are generated by 'more complex organisations of experience and senses of self' (Mitchell and Black, [1995]/2016, p. 91).

Klein's view of the aim of the impulse also differed from that of Freud, who saw the aim of the impulse as discharge, with the 'object' being a means to that end which was accidentally discovered. For Klein, objects were part of the experience of the impulse itself, with the object of desire being implicit in the very experience of the desire. In Klein's delineation of early experience, the ego vacillates between a loving orientation towards other individuals who are loving and lovable and a hateful orientation towards others who are hating and hateful. The mind is envisaged as less about impulses and more about relationships. Infant experience is portrayed as two very different states. A paradigm of these states is the infant at the mother's breast experiencing in one state the good and in another state the bad breast.

Importantly, the infant's divided world is formed prior to any capacity for testing reality. Consequently, the infant believes that his or her fantasies (loving or hating) powerfully and directly influence the objects of the fantasies. Emotional equilibrium requires that the infant keep the two worlds apart. It is important that the infant's fantasies of destroying the bad breast are contained in the relationship to the bad object. Confusion between the good and bad object could result in the annihilation of the good object (the good breast), leaving the infant unprotected from the hatred of the bad breast.

Why is this called the 'paranoid-schizoid position'? It refers to a paranoid anxiety – a fear of external malevolence. It is characterised by a schizoid splitting of the good and the bad breast. It is a 'position' in that is an organisation of the experience of internal and external reality in which the world of good and bad is a basic form for organising experience and an approach to locating different versions of oneself in relation to various others. The conception of the paranoid-schizoid position developed from Klein's work with psychotic patients and children. The malevolence of the position begins with constitutional aggression, but 'a good environment can ameliorate it terrors' (Mitchell and Black, [1995]/2016, p. 94).

Klein and the 'depressive position'

A tendency towards integration in arranging experience encourages the infant to reach a sense of the whole object that is neither completely good or solely bad but is sometimes good and sometimes bad. The good-and-bad breast comes to be understood as different features of the mother, who exists as another entity with her own subjectivity. Paranoid anxiety is thus reduced, but other fears replace it relating to the containment of aggression. In the infant's aggressive fantasies, the whole mother who 'fails' the infant, bringing about longing and desperation, is destroyed. Being the provider of both goodness and frustration, the external mother and the corresponding internal whole object are destroyed in these infant fantasies.

In destroying the frustrating whole object, the infant also destroys the good protective object. Klein calls the fear and guilt brought about by damage done to the loved object by the child's destructiveness 'depressive anxiety'. The more integrated and developmentally more advanced organisation of experience in which the infant relates to the whole object with both love and hate she calls the 'depressive position'. This state involves deep remorse, generating fantasies of reparation in the effort to repair the damage and bring the mother back to wholeness. Ideally, cycles of loving, frustration, destruction and reparation are positive. They develop the child's feeling that reparation can compensate for destructiveness.

However, such fantasies continue in life where destructiveness towards loved others generates continuing depressive anxiety and the need for reparation. On occasions when the destructiveness is overwhelming, fleeting security may be found in a return to the paranoid-schizoid position. Another solution to the pain of depressive anxiety is 'manic defence'. Here, the uniqueness of the loved object, and one's dependence on it, is denied. For Klein, a relative state of mental well-being is not secure and lasting but is a position that is continually lost and reacquired. Depressive anxiety is therefore a continuing feature of human existence, and in highly challenging periods, there is a retreat into the security of the paranoid-schizoid position and manic defence.

In unideal circumstances, the child experiences rage as more powerful than reparative love. The splitting of the paranoid-schizoid position, in which good and evil are distinctly separate, becomes the only way of keeping remnants of love and security.

Klein's influence

Klein's influence has been widespread, and her ideas and approaches have perhaps been most extensively developed by Wilfred Bion (1897–1979), who was a student of Klein's and was analysed by her. Bion's own work was influenced strongly by his work with schizophrenic patients. In her later work, Klein had formulated ideas concerning 'envy' as an attack on an object. In the paradigm of the infant, this was a destruction of the breast. For Bion, what was attacked was not just the object itself but also the part of the child's psyche that was attached to the object and to reality generally.

This, it seemed to Bion, shed light on the origins and experience of schizophrenia, in which thought and language were so fragmented and apparently meaningless. In Bion's theories, the infant in his or her envy, experiences his or her link with the object as very painful. The infant therefore attacks not only the breast but his or her own mental capacities that bind him or her to the breast. The fantasised attack is on both object and the infant's cognitive and perceptual apparatus. This destroys both the capacity to perceive and make sense of reality generally and the ability to make meaningful contact with others. The parallel with schizophrenia and psychosis is evident in this picture. Envy, as understood in this psychoanalytical context, becomes an attack on the self. (Please also see Bion, 1955; [1967]/1988.)

Kleinian language

Klein speaks of primitive, phantasmagoric images and of fantasies and terrors. Rather than Freud's descriptions of developmental stages, Klein focuses more on accounts of threatening and more fluid 'positions'.

Among issues arising in Klein's use of language are those concerning her attempts to understand and delineate supposed very early infant experiences, such as those of the good and bad breast. The account refers to preverbal infancy and, in attempting to convey views about it, uses adult language. The dilemma is double, in having to use language to convey ideas and observations about states that arise before language, and in trying to convey infant experience in adult terms. Klein and her collaborators tried to express themselves in clear language but recognised, as Mitchell and Black ([1995]/2016) suggest, that the child's experiences were 'neither clear nor verbal, but amorphous and phantasmagoric, at some distance from what adults are able to remember or experience themselves' (Ibid., p. 92). In Bion's work, his own language is often obscure. It has been described as 'extremely opaque and abstruse' and, in some respects, veering off into a 'somewhat mystical direction' (p. 102).

Yet for any theorist or practitioner wishing to try to understand early infant development, it is difficult to see how one can avoid the challenges of the ultimate inaccessibility of infant experience being as it is prelanguage. Responses to this challenge include close observation of mother-child interaction and to some extent an intuitive exploration of one's own and others' experiences. The language in which findings from such explorations is ultimately clothed is unlikely to always be clear and simple, given the complexities of the task. Some psychoanalytic writers have the skill of presenting complex ideas and findings with clarity which does not distort the complexity of the discourse, but not all. It is then down to interpreters of the original concepts and approaches to try to clarify them, often by setting the work in a historical and cultural context that may have been unavailable to the original writer.

Lacan on psychosis

Lacan's work

Where Freud laid the groundwork which others built on or modified, Lacan, although trained in psychoanalysis, took such a different approach that any implications for clinical work are unclear. However, given that our focus is on language and psychosis, and Lacan's work purports to shed light on psychosis in terms of language, it is possible to justify his inclusion. Here, we look briefly at Lacan's broad ideas, then at his view of psychosis and finally at aspects of the language that he uses.

Lacan's broad ideas

Lacan ([1955–1956]/1997), in a series of talks, develops an interpretation of psychoses, making extensive reference to Schreber's ([1903]/1955 and 2000) *Memoirs* and Freud's interpretations of them. In doing so, Lacan identifies important differences, according to his scheme, between psychosis and neurosis.

In typical development, the father, in his role standing for law and order and other aspects of the symbolic world, is instrumental in the process that helps a child separate from the mother into an entity in his or her own right. The realms of the 'real', the 'imaginary' and the 'symbolic' are brought together, enabling meaning and meaningful communication.

With a person experiencing psychosis, the 'name of the father' (as a primordial signifier) is 'foreclosed' and not integrated into the symbolic order. This is brought about when some signifier which the individual cannot assimilate is triggered, leaving a 'hole' in the symbolic order. When the foreclosed 'name of the father' appears in the 'real', the subject is unable to assimilate it, precipitating the onset of psychosis with delusions and/or hallucinations. The realm of the symbolic is not bound sufficiently to the realm of the imaginary, which can lead to failures in meaning.

PAUSE FOR REFLECTION: FORECLOSURE

Search the Internet for the video 'INTDC English Alastair Black' (https://vimeo.com/52166370).

How does foreclosure help to distinguish between neurosis and psychosis in Lacan's scheme?

Lacan and psychosis

Lacan draws on his previously developed terminology in discussing psychosis. He refers to the 'other' (with a small *o*) as a reflection of the ego and as being inscribed in the 'imaginary order'. This is distinguished from the 'Other' (with a large *O*), which equates with language and the law and which is inscribed in the symbolic order. The 'Other' is both another subject and the symbolic order which mediates the relationship with that subject (Lacan, [1955–1956]/1997, pp. 14–15). Referring to delusions, Lacan emphasises the importance of the distinction between 'Other' and 'other'. Indeed, he maintains that it is in the 'gap' opened between these two relations that 'the entire dialectic of delusion has to be situated' (Ibid., p. 40).

A function of the signifier is that it 'polarizes meanings' in grouping them (Lacan, [1955–1956]/1997, p. 291). In the case of Schreber, the 'fundamental signifier' that was incompletely assimilated was 'being a father' (Ibid., p. 293). In the resulting confusion leading him to the point of 'thinking of acting like a woman', Schreber had to imagine himself a woman and 'bring about in pregnancy', the second part of the route that, when added to the first, was necessary for the realisation of being a father (Ibid.).

Regarding psychosis, Lacan argues that prior to all symbolization, there is a stage at which a 'portion of symbolization' may not take place. It can happen that 'something primordial' regarding the subject's being 'does not enter into symbolization' and is 'rejected' (Lacan, [1955–1956]/1997, p. 81). Here, the psychotic phenomenon is 'the emergence in reality of an enormous meaning that has the appearance of being nothing at all'. It apparently lacks meaning because it has not entered the system of symbolization. However, under certain conditions, this intrusion can 'threaten the entire edifice' (Ibid., p. 85).

Language and Lacan's theories

Lacan can write with insight and subtlety. But he is often criticised for obscurantism, including his extensive use of new terminology: the 'imaginary', the 'mirror stage', 'Phallus', 'Law of the father', 'object little a' and so on. Yet, Lacan's working out of the implications of pre-Oedipal and Oedipal stages and their interpretation in relation to language (Lacan, [1966]/2006) has generated speculation about areas including psychoanalysis itself, literary theory, philosophy, feminism and disability.

Dawkins (1998), in a review, suggests that Lacan's writing is full of scientific pretensions. Similarly, Sokal and Bricamont ([1997]/1998) argue that Lacan's use of mathematical symbols, while presented as meaningful (rather than suggestive or metaphorical), is nonsense. Providing examples of Lacan's misuse of mathematical and scientific concepts, they criticise Lacan for the privilege he accords theory over observation and experiment. The authors point out that even if one assumes psychoanalysis has a scientific basis, it is a still a 'young science'. They suggest that, before anyone launches into 'vast theoretical generalisations' about psychoanalysis, they should 'check the empirical adequacy of at least some of its propositions'.

However, Lacan's writings instead comprise 'mainly quotations and analyses of texts and concepts' (Ibid., p. 34).

Others defend Lacan. Bruce Fink, the main translator of the complete *Écrits*, suggests that Sokal and Bricamont miss the point that Lacan is using mathematical terminology metaphorically. Fink (2004, p. 130) criticises them for expecting 'clear meanings' as the only standard of serious writing. This suggestion is difficult to sustain, however. Sokal and Bricamont ([1997]/1998) carefully consider whether Lacan is writing metaphorically, concluding that he is not. Even metaphor should convey something. There is no indication as to what the mathematical metaphors are supposed to mean or suggest, raising the suspicion that they are there solely for effect. Also, it is difficult to know what Fink means when he criticises the requirement for 'clear meanings' as the only standard of serious writing. Surely, if a writer is introducing a theoretical framework as Lacan seeks to do, then one can expect him to try to express his meaning clearly. In this Lacan often disappoints, and all the talk that the reader should be cleverer in order to understand the seminars or essays has a defensive tone and rings false.

Lacan moved away from most recognisable routes leading from psychoanalysis in his pursuit of a language-related theory. Deleuze and Guattari, as we shall see, go even further in their development of a social criticism relating to psychoanalysis (and capitalism). A trajectory of language goes in a tentative thread from Freud, through Klein and Lacan, and to Deleuze and Guattari, where it leads ultimately into social criticism rather than clinical understanding.

Deleuze and Guattari

Anti-Oedipus

Here, we briefly consider Deleuze and Guattari's work *Anti-Oedipus*, looking at their conception of schizoanalysis in relation to emancipation and at the nature of their language. This leads us a long way from the field of psychoanalysis and points towards later developments in 'anti-psychiatry', which are pursued in a later chapter (Chapter 7).

Collaboration between philosopher Gilles Deleuze (1925–1975) and French psychoanalyst and psychiatrist Felix Guattari (1930–1992) included producing *Anti-Oedipus: Capitalism and Schizophrenia* (Deleuze and Guattari, [1972]/1983). In this work, they present a conception of desire and a view of how Freudian notions of Oedipus and the forces of capitalism delude participants (subjects). On the way, the authors introduce or borrow terms such as 'codes' (structures), 'desiring machines', 'desiring production', 'body without organs' and 'deterritorialization'. Deleuze and Guattari often use examples from physics to convey the material nature of 'desiring machines'. They suggest how such entities might gather together, how they are both producers and products and how an apparent reality might be misconceived. From this context, they propose a communal form of analysis (schizoanalysis) which recognises and productively deploys desire in individual and political spheres. (Please also see Buchanan, 2008.)

Schizoanalysis and emancipation

Whereas psychoanalysts force on their client's complicity with capitalist structures, schizoanalysis represents a political analysis of desire, marshalling capitalist and psychoanalytic modes of production to revolutionary ends. A schizophrenic is a revolutionary. Schizophrenia concerns what cannot be (or refuses to be) coded, assimilated or structured, expressing desire as flow. A schizophrenic ego functions not as a whole but as the aggregate of individuals that compose it. It is the task of schizoanalysis to become multiple, destroying Oedipus by fracturing and not reforming. The revolutionary learns from the psychotic how to evade the Oedipal constraint and the influence of power to form a radical politics. But this does not suggest an individual approach to the schizophrenic. Desire, insofar as its aim is to disconnect and connect desiring machines, is always social. It follows that the task of schizoanalysis is to de-Oedipalize people, not individually but en masse, to allow the potential to be everyone and everything.

Language and Deleuze and Guattari

Deleuze and Guattari's work as political emancipatory theory was popular in combining threads of Freudian thinking and Marxist theory, using the image of schizophrenia as creating thought in a personal and political sense. As a contribution to the clinical understanding of schizophrenia, their work is unilluminating. The idea that schizophrenia is a creative state is romanticised. Similarly, the notion that the revolutionary learns from the psychotic how to evade Oedipal constraint and the influence of power to form a radical politics seems far-fetched. Sokal and Bricamont ([1997]/1998) criticise Deleuze and Guattari for obscure language and using scientific terms meaninglessly, such as with their examples from physics to convey the material nature of 'desiring machines', which obscure rather than illuminate. Regarding *Anti-Oedipus*, Elliott (2002) rejects that 'desire is naturally rebellious and subversive'. He believes that Deleuze and Guattari see the individual as 'no more than various organs, intensities and flows', whereas a more accurate picture of the individual is as 'a complex, contradictory identity'. They make false emancipatory claims for schizophrenia, providing 'little more than a romantic, idealized fantasy of the "schizoid hero"' (Ibid., pp. 157, 161–163).

Conclusion

Among key aspects of Freud's theories are the id, ego and super ego (Freud, [1940]/2003). Sexual phenomena are envisaged in stages, including oral, sadistic-anal and phallic (Oedipal) phases. Psychoanalysis allows clients to express uncensored self-observations, enabling the analyst to deduce and reveal 'repressed unconscious material' (Ibid., p. 202). Freud ([1923/1924]/2001) proposes that psychosis results from a disturbance in the 'relations between the ego and the external world' (Ibid., p. 149). Furthermore, Freud ([1924]/2001) suggests that psychosis first 'drags the ego away . . . from reality', then attempts to rectify the loss of reality by creating 'a new reality' which avoids the objections of the old one (Ibid., pp. 184–185). His reading of Schreber's *Memoirs* (Schreber, [1903]/1955 and 2000) led to a psychoanalytical interpretation (Freud, [1911]/2001). His psychoanalytic writing, including that on psychosis, has been criticised for appearing in scientific mode yet rarely being amenable to scientific testing. Broadly, Freud's language and tone has been likened to religious exegesis rather than scientific exposition.

In the 1950s and 1960s, Klein and her followers applied the understanding they had gained from work with young children to adult psychotic patients. Klein understood the withdrawal and bizarre behaviour of psychotic adults as desperate efforts to fend away the terrors she had seen in children's play. Her psychic vision was of a succession of primitive, phantasmagoric images, fantasies and terrors. Among important concepts in Kleinian psychoanalysis are the 'paranoid-schizoid position' and the 'depressive position'. Kleinian language faces challenges where it attempts to delineate supposed very early infant experiences. Klein's account refers to preverbal infancy and, in attempting to convey views about it, uses adult language. Language is inevitably and unavoidably used to convey ideas and observations about pre-states and to convey infant experience in adult terms. The child's experiences are neither clear nor verbal and distant from what adults can remember or experience. Bion's writings themselves are often obscure and sometimes almost mystical. Yet it is difficult to see how one can avoid the challenges of the ultimate inaccessibility of infant experience, being as it is prelanguage. Responses include close observation of mother–child interaction and to some extent an intuitive exploration of one's own and others' experiences. The language in which findings from such explorations is ultimately clothed is unlikely to always be clear and simple given the complexities of the task. Where original psychoanalytic writers lack the skills of presenting complex ideas and findings lucidly, interpreters are sometimes able to clarify them, perhaps by setting the work in a historical and cultural context.

In *Écrits*, Lacan ([1966]/2006) reconsiders Freudian theories and their possible relationships with language. Lacan ([1955–1956]/1997) develops an interpretation of psychoses, making extensive reference to Schreber's ([1903]/1955 and 2000) *Memoirs* and Freud's related interpretations. For Lacan, with a person experiencing psychosis, the 'name of the father' (as a primordial signifier) is 'foreclosed' and not integrated into the symbolic order. This is brought about when some signifier which the individual cannot assimilate is triggered, leaving a 'hole' in the symbolic order. When the foreclosed 'name of the father' appears in the 'real', the subject is unable to assimilate it, precipitating the onset of psychosis. The realm of the symbolic, being insufficiently bound to the realm of the imaginary, leads to failures in meaning. Lacan's language has been criticised for being unnecessarily obscure, as well as pretentious and vacuous in its misuse of scientific and mathematical vocabulary.

Regarding Deleuze and Guattari, *Anti-Oedipus* ([1972]/1983) as an emancipatory theory brings together threads of Freudian and Marxist thinking. Deleuze and Guattari's work uses the image of schizophrenia as creating thought in a personal, as well as a political, sense. Concerning the clinical understanding of schizophrenia, their idea that it is a creative state seems romanticised. The notion that the revolutionary learns from the psychotic how to evade Oedipal constraint and the influence of power to form a radical politics stretches credulity. Their language includes scientific analogies that confuse rather than explain.

Thinking points

Readers may wish to consider:

*   differences in the ways in which Freud's theories and those of Klein seek to explain and illuminate psychosis, as well as the relative strengths of each perspective;
*   the extent to which Lacan's theories have relevance to understanding and clinical practise regarding psychosis.

Key texts

Gurman, A. S. and Messer, S. B. (Eds.) (2003) (2nd. Edition) *Essential Psychotherapies: Theory and Practice* New York and London, The Guilford Press.

In this skilfully edited book, the chapter by David Wolitzky is one of the best concise accounts of Freudian psychoanalysis available.

Klein, M. ([1932 and 1975]/1998) *The Psychoanalysis of Children* London, Karnac Books (Translated from the German by A. Strachey and revised in collaboration with A. Strachey and H. A. Thorner).

A pioneering book in which Klein proposes an approach to the psychoanalysis of young children and sets out implications for the understanding and treatment of neurosis and psychosis.

Lacan, J. ([1955–1956]/1997) *The Psychoses 1955–1956: The Seminar of Jacques Lacan Book III* New York and London: W.W. Norton (Edited by J.-A. Miller; translated from the French by R. Grigg).

In this series of talks, Lacan discusses the psychoses in relation to the symbolic processes of language, referring to the case of Schreber and Freud's interpretation of it.

Mitchell, S. A. and Black, M. J. ([1995]/2016) *Freud and Beyond: A History of Modern Psychoanalytic Thought* Philadelphia and New York, Basic Books/Perseus Books.

A systematic presentation of the development of Freudian and other ideas which covers many contributions including those of Freud himself, Harry Stack Sullivan, Melanie Klein and Wilfred Bion.

6
ADVOCACY

Introduction

In general terms, advocacy involves putting a view forward and trying to ensure that it gets a fair hearing. Of the different types, peer advocacy may involve the networking and coordination of people with similar views and aspirations. Independent advocacy concerns the representation of people by others who may not share their experiences but can present their case. 'Self-advocacy' is self-explanatory (Newbigging, Ridley and McKeown et al., 2015).

Sometimes linked with the aim of advocacy is a desire to act to improve matters for people with mental disorders. This may be clothed in the language of human rights (sometimes said to be 'fundamental' or 'basic' human rights), linked with a claim that certain rights are being ignored unjustifiably. Naturally, advocating for individuals and claiming human rights can be linked so that a perceived violation of human rights can motivate and channel the drive for getting a fair hearing.

Mad Pride

An early rights activist and advocacy group was Mad Pride (Lewis, 2010). This is described as an 'activist group' which is 'devoted to resisting and critiquing physician-centred psychiatric systems'. It seeks to find 'alternatives and peer run approaches to mental health recovery'. The group also helps people who wish to do so to 'minimise their involvement with current psychiatric institutions' (Ibid., p. 160). Accordingly, the name 'Mad Pride' indicates a desire to subvert 'traditional distinctions and hierarchies' and reverse 'standard pathological connotations of "madness"'. It signifies a position of 'respect, appreciation and affirmation' (p. 161). Epistemological issues, as well as political issues, are considered important.

Lewis (2010) identifies similarities to disability studies. For example, central to the Mad Pride movement is the task of 'undermining stereotyped representations of individualism, medicalisation and normality'. It is argued that 'individualistic approaches to mental difference and distress blame and punish the victim for structural problems' (Ibid., p. 162). Alternatively, it is suggested that the problems are better understood as 'located in families, communities and society'. Medicalisation or 'psychiatrisation', it is maintained, 'legitimises the medical community's expert authority over the domain of mental difference' (pp. 161–162).

Legal structures and guidance exist in different countries, including the United States and the United Kingdom, that aim to ensure that people with mental disorders and others have their views heard. For example, in the United Kingdom, the Mental Capacity Act of 2005 was intended to protect and restore some control to vulnerable people who may lack the capacity to make decisions. Within the framework, independent mental capacity advocates act as a safeguard for those who have no one independent of the services that are being used to represent them. Rather than review these legal structures, and the support provided within them, this chapter instead concentrates on the language employed by advocacy groups to argue their case using particularly the examples of Mad Pride and MindFreedom.

Advocacy groups for individuals with mental disorders often criticise a so-called medical model of disability. In an early example of such criticism, Goffman ([1961]/1981) points to the limitations of 'the medical model and mental hospitalisation'. Mental health advocacy groups tend to take a more social view. Key in the formation of the social approach (or social model) are historical materialism and symbolic interactionism, articulating the view that reality is socially produced. Emerging from symbolic interactionism and other sources, 'labelling theory' is part of the social perspective and informs discussions of potentially negative labelling of individuals.

As already indicated, among examples of advocacy is the work of Mad Pride. Relatedly, the MindFreedom website provides instances of the language associated with advocacy and mental disorder. It raises concerns about the medical model, pointing to the risks of negative labelling and to the possibility of discrimination. MindFreedom argues against a 'medical model' and the use of associated language such as 'mentally ill'. The organisation calls for the use of alternative terms, such as 'service users', and signals reservations about other expressions, for instance by putting them in quotation marks. But do such alternatives and the language associated with them have their own limitations?

'The Medical Model and Mental Hospitalization'

In an earlier chapter (on 'Psychiatric terminology') we looked at how discussions about disorders can be polarised between individual, 'within person' perspectives and social (and socially constructed) views of disability (Farrell, 2010, 2012). Critics of the scientific leanings of psychiatry sometimes refer to a 'medical model' or 'illness model' (e.g. Read and Dillon, 2013) to indicate a perceived overemphasis on individual, 'within person' factors. Sometimes a medical model may be represented as rigidly biological, simplistic and out of date. By contrast, a 'social model' tends to focus on environmental factors in relation to mental disorders.

An early critical discussion of a so-called medical model was presented by Goffman ([1961]/1981), and we look briefly at this before considering aspects of a social model so often preferred by advocacy groups. (His *Asylums* is further discussed in the subsequent chapter on 'Anti-psychiatry'.) In 'The Medical Model and Mental Hospitalization: Some Notes on the Vicissitudes of the Tinkering Trades', Goffman ([1961]/1981) considers the role of the medical perspective 'in presenting to the inmate, the facts of his situation' (Ibid., p. 12).

Goffman wryly compares aspects of car repair and medicine as 'tinkering trades', for example, as both have a client relationship and an expectation of practitioner expertise (Goffman, [1961]/1981, pp. 285–286). Such tinkering also implies 'a belief in rationalism, empiricism, and mechanism' (Ibid., p. 287). However, any 'free agent' aspect of such a model does not fit as well with those who might not realise that they need a service. These include 'the very young, the very old, and the mentally ill' who may have to be brought to medical attention (as Goffman puts it in mistrustful quotation marks) 'for their own good' (p. 300).

In a mental hospital, it is apparent that some of the routines exist for the 'convenience and comfort of staff', not primarily for the direct benefit of patients (Ibid., pp. 302–303). A client, where he or she is willing to comply with the server in regarding the client's disorder, 'impersonally' attests to the 'validity of the physician's claims' and consequently to the validity of the medical model (p. 304).

In applying the medical model to 'institutional psychiatry', Goffman ([1961]/1981) sees it as part of 'the interpretation of persons who seem to act oddly'. A shift was made from superstitious explanations of mental disorder to a 'medical mandate' over 'offenders'. Accordingly, 'inmates were called patients, nurses were trained, and medically styled case records were kept'. 'Madhouses' became 'mental hospitals' (Ibid., p. 305). On entry into the system, the medical-service model is applied as a 'technical-psychiatric' view irrespective of the patient's social circumstances and social context (Ibid., p. 306).

However, the applicability of a service model to institutional psychiatry is compromised by the 'custodial role' of the hospital (Ibid., p. 308). There is a feeling of 'stigmatization' and 'sensed deprivation' that the patient experiences on entry into the hospital, leading to feelings of alienation (Ibid., p. 310). Also, the psychiatric role (unique among servers) is accorded great power. Difficulties arise with treatment because treatment is unlikely to be 'specific to the disorder' (pp. 313–314). In 'functional psychosis', diagnosis may have cultural influences and not simply be located in an individual (pp. 316–317, paraphrased). In total, 'mental hospitals institutionalize a kind of grotesque of the service relationship' (p. 321). A psychiatrist can 'admit some of the weaknesses of individual therapy' and try more socially orientated approaches such as family and milieu therapy (pp. 323–324). But these can descend into turning every problem back to the patient (p. 327).

Certain 'translations' are made to try to justify the regime. For example, 'dormitories are called wards', women 'long since unable to perform such routine tasks as taking blood are called nurses and wear nursing uniforms', and work assignments are defined as 'industrial therapy' (Ibid., pp. 331–332). In all, 'medical action is presented to the patient and his relatives as an individual service, but what is being serviced here is the institution' (p. 333).

Such is one conception of the medical model, but what of the social model?

A social approach

Social perspectives and social model

A useful place to begin looking at a social approach is in areas where it differs from alternatives. Where a social approach is contrasted to a 'medical model', it is then itself often referred to as a 'social model'. A social model tends to deemphasise illness and considers a range of responses to disorder, including physical ones like medication. It takes account of the content and meaning of the individual's experiences and encourages a sense of control (agency). The model avoids negative categorising and labelling and tries to respond to the complexity of a person's life and to demonstrate that it is valued. Among variations in broad social approaches are ones that explore the material influences that are exerted on society and culture, and ones that examine symbolic phenomena in relation to the way that 'reality' is seen.

A historical-materialist account

Oliver (1990) developed a historical-materialist account of disablement which, although tending to focus on physical disabilities, has some relevance for mental disorders. In his view, disabled people experience disability as a 'social restriction' (Ibid., p. xiv). Among factors leading to these restrictions are 'hostile public attitudes' to individuals whose disabilities are not visible and obvious (Ibid.). Differences in the ways that people are treated, including discrimination, are considered to be culturally produced through the relationship between 'the mode of production' and the 'central values' of a particular society (p. 23). Marx ([1859]/1981, pp. 20–21, preface) had said that social existence determines people's consciences, and Oliver concurs. Indeed, Oliver (1990) sees disabled individuals as 'an ideological construction', related to 'the core ideology' of individualism, medicalisation and normality. It is the 'discursive practices' emerging from these ideologies that structure an individual's experience of disability (Ibid., p. 58).

Oliver's (1996) definition of disabled people comprises three characteristics: 'the presence of impairment', 'experience of externally imposed restriction' and 'self-identification as a disabled person' (Ibid., p. 5). Through political economy, phenomena including social categories are produced by the 'economic and social forces of capitalism itself'. The forms in which they are produced are dependent ultimately on 'their relationship to the economy' (p. 31). It is economic and social forces then that 'produce' disability in the form in which it appears (Ibid.).

Given these views, it is unsurprising that Oliver (1999) regards the production of disability as no different from the production of material goods like cars and hamburgers (Ibid., p. 83; page numbers here refer to the reprint of Oliver's [1999] essay in Mitchell). Disability is produced as an economic problem because of changes in the nature of work and the 'needs of the labour market within capitalism' (p. 84). As capitalism rose, disabled people experienced social and economic exclusion, so that disability was 'produced' as an individual problem requiring medical treatment. The institution was at the heart of this exclusion (p. 86). Community care came as a response to the increasing cost of institutional care. Yet the continuation of community-based care is only an extension of 'the process of control within a capitalist state' (p. 87). Power relationships between professionals and disabled people have stayed the same with the social structure under late capitalism being characterised by 'difference' based on features such as abilities and gender (p. 88).

Barnes (1998) regards the social model of disability as focusing on the 'environmental and social barriers which exclude people with perceived impairments from mainstream society'. Impairment is seen as the 'biological characteristics of the body and mind', while disability is presented as 'society's failure to address the needs of disabled people'. It follows that policy should focus on those aspects of the lives of disabled people which can (and should be) changed (Ibid., p. 78). For Corker and Shakespeare (2002), the social model concerns the 'political project of emancipation' and, in some forms, has to do with shaping 'an oppositional politics of identity' (Ibid., p. 3).

In a similar way, Thomas and Corker (2002) draw on 'historical materialist premises' in seeking to understand the nature of social and cultural systems. Disability and disablism in today's society is seen as related, firstly to society's economic foundations of 'capitalist and social relations of production', and secondly to 'cultural forms and ideological phenomena'. Both of these factors are seen as being shaped by and having an influence upon the economic foundations (Ibid., p. 19). Accordingly, a material perspective can 'engage richly' with 'the cultural, ideological and the psychosocial (for example identity)' (p. 20).

On the face of it, a historical-materialist analysis has clearer resonance with physical disabilities than with disorders such as autism or intellectual disability. However, it has been argued that a historical-materialist perspective embraces such disorders too. There appear to be several points of contact between the historical-materialist views just outlined and social views of mental disorder. Among these are the possible influence of hostile public attitudes, discrimination and exclusion. Also, both might challenge a 'core ideology' of individualism, medicalisation and normality and could inform discussion of broad changes from institutional care to more community-based care.

Symbolic interactionism and the social production of reality

In addition to a historical-materialist account of mental disorder, symbolic interactionism also has relevance. Symbolic interactionism developed from many sources, typified by the work of several contributors. American sociologist Charles Cooley (1864–1929) proposed the notion of the 'looking glass self'. This suggests that individuals partly regard themselves as they believe others see them, with implications for the development of the self-concept (Cooley, [1902]/1983). American philosopher George Herbert Mead (1863–1931) considered that social processes were prior to the processes of individual experience, with 'mind' arising within the social processes of communication (Mead, [various dates and 1934]/1967). Herbert Blumer (1900–1987), the American sociologist, first coined the term 'symbolic interactionism', citing three premises. These were (a) that individuals act towards things according to the meaning that those things have for them; (b) that those meanings derive from social interactions with other people; and (c) that those meanings are dealt with and modified through an interpretative process used by the individual (Blumer, 1986, p. 2, paraphrased).[1]

In comparison with the historical-materialist perspective, the relevance of symbolic interactionism to a social view of mental disorder is readily apparent. In broad terms, symbolic interactionism is a sociological view of the self and of society. People live in a symbolic environment. The meaning of symbols (seen as social objects derived from human culture) is shared and developed in interaction with others. Language and communication enable symbols to be the means by which reality is constructed, so that reality is largely a social product. A sense of self, culture and society emerge from symbolic interactions, and indeed they are dependent on symbolic interaction for their very existence. In the way that it is made relevant to human behaviour, the physical environment too is interpreted through symbolic systems. Individual experiences are given meaning by being socially formed, and meaning is constructed in the process of being shared. Individuals respond to another person in line with the meaning that they put on that person's actions. Symbols, interpretation and efforts to figure out meaning all mediate human action, with better interpretations being retained and poorer ones rejected. In social interaction, meanings are negotiated, challenged and modified, giving them a rational basis. In this perspective, the language that people use about mental disorders and the interactions between those having mental disorders and others are clearly important. (Please also see Farrell, 2012, pp. 145–148.)

Labelling theory

Labelling theory is also seen as relevant to a social view of disorders. It is informed by symbolic interactionism, which has just been discussed, and by phenomenology. Very briefly, phenomenology is a philosophical perspective with different emphases. For example, the transcendental phenomenology of Husserl ([1913]/1982, [1913]/1989, [1913]/1980) maintains that although the independent existence of things can be questioned, what cannot be doubted is how things appear to us immediately in consciousness. Accordingly, knowledge should be based on these phenomenal experiences. (Please also see Farrell, 2012, pp. 49–53.)

Labelling theory applied these ideas from symbolic interactionism and from phenomenology to deviance and crime, specifically to deviant acts and identities. This led to an emphasis on the ways in which acts and identities are constructed, interpreted, evaluated and controlled over time. In labelling theory, language is crucially important in the process of developing a 'career' of deviance. Labelling taking place in the criminal justice system is believed to have particular power and authority. An individual commits an initial delinquent act (the so-called primary deviance) and then experiences the reactions of others identifying him or her as deviant. The individual may respond in a deviant role, for example as a means of defence or attack. If so the deviance becomes 'secondary'. That is, it incorporates the knowledge, stereotypes and experience of others in shaping identity and future behaviour (Becker, 1963).

Having laid some of the groundwork of the influences on a social view of disorders of historical materialism, symbolic interactionism and labelling theory, we are now able to look at advocacy and mental disorder.

Advocacy in action

PAUSE FOR REFLECTION: ASPECTS OF ADVOCACY

Search the Internet for the video 'What Is Advocacy?' (www.youtube.com/watch?v=NnOk2tTz468).

Twelve aspects of advocacy are listed. Is there any order of importance of these in your view?

Writing in the context of a Mad Pride perspective, Lewis ([2006]/2010), in what might be an allusion to the binary ideas of French philosopher Jacques Derrida ([1967]/1997), suggests that 'the binary between normal and abnormal' bolsters the psychiatrisation. It does so by giving 'tremendous social and psychological pressure to stay on the side of normality' (Ibid., p. 162). The social stigma and oppression against 'mental difference' is described as 'sanism'. Many in Mad Pride, it is stated, see their 'mental difference' as a 'valued capacity'. Activists have to deal with 'state sponsored coercion in the forms of involuntary commitment and forced medication laws' (Ibid.). An example is that biomedical science has been 'able to justify a broad range of subordination practices' (p. 162).

While there are earlier antecedents, the more recent ones of the 1970s are identified as being relevant to the development of Mad Pride. Activists were motivated by their 'negative treatment within the psychiatric system' and by being treated with 'disrespect, disregard and discrimination' (Ibid., p. 163). Many suffered from 'unjustified confinement, verbal and physical abuse, and exclusion from treatment planning' (Ibid.).

Peer-run alternatives were given a boost by the publication of the book *On Our Own* (Chamberlin, 1977) describing ex-patients who had set up alternatives to the mental health system. The early period of the Mad Pride movement was, states Lewis ([2006]/2010), 'the most radical in its epistemological critique' (Ibid., p. 165). Early leaders of the group drew ideas from writers who came to be known as being 'anti-psychiatry'. Since that early period, Mad Pride, it is said, has 'increasingly infiltrated the health system', whereas before it criticised the system from the outside (p. 166). It is stated that 'institutional psychiatry continues to ignore and denigrate' the efforts of Mad Pride. However, some 'important government agencies involved in mental health policy' have begun to take notice, for example the national Center for Mental Health Services (CMHS). This has led to 'increasing consumer participation' in planning treatments and the governance of facilities and developing 'peer run treatment alternatives' (Ibid.).

Lewis ([2006]/2010) suggests that developments in psychiatry have led to a 'scientific revolution' that primarily values 'quantitative positivistic' protocols for research (Ibid., p. 167). An associated emphasis on objective data has led to a preference for 'neuroscience and genetics'. At the same time, 'cultural and humanistic styles of enquiry' have been comparatively neglected. This new psychiatry 'working in tandem' with pharmaceutical funding has led to a dominant 'biopsychiatry' emphasising 'biomedical style diagnoses' and 'pharmaceutical treatments' (Ibid.). Drawbacks of drug treatments have not always been made clear. For example, treatments are expensive, may not be effective and can have side effects. Drug treatments have been given priority, and alternatives such as 'psychotherapy, peer-support, and personal and political activism' have been less considered (p. 168). Mad Pride 'continues to have some success in destabilising psychiatry's biomedical model' (p. 169).

Regarding the infrastructure of Mad Pride, the Conference of Human Rights and Psychiatric Oppression was replaced by the Alternatives Conference. This signalled a shift of emphasis from focusing on oppression to focusing on support, although both are relevant. Members are connected through Support Coalitions International, which brings together local groups from across the world. Their website is called MindFreedom. (An example of their views on language relating to mental disorder is discussed later in this chapter.)

Summarising, Lewis ([2006]/2010) maintains that the Mad Pride movement has 'worked impressively to expose psychiatry as a limited field of enquiry, to open up services to more peer-run alternatives, and to reduce coercive connections between psychiatry and the state' (Ibid., p. 173). The fight has also been to 'reduce individualisation, psychiatrisation, and sanist approaches' (Ibid.). There is reference to 'active biocultural citizenship regarding mental difference and distress' (Ibid.). Mad Pride's language, to the extent that it is reflected in Lewis's article, emphasises the perceived oppressive nature of psychiatry. There is resistance to 'traditional distinctions and *hierarchies*'. The traditional approach is said to '*blame and punish* the *victim* for structural problems'. There is said to be 'state sponsored *coercion*' in the forms of '*involuntary* commitment and *forced* medication laws'. There is 'a broad range of *subordination* practices' (emphasis added). One response to this is reflected in the language of subversion and military operation or espionage, where there are efforts aimed at '*undermining* stereotyped representations of individualism, medicalisation and normality' that have 'increasingly *infiltrated* the health system'.

Advocacy and its sources

Sources of advocacy in relation to psychosis include charities or other organisations run by people who have experienced mental disorders, including psychosis. Advocacy is not necessarily the only or the main purpose of such groups. Some such organisations also provide services independently or contribute to already-existing health services.

In the United Kingdom, for example, one body is the National Service User Network (NSUN, www.nsun.org.uk) established in 2007. This charity is led by 'service users' and connects 'people with experience of mental health issues' to provide a voice to influence policies and services. The network publishes a *Members' Manifesto* on their website (accessed August 2016). One item is to 'provide alternatives to medication, and reflect the social model of disability, in better person-centred support'. The manifesto states the view that 'mental health continues to be understood within a medical framework'. The approach is 'led by professionals', it puts people into 'medicalised diagnostic categories' and its treatments are 'based on drugs and hospital treatment'. The 'medical model' is one of 'mental illness'. The work of the NSUN is 'underpinned' by a 'social model' that seeks alternatives to the medical model. The organisation calls for the next government to move towards integrating physical and mental health services 'to create a more holistic model of care and reduce stigma' (Ibid.).

In the United States, a nonprofit organisation, MindFreedom International, brings together some one hundred sponsor and grass-roots groups with individual members. The aim is to 'win human rights and alternatives for people labelled with psychiatric disabilities' (www.mindfreedom.org). Goals include challenging 'abuse by the psychiatric industry', supporting 'the self-determination of psychiatric survivors and mental health consumers' and advocating for 'safe, humane and effective options for mental health'. The MindFreedom mission statement brings together some of these aims and goals, expressing 'a spirit of mutual cooperation' and stating that it 'leads a nonviolent revolution of freedom, equality, truth and human rights that unites people affected by the mental health system with movements for justice everywhere'. The website states that the majority of members of MindFreedom are 'people who have experienced human rights violations in the mental health system' or 'psychiatric survivors'. The site further states that MindFreedom is where 'the power of mutual support combines with the power of human rights activism' ('Who we are' page accessed August 2016).

MindFreedom and views about language use

An example of an argument about the importance of language in relation to activ-ism and advocacy is provided by an essay on the MindFreedom International website accessed in 2016 (www.mindfreedom.com). Written by David Oaks, the essay is called 'Let's Find Language More Inclusive Than Mentally Ill' (Oaks, 2016). It asks several questions concerning being more 'inclusive with our language' in the 'mental health field' and showing those who have been 'marginalised' by 'psychiatric labels' that they are listened to and welcomed. The author indicates that this is not about being 'politically correct' but does make a call to stop the use of the terms 'mentally ill' or 'mental illness' and find replacements. Relatedly, concerns are raised about the 'medical model'.

Concerns about the 'medical model'

On the MindFreedom website, Oaks (2016), referring to a book by Ann Goldberg (2001), *Sex, Religion and the Making of Modern Madness*, states that 'her research seems to show we have been some of the people who have not "fitted in" to a modernis-ing society, a society that has some major problems itself'. The 'medical model' is described as 'psychiatry's dominant ideology', which in the 1800s was 'simply a kind of rallying flag to consolidate the power of the dominant psychiatrists'. It was 'about setting boundaries for power, and it was not about science'. Referring to another book, *The Masters of Bedlam* (Scull, MacKenzie and Hervey, 2014), the essay says that this will help readers to understand 'how a few hundred elites in England in the 1800s helped construct the medical domination system we see today'. It is recognised that the *DSM* of the American Psychiatric Association, which is seen as 'psychiatry's own official bible', does not use the phrase 'mental illness'. From this, the essay concludes, 'so it is actually scientifically impossible, by psychiatry's own standards, to be officially "diagnosed mentally ill"'. There is a video link to see people led by MindFreedom marching in front of the American Psychiatric Asso-ciation meeting in Philadelphia in 2012 'protesting the *DSM*'.

Concerns about secrecy and power

Referring to work on the *DSM-5*, which was being developed at the time, Oaks (2016) states that 'USA psychiatrists are currently working behind closed doors on their fifth revision of the *DSM*, which has international implications'. The organisers of the early meetings discussing possible changes to the *DSM* 'despite our many requests' have 'refused to open those doors or even respond to our civil inquiries'. However, following 'public pressure', the American Psychiatric Association has 'opened up a bit' and created as *DSM-5* website to gather public comments about its draft. But the essay states that 'we want far more than input on a website to the few hundred privileged professionals who literally vote on our labels'. Oaks (2016) refers to psychologists, psychiatrists and others working as specialists on diagnostic procedures and seeking majority agreement on contentious issues. This he regards as 'literally voting on what courts and legislatures consider "normal"' and is an 'unfair legal power'.

Risk of negative labelling

Where categorisation risks becoming the sole way of seeing a person, it may give rise to problems of negative labelling and lowered expectations (Farrell, 2010, pp. 74–83). Of course, categories refer to disorders rather than to individuals. Saying that a person has 'schizophrenia' does not categorise the individual solely in these terms. There will be many other ways in which the individual will be seen in relation to other possible groupings, such as gender, ethnic group, age and interests, as well as individual characteristics. On the other hand, some individuals and those close to them welcome a label such as a 'delusional disorder' as an aid to understanding previously bewildering aspects of their experience.

MindFreedom takes the view that labelling can be negative, although the point of labelling theory from which much of the unease about labelling stems is sometimes overlooked. As indicated earlier, labelling theory is informed by phenomenology (Husserl, [1913]/1982, [1913]/1989, [1913]/1980) and by symbolic interactionism (Cooley, [1902]/1983; Mead, [various dates and 1934]/1967; Blumer, 1986). It developed in relation to a view of deviancy and crime with notions of a 'deviant career' and of primary and secondary deviance being central (Becker, 1963).

When negative labelling is discussed in relation to mental disorders, it is not always made explicit how these labels apply. Consequently, it is not clear how labelling theory transfers to mental disorder. It may be argued that similar processes apply to the construction of psychotic behaviour and identity and the way that identity is constructed, interpreted, evaluated and controlled over time. It could be suggested that language powerfully influences the process of developing a 'career' of psychosis, although the parallels between crime and psychosis seem rather stretched in this aspect. Nevertheless, it may be maintained that labelling taking place in the health care system may have particular power and authority. An individual behaves in a way that is seen as psychotic (perhaps equated with 'primary deviance') and then experiences the reactions of others identifying him or her as psychotic. The individual may respond in a psychotic role, for example, as a means of defence or attack. If so the psychosis becomes 'secondary', incorporating the knowledge, stereotypes and experience of others in shaping identity and future behaviour. It is the last part of the parallel that does not seem convincing. It is as if the individual is choosing to be psychotic because others expect it. Such issues are not always considered sufficiently, and instead a rather glib and watered-down version of labelling seems to be adopted in which it is simply assumed that certain labels are negative and harmful.

Discrimination

Diagnosis and discrimination

Oaks (2016) argues that diagnoses such as 'psychosis' are like being 'officially labelled'. Worries may be expressed about discrimination, such as when it is stated that 'the discrimination against those with that "p-word" label is so immense'. Discrimination where it is unfair can be challenged and changed, 'such as through legislation'. Dislike of the *DSM* is reflected in comments that compare it to the guidance provided to identify witches in medieval times. It is said that 'the pseudo-scientific aura around the composition and organisation of the *DSM* is reminiscent of the book once used to "diagnose" witches, the infamous, *Malleus Maleficarum*'. Relatedly, the medical perspective, 'the medical model approach', is seen as 'narrow'. Those who benefit from seeing 'mental and emotional problems' as 'primarily a biologically based issue', for example 'pharmaceutical companies', are the ones who 'benefit by medical model language'.

'Sanism' as discrimination

As Oaks (2016) points out, the word 'sanism' is sometimes used to convey the idea of people who are sane discriminating against those with mental disorders. The parallel is with other terms such as 'sexism', 'racism' and 'ageism', to suggest negative and unfair discrimination against individuals because of respectively their gender, race or age. If there is negative and unfair discrimination against someone because, for example, they have experienced psychosis, then this would be regarded as 'sanism'. If it could be demonstrated that someone was rejected for a job that they were capable of fulfilling because they had experienced psychosis and this was irrelevant to their job application, then negative discrimination could conceivably be claimed.

Rejecting medical terminology

'Mentally ill' and other medical terms

A term that Oaks (2016) rejects is 'mentally ill' because it reflects 'very much a narrow medical model'. Others are free to use the term about themselves, but where it is used about others, including 'psychiatric survivors', there are unwelcome implications. For example, it could suggest that 'since "illness" is the problem, then a physician ought to be part of the solution'. Also, if 'mental illness' is 'like a materialistic physical illness', then the implication might be that 'the solution ought to be physical too, such as a chemical or a drug or electricity'. However, the intention, it is stated, is not to oppose the medical model as such but to resist 'domination by any model in this complex field' and to oppose 'bullying in mental health care'. The response, it is said, should be to 'drop the use of other words that tend to confine us in the dominant model', such as 'patient', 'chemical imbalance', 'biologically based', 'symptom', 'brain disease' and 'relapse', when speaking of 'those who have been labelled with a psychiatric disability'.

Reasons for replacing the term 'mentally ill'

Oaks (2016) argues for the replacement of the expression 'mentally ill'. One reason for this is to show that 'we are listening to psychiatric survivors' who have 'strong preferences' about what they are called. Another is to demonstrate that a 'wide range of perspectives' is heard, including those of people who have been shut out because of the 'current paradigm in mental health'. A further reason for replacing the term 'mentally ill' is 'to show we are trying to care'. Here, the rationale is that words and social reality itself are constructs that we 'co-create'.

Changing language

Oaks (2016) suggests that a response to the unwanted labelling by *DSM* professionals would be to aim to alter the language 'we personally use'. Some people in our 'mad movement' use the term 'mentally ill' because they think it is more recognised by the public. Others define themselves as 'mentally ill' and accept the medical model. But, it is objected, the medical model has become the 'bully in the room'. Language that reflects a medical model is seen as encouraging 'domination'. It is regarded as unhelpful to the 'nonviolent revolution in the health system we need'. This is a revolution of 'choice, empowerment and self-determination'. What also has to be taken into account, the essay suggests, is people who 'define their problems from a social, psychological, spiritual or other point of view'. Others do not see 'their differences' as problems, just as 'differences' or as 'qualities'. Oaks (2016) recognises that it is not going to be possible to find 'perfect' or 'correct' language. There is no consensus, and there may never be. But it is suggested that 'diverse speculation is a wonderful antidote to the falsehood of certainty'.

Alternatives to rejected terms

Highlighting the label

Oaks (2016) discusses alternatives to undesired terms. Some alternatives point out the labelling nature of the terms, either directly or with reference to diagnosis.

These are 'person labelled with psychiatric disability' and 'person labelled with psychosocial disability', as well as 'person diagnosed with a mental disorder', 'person diagnosed with a psychiatric disorder' and 'psychiatrically diagnosed'. There are difficulties with what Oaks suggests here. The implication of preferring such terms seems to be that the person with the label can point to the label as a label and can agree or not agree that it applies to them. Thus, the individual may claim to have a psychiatric or psychosocial disability or merely be labelled in that way. Similarly, the person may have a mental disorder, a psychiatric disorder or simply be diagnosed by someone else as such. These terms can draw attention to the labels, helpfully conveying to others that labels are not everything. However, they face a difficulty of being unclear whether the diagnosis or the label is accepted or not. Do the phrases mean that the person has been labelled and they accept the label? Or do they mean that the label was applied and they do not accept it? If so, why mention the label in the first place? Perhaps one response to this is the slogan 'I have a name not a label . . . John' (or whatever the name is).

Users, survivors and 'experience of'

Oaks (2016) refers to a range of expressions. One cluster of phrases highlights that the person has used mental health services. Examples are 'mental health consumer', 'user of mental health services' and 'mental health client'. It may need further clarification if anyone was interested in why the individual used mental health services. Was it because of psychosis? Depression? Anxiety? The emphasis on 'use' avoids such direct references. A 'mental health peer' perhaps means that the person is a peer to others whether those others have mental disorders or not. If so, it suggests a dislike of labelling.

Some expressions seem to convey resentment or negative experiences of treatment and a view that, far from helping, psychiatric intervention was something that one was fortunate to survive. Examples are 'psychiatric survivor', 'person who identifies as a survivor of psychiatric atrocities', 'person in mental health care who is on the sharp end of the needle', 'survivor of forced psychiatry', 'psychiatrised' and terms that combine being a consumer with resenting the system: 'Consumer/Survivor/eX-inmate', which is abbreviated as CSX.

Experience rather than use is suggested by a 'person who has experienced the mental health system' and 'person with lived experience of mental health care'. A set of phrases that seem to emphasise that any mental disorder is in the past and that the individual now has no such disorder include 'person with a mental health history' and 'person with a psychiatric history'.

Euphemism

Perhaps the most direct alternative to 'mentally ill' mentioned by Oaks (2016) is 'person with a psychosocial disability'. Other terms, however, are more indirect, conveying various positions, some of them euphemistic. One can avoid any suggestion that there might be a difficulty or a problem if one uses terms such as 'person with mental and emotional *challenges*', 'person with mental health *issues*' or 'person with psychiatric *vulnerabilities*'. One can use the word 'problem' but avoid stating what the problem might be as with 'person who experiences problems in living', which surely applies to everyone and consequently is not a very useful expression. Doubly euphemistic is 'person our society considers to have very different and unusual behaviour'. The 'unusual behaviour' given as an example is 'not sleeping', although this is surely not an unusual behaviour at all. Here, the nature of the behaviour that might be widely considered to be very different or unusual is avoided, as well as any judgement on whether it is in fact very different or unusual or just something that society considers so and may have got wrong.

The mental state of the person might be described. Among the more direct of these are 'person experiencing severe and overwhelming mental and emotional problems (e.g. despair)' or simply 'in despair'. The expression 'in crisis' suggests a difficult situation, as well as someone having difficulty responding to it. But it is not specific enough to be clear about what the crisis is and why there might be a difficulty responding to it. For example, someone with insufficient money with which to live is 'in crisis' financially. Other terms are more evasive. 'Distressed' hardly conveys mental disorder and can be used quite casually as in 'I was distressed to hear you had a nasty cold last week'. Similarly, a 'person with lived experience of the extremes of human experience' could be any number of artists, mountaineers or others who experience great joy or challenge in their work. 'In ecstasy' might describe a happy wedding night. 'Overwhelmed' and 'extremely overwhelmed' might suggest a busy working week, while 'upset' could describe someone who has just lost a house key.

A few examples are even more nebulous. It is unclear what 'neurodiverse' means, but if it suggests that different people have different neurological connections, it conveys little. Also, 'different' might describe anyone. Is not everyone different in some way or another? Therefore, as an alternative to terms describing mental disorders it is evasive. That someone is a 'citizen', a 'person' or 'a human being! Period!' perhaps conveys that the individual does not want to be labelled or seen exclusively {or too much} in terms of any mental disorders that he or she may experience. But as alternatives they are unhelpful. If someone, for example, was discussing their mental health and stated that he or she received treatment, someone might ask the reason for this. If the answer was 'because I am citizen', it becomes clear that the term is too broad to be meaningful in this context.

Quotation marks and other approaches

Among the ways of indicating that certain words are unacceptable or need to be questioned is the use of quotation marks. 'A person with schizophrenia' then becomes 'A person with "schizophrenia"'. Oaks (2016) suggests that even better is the use of expressions such as 'people diagnosed with "schizophrenia"' or as 'people labelled with "schizophrenia"'. Some 'activists' do not 'want to give legitimacy to this process by using the word *diagnosis*, a word that can mean identifying an illness based on science and medicine'. This is explained by stating, 'Exploring the complexities of language – even if it takes a few extra words – is far better than tagging people with a judgemental and harmful label'.

Conclusion

Background influences informing advocacy and the importance of language in relation to mental disorders include criticisms of a medical model of disability and a preference for a social perspective.

Goffman ([1961]/1981), applying the medical model to 'institutional psychiatry', sees it as part of 'the interpretation of persons who seem to act oddly'. Regarding a social view of disability, Oliver (1990) developed a historical-materialist account of disablement which, although tending to focus on physical disabilities, has some relevance for mental disorders. Barnes (1998) regards the social model of disability as focusing on the 'environmental and social barriers which exclude people with perceived impairments from mainstream society'. Impairment is regarded as the 'biological characteristics of the body and mind' while disability is seen as 'society's failure to address the needs of disabled people'. For Corker and Shakespeare (2002), the social model concerns 'the political project of emancipation'. Other influences on the relevance of language and mental disorder are symbolic interactionism and phenomenology, which has informed labelling theory. Symbolic interactionism developed from sources including Cooley ([1902]/1983), who proposed the notion of the 'looking glass self'; Mead ([various dates and 1934]/1967), who considered that social processes were prior to the processes of individual experience; and Blumer (1986), who coined the term 'symbolic interactionism'. Labelling theory is informed by symbolic interactionism and by phenomenology, including transcendental phenomenology (Husserl, [1913]/1982, [1913]/1989, [1913]/1980).

An example of an advocacy movement is Mad Pride (Lewis, [2006]/2010). This movement, it is said, has worked to 'expose psychiatry as a limited field of enquiry, to open up services to more peer-run alternatives, and to reduce coercive connections between psychiatry and the state' and to 'reduce individualisation, psychiatrisation, and sanist approaches' (Ibid., p. 173). The importance of language in relation to activism and advocacy is reflected in an essay on the MindFreedom International website called 'Let's Find Language More Inclusive Than Mentally Ill' (Oaks, 2016). The essay expresses concerns about the medical model and the supposed secrecy and power in the development of *DSM-5*. It discusses negative labelling, discrimination and medical language. Alternatives to medical-type terms are suggested, but these present their own difficulties, and some alternatives can appear euphemistic, unclear and evasive.

Thinking points

Readers may wish to consider:

- possible reasons for wanting to change the language used by wider society about mental disorders and psychosis;
- the extent to which such language can be changed in wider society, and what factors support and resist such moves.

Note

1 Please also see the Society for the Study of Social Interactionism website at www.socialinteractionism.org.

Key text

Newbigging, K., Ridley, J., McKeown, M., Sadd, J., Machin, K., Cruse, K., De La Haye, S., Able, L. and Poursanidou, K. (2015) *Mental Health Advocacy – the Right to be Heard: Context, Values and Good Practice* London and Philadelphia, Jessica Kingsley Publishers.

The first part of this book contextualises mental health advocacy and provides a historical background. The second part concerns the practise and experience of independent mental health advocacy services.

Internet resources

MindFreedom International website (www.mindfreedom.com)
The National Service User Network (www.nsun.org.uk)

7

ANTI-PSYCHIATRY

Introduction

Some commentators consider the history of anti-psychiatry quite broadly to refer to the resistance to psychiatric ideas that can be traced back to the origins of psychiatry itself. For others, it refers more aptly to a movement that coalesced in the 1960s and 1970s and was associated with writers such as Erving Goffman, Thomas Szasz and R. D. Laing. Consensus is also lacking on the influence of anti-psychiatry and whether its day is over or whether in modified forms it persists to the present time. In examining such issues, we first need to provisionally specify what anti-psychiatry is. This allows us to examine the views and language of some of the people associated with its development and what may be seen as modern-day anti-psychiatry messages. Finally, we can consider examples of the issues raised and the language that is used to convey them.

What is anti-psychiatry?

To be against a discipline or a way of doing things implies a particular view of what it is that one opposes. To be 'anti' psychiatry implies holding a certain view of psychiatry which one strives against. Such a view of psychiatry may or may not be the same as that of others.

In an earlier chapter concerning the language of psychiatry, I suggested that medical terminology typifies psychiatric discussions, including those to do with psychosis and schizophrenia. Terms like 'prevalence', 'development and course', 'risk factors', 'aetiology' and 'treatment' are the same as the ones used when referring to physical illnesses, and many such expressions reflect a scientific stance. However, a psychiatric view as reflected, for example, in the guidance in *DSM-5* (American Psychiatric Association, 2013) not only is biological but also takes account of environmental and other factors. An example is that assessment criteria for schizophrenia specify that for younger people, there is 'a failure to achieve expected levels of interpersonal, academic or occupational functioning' (Ibid., p. 103). There is no implication that the condition is incurable, and it is observed that 'course and outcome may not be reliably predicted' (Ibid.). There is no talk of 'disease' or 'disease of the brain'. Nor is it claimed that the inevitable response to psychosis is medication. This is not the depiction of psychiatry that anti-psychiatrists are against.

Essentially, anti-psychiatry is an opposition to psychiatry and psychiatric interventions on various grounds. Psychiatry is seen as doing more harm than good. It is regarded as oppressive and coercive in part because of the unequal relationship that exists between physician and patient. The identification and assessment of mental disorders are challenged. The *Diagnostic and Statistical Manual of Mental Disorders* (American Psychiatric Association, 2013) is sometimes a focus for such questioning, to the extent that its classifications are seen as unreliable and invalid. This relates to concerns about negative labelling that is seen as based on inadequate grounds and likely to inhibit the life chances of those who are labelled. Critics point to the great expansion of perceived mental disorders in the various editions of the *DSM* and question whether the remit is so wide that everyone it seems has a mental disorder.

Treatments are criticised as being at worst harmful, while historically such interventions as lobotomy may be cited as being excessively used or inhumane. Shoddy conditions in some 'mental asylums' in the past are also raised as indications of the poor treatment of 'inmates'. In more current practise, the use of drugs is questioned. This includes worry about the side effects and the perceived overuse of medications, including those for children. Reference may be made to the great influence of pharmaceutical companies and the profits made from drugs. Concern is also expressed about the involuntary treatment and commitment of individuals with certain mental disorders.

In its rejection of psychiatry, anti-psychiatry seeks to develop other explanations for mental disorders other than that they are medical conditions. Among the alternative explanations of psychosis is that it is a response to the wrongs of civilisation and that it is a misunderstood creative force. As Shorter (1997) summarises the view, 'psychiatric illness is not medical in nature but social, political and legal' (Ibid., p. 274). Furthermore, 'society defines what schizophrenia and depression is, and not nature. If psychiatric illness is thus socially constructed, it must be deconstructed in the interest of freeing deviants, free spirits, and exceptional creative people from the stigma of being "pathological"'.

Nasrallah (2010) suggests that anti-psychiatry sentiment has been evident for two centuries. A more common view is that something of a surge in antipathy took place in the 1960s. For example, David Cooper (1931–1986), a South African born psychiatrist, coined the term 'anti-psychiatry'. Having worked in in several London hospitals, he ran in the early 1960s an experimental unit for schizophrenics. His book *Psychiatry and Anti-Psychiatry* was published in 1967. Being existentialist and Marxist, Cooper regarded psychotherapy as a sort of social control that developed hand in glove with capitalism as a further form of repression. Given this link, he believed that psychiatry could be demolished through the political transformation of society (Cooper, 1980).

Furnham (2015) observes that supporters of anti-psychiatry questioned three features. These were 'the medicalisation of madness; the existence of mental illness; and the power of psychiatrists to detain and treat certain individuals'. The loose coalition of people involved in the anti-psychiatry movement tended to be interested in 'authenticity and liberation', 'empowerment and personal management' (as opposed to the use of drugs), 'social power and control' and the problems of 'stigma and discrimination'. Pharmaceutical industries came in for heavy criticism. The movement is also concerned with the 'power of diagnostic labels'. Among those who influenced the positions that are expressed in anti-psychiatry is Erving Goffman, whose work is discussed in some detail given its wide influence. Other important figures are Thomas Szasz and Ronald David Laing (Nasser, 1995). It is to the views of these figures that we now turn.

Erving Goffman's *Asylums*

Total institutions

Sociologist Erving Goffman (1922–1982) contributed to a trend that led to many mental 'asylums' being replaced by community-orientated alternatives (Weinstein, 1994). In *Asylums*, Goffman ([1961]/1981) discusses the effect of 'total institutions' through the roles and practises in asylums and other institutions, such as boarding schools, sanatoria, brainwashing camps and prisons (p. 16). Such institutions, in efforts to maintain and regulate behaviour, create rituals so that different groups know and follow their expected roles. Goffman gathered material working undercover from 1955–1956 as the supposed 'assistant to the athletics director' at St. Elizabeth's Hospital in Washington, DC (p. 7).

A total institution is defined as 'a place of residence and work where a large number of like-situated individuals, cut off from the wider society for an appreciable period of time, together lead an enclosed, formally administered round of life' (p. 11). It is something of a hybrid, being 'part residential community, part formal organisation', as well as being a 'forcing house' for changing persons (p. 22). These institutions break down normal barriers between spheres of sleep, play and work (p. 17).

Bureaucratically managing many people leads to a split between a 'large managed group' (inmates) and a 'small supervisory staff' (p. 18). Talk across the staff-inmate 'boundary' is restricted, helping to maintain 'antagonistic stereotypes' (pp. 19–20). There is incompatibility between total institutions and the 'basic work-payments structure of our society', as well as between the institutional 'batch living' and family life (p. 21). *Asylums* comprises four 'papers', three of which are considered here (the paper on a medical model was discussed in the 'Advocacy' chapter earlier).

Characteristics of total institutions

'On the Characteristics of Total Institutions' examines the social life of such places, especially those of involuntary membership: mental hospitals and prisons, drawing on a 'symbolic interaction framework' (p. 50). An inmate, on entering, begins a series of 'abasements, degradations, humiliations, and profanations of self' (p. 24). He or she begins 'radical shifts' in his or her 'moral career'. Admission procedures program the person to be 'fed into the administrative machinery of the establishment' (p. 26). Also shaping the inmate's life is the privilege system, including house rules, rewards and punishments (pp. 51–53). Supposedly more advanced psychiatric establishments turn didactic feedback into a 'basic therapeutic doctrine' (p. 42). A permissive atmosphere encourages the inmate to act out his 'difficulties in living', which are then 'brought to his attention' during group therapy (Ibid.). Induction and provision constitute a stripping process and reorganising process (p. 69).

Inmate responses might include 'situational withdrawal', which can be labelled 'regression' in mental hospitals (p. 61). Another adaptation is the 'compensative satisfaction' involving 'the middle-class vocabulary of group psychotherapy and the classless ideology of psychodynamics'. These give 'some socially ambitious and socially frustrated lower-class mental patients' contact with the 'polite world' (Ibid., p. 65). Effects of the stripping and reorganisation processes are partly counteracted by inmates' opportunities for 'secondary adjustments' and the presence of 'counter-mores' (pp. 78–79).

In institutions, it is suggested, 'concern about words and verbalised perspectives' plays 'a central and often feverish role' (p. 81). Accordingly, the 'automatic identification of the inmate' is essentially a 'means of social control', helping to provide for staff and others the 'institutional perspective' (Ibid., pp. 81–82). Goffman is cynical about the provision of therapy such as group psychotherapy, psychodrama or art therapy. These are introduced with strong hospital management support but are soon 'given only token support except when visitors come to the institution'. In such situations, higher management is keen to demonstrate 'how modern and complete the facilities are' (pp. 87–88). Group therapy is merely an opportunity for inmates to be shaped in the image that staff have for them. In return for spending time in a comparatively 'equalitarian milieu', inmates are expected to become 'more receptive to the ideal-for-self that the staff defines for them' (Ibid., p. 92).

Moral career

'The Moral Career of the Mental Patient' looks at the 'initial effects of institutionalisation' on inmates' previous social relationships (p. 12). 'Career' refers to life course, while 'moral' conveys developing a framework for judging oneself and others (p. 119). For Goffman, 'the perception of losing one's mind is based on culturally derived and socially engrained stereotypes'. These concern the significance of symptoms such as 'hearing voices, losing temporal and spatial orientation, and sensing that one is being followed'. In fact, states Goffman, many such symptoms sometimes psychiatrically signify 'merely a temporary emotional upset in a stressful situation, however terrifying to the person at the time' (pp. 123–124). For some individuals, hospitalisation makes things worse by confirming their 'private experience of self' (p. 124).

The 'pre-patient' starts out with at least some of the 'rights, liberties, and satisfactions of the civilian' but ends up 'on a psychiatric ward stripped of almost everything'. From the pre-patient's viewpoint, the 'circuit of significant figures can function as a kind of betrayal funnel'. In recalling admission, the new patient may feel that while the comfort of everyone else was being maintained, 'his long-range welfare was being undermined' (pp. 130–131). In the 'inpatient phase' after being 'conned' and 'betrayed' into the mental hospital, the individual may show apparent 'manic' behaviour 'to avoid ratifying any interaction that presses a politely reciprocal role upon him and opens him up to what he has become in the eyes of others' (p. 136).

The new patient is subjected to 'mortifying experiences: restriction of free movement, communal living, diffuse authority of a whole echelon of people', which likely affects the individual's sense of self (pp. 137–138). A patient can depict the ward on which he or she is placed as a reflection of his or her own 'general level of social functioning' and his or her personal status so that being with others with 'organic brain damage' can have a negative 'mirroring effect' (p. 139). At least in concentration camps 'self-insulation from the symbolic implications of the settings may be easier'. Self-insulation in mental hospitals may be so hard that 'patients have to employ devices for this which staff interpret as psychotic symptoms' (p. 139, footnote 30). The self-stories of patients, which may make light of problems, are undercut by 'stories already constructed along psychiatric lines', such as the 'official sheet of paper' affirming that 'the patient is of unsound mind, a danger to himself and others'. They are also contested by the 'degrading conditions' of the hospital (p. 142).

Underlife

'The Underlife of a Public Institution' concerns the attachment that 'the inmate is expected to manifest to his iron home' and the way inmates can distance themselves from these expectations (p. 12). A 'formal instrumental organisation' sets out 'officially appropriate standards of welfare, joint values, incentives, and sanctions' which define the participant's 'nature and social being' (p. 164). Every organisation involves a 'discipline of activity' and a 'discipline of being', forming an 'obligation to be of a given character' and to inhabit a 'given world'. But some people default from this (p. 171).

Two kinds of adjustments to settings are envisaged. Primary adjustments are 'congenial', and the individual and institution are adapted satisfactorily, while in secondary adjustments, individuals 'stand apart' from the role and the self that the institution allocates (p. 172, paraphrased). Secondary adjustments may be 'disruptive', aiming at radical change, or 'contained', as an established part of an organisation's 'underlife' (pp. 180–181). Patients' secondary adjustments involved negotiating the hierarchical 'ward system' and services (e.g. 'back wards') through which 'drastically reduced living conditions are allocated via punishments and rewards'. This framework is operated by 'attendants' and by 'higher staff' (p. 186).

The hospital underlife comprises sources, places, facilities and social structures. For example, sources of materials that patients employ in their secondary adjustments include 'make-do's' such as 'working the system' through scavenging (p. 192) or (in the longer term) through getting a job in the laundry and so getting clean clothes more often (p. 198). Staff-patient relationships might involve patronage and 'indulgences' such as treats of food or tobacco or gaining extra access to recreation areas (pp. 242–243). A staff member might give a patient a lift in his or her car to another part of the campus for an appointment (p. 254). The 'paternalistic old-line attendants' might teasingly require 'abject begging signs' from patients for the indulgence of a cigarette (pp. 260–261). So-called removal activities for patients include gambling and enthusiastically pursued supervisory work (p. 273). Such practises suggest that the participant 'has some selfhood and personal autonomy beyond the grasp of the organisation' (pp. 275–276).

Thomas Szasz and the myth of mental illness

Born in Budapest, Thomas Szasz (1920–2012) trained as a psychoanalyst in Chicago and developed the view that mental disorders could be understood as communications and rule-bound 'games'. In *The Myth of Mental Illness*, Szasz ([1960]/2010) argues that it makes no sense to speak of 'mental illness'. Psychiatry is usually defined 'as a medical speciality concerned with the diagnosis and treatment of mental diseases' (Ibid., p. 1). But this, in Szasz's view, confines it to the role of a 'pseudoscience' because there is 'no such thing' as mental illness. He therefore challenges the view that psychiatry should be seen as concerned with 'illness, neurosis, psychosis, treatment'. Instead, Szasz argues for an alternative of focusing on 'interventions or processes' by developing 'the foundations of a process theory of personal conduct' (Ibid., p. 2).

Szasz ([1960]/2010) voiced concerns, held by others to this day, about the expansion of the number and range of supposed mental disorders. Not just physicians and psychiatrists but also philosophers and journalists, lawyers and others became involved in the labelling of 'mental illness'. They labelled as such 'any and every kind of human experience or behaviour in which they could detect, or to which they could ascribe, "malfunctioning" or suffering'. In this environment, 'divorce became an illness because it signalled the failure of marriage; bachelorhood, because it signalled the failure to marry' (Ibid., p. 41).

Rejecting what he calls the 'medical model' as a 'false perspective', Szasz ([1960]/2010) proposes replacing it with new approaches suitable to 'the ethical, political, psychological and social problems from which psychiatric patients suffer and which psychiatrists ostensibly seek to remedy' (Ibid., pp. 78–79). If what is referred to as mental disorder is not an illness, then what is it? For Szasz

([1960]/2010), '"mental illness" is a metaphor' (Ibid., p. 267). Psychiatric diagnoses are 'stigmatising labels, phrased to resemble medical diagnoses'. They are applied to 'persons whose behaviour annoys or offends others'. For example, psychosis is a convenient label for dealing with unwanted behaviour. Szasz states that 'it is a fundamental characteristic of the *language of psychiatry* that imperative sentences habitually masquerade as indicative ones' (emphasis added). To take an example, to say that someone 'is psychotic' is, on the face of it, 'indicative and informative' (Ibid., p. 120). In fact, Szasz believes, such a statement is 'promotive and prescriptive' (Ibid.). If one makes explicit who is the speaker (the 'sign users', as Szasz calls them), such statements can be translated to put the situation in a different light.

To take an example, assume that

> Mrs. John Doe does not like the way her husband is acting. Dr. James Smith believes that men preoccupied by jealousy are mentally ill and potentially dangerous. Hence, both Mrs. Doe and Dr. Smith want Mr. Doe to be confined in a hospital.
>
> *(Ibid., pp. 120–121)*

Such 'indicative sentences' lack the 'promotive impact' of the brief assertion that 'John Doe is psychotic' (Ibid., p. 121). Because mental illnesses are idioms, psychiatry deals not with illnesses but with communications. Szasz points out that, 'although the idea that psychiatry deals with the analysis of communications is not new, the view that so-called mental illnesses are idioms rather than illnesses has not been adequately articulated, nor have its implications been fully appreciated' (Ibid., p. 145).

Psychiatrists 'create diagnoses of mental diseases by giving disease-names to (mis) conduct', and in this regard, they act as 'legislators, not scientists' (Ibid., p. 280). Szasz puts the view that 'the old quacks peddled fake cures to treat real diseases. The new quacks peddle fake diseases to justify chemical pacification and medical coercion'. He adds that 'theocracy is the alliance of religion with the state. Pharmacracy is the alliance of medicine with the state' (Ibid., p. 300).

It follows that, if there is no mental illness, there can be 'no hospitalization, treatments, or cure for it' (Ibid., p. 267). Treatment is seen as 'psychiatric slavery' (Ibid., p. 278). Accordingly, Szasz states that 'there is no medical, moral, or legal justification for involuntary psychiatric interventions'. These are considered 'crimes against humanity' (Ibid., p. 268).

In more recent times, Szasz is still remembered. Oliver (2006), while recognising that Szasz's criticisms 'often became a caricature', notes that one cannot ignore his 'intuition about the limits and deformations of modern psychiatry'. Benefits of psychiatric treatment are evident, including those of talk therapy and drugs, but psychiatry's, 'long history of error', such as snake pits and lobotomy, 'should give us pause'. In short, Oliver suggests, 'scepticism is not backwardness, even if Szasz often took his scepticism to rhetorical extremes' (Ibid.). Buchanan-Parker and Barker (2009) review aspects of Szasz's work and criticisms of it and make a plea that, at the very least, critics might read what he in fact says. Poulsen (2011), writing soon after Szasz's death, described him as 'a critic of our enchantment with psychiatry' and suggests that *The Myth of Mental Illness* 'provided the philosophical basis for the anti-psychiatry and patient advocate movements that began in the 1960s and have flourished ever since'.

PAUSE FOR REFLECTION: SZASZ ON PSYCHIATRY

Search the Internet for the video 'Dr Thomas Szasz on Psychiatry' (www.youtube.com/watch?v=Qj7GmeSAxXo).

What do you consider the most convincing and least convincing aspects of his brief outline?

Ronald David Laing

Ronald David Laing (1927–1989), usually cited as R. D. Laing, qualified in psychiatry in Glasgow, Scotland, and trained in psychoanalysis in London. In his book, *The Divided Self* (Laing, [1960]/1965 and 1969), he presents an existential view in which psychotic delusions can be interpreted as meaningful descriptions of experience offering possibly prophetic insight. He states, for example,

> I am aware that the man who is said to be deluded may be in his delusion telling me the truth, and this in no equivocal or metaphorical sense, but quite literally, and that the cracked mind of the schizophrenic may *let in* light which does not enter the intact minds of many sane people whose minds are closed.
>
> *(Ibid., p. 27, emphasis in original)*

Notable here is how Laing uses a metaphor 'cracked' and from it suggests illumination, 'letting in light', which is not really explained. Laing adds an observation relating to Ezekiel, the Hebrew prophet, and Karl Jaspers (1883–1969), a Swiss psychiatrist and philosopher. Laing notes that 'Ezekiel, in Jaspers' opinion, was a schizophrenic' (Ibid.). Given the difficulty of being confident about psychiatric diagnosis even after extensive discussion with an individual and those close to them, the fact that Laing appears to concur with Jaspers's fanciful 'diagnosis' of someone from history based on a few lines of biblical text is perhaps a little too ambitious.

Laing describes a 'schizoid existential position'. In this, the self is responding 'in order to develop and sustain its identity and autonomy, and in order to be safe from the persistent threat and danger from the world'. In doing this, the self has 'cut off from direct relatedness with others, and has endeavoured to become its own object; to become, in fact, related directly only to itself'. Indeed, the 'cardinal functions' of the self become 'fantasy and observation' (Ibid., p. 137).

The self has difficulty sustaining a sense of reality because it does not come into contact with reality. Instead, 'relationship with others and the world . . . is delegated to false-self system whose perceptions, feelings, thoughts, actions, possess a relatively low "coefficient" of realness' (Ibid., p. 138). The 'inner self' undergoes various changes, for example becoming 'unreal' (Ibid., p. 139). Also, the false-self system undergoes changes, for example becoming 'more autonomous' (Ibid., p. 144).

In summarising, Laing ([1960]/1965 and 1969) states that 'the divorce of the self from the body is both something which is painful to be borne, and which the sufferer desperately longs for someone to help mend, but it is also utilised as the basic means of defence'. The dilemma is that 'the self wishes to be wedded to and embedded in the body'. At the same time, it is constantly afraid to lodge in the body 'for fear of there being subject to attacks and dangers which it cannot escape'. However, the self finds that 'though it is outside the body it cannot sustain the advantages that it might hope for in this position'. Various consequences follow; for example, 'the "inner" self becomes itself split, and loses its own identity and integrity' (Ibid., p. 161). Another outcome for the inner self is that it is 'persecuted . . . by split concretised parts of itself or by its own phantoms which have become uncontrollable' (Ibid., p. 162).

Laing ([1960]/1965 and 1969) says of schizophrenic speech, 'A good deal of schizophrenia is simply nonsense, red-herring speech, prolonged filibustering to throw dangerous people off the scent, to create boredom and futility in others'. Often 'making a fool of himself and the doctor', the schizophrenic is 'playing at being mad to avoid at all costs the possibility of being held *responsible* for a single coherent idea of intention' (Ibid., p. 164, emphasis in original). Laing supports the view of Jung, the Swiss psychoanalyst, that 'the schizophrenic ceases to be schizophrenic when he meets someone by whom he feels understood'. Laing concurs that when this happens, 'most of the bizarrerie which is taken as the, "signs" of the, "disease" simply evaporates'. Furthermore, 'the main agent in uniting the patient, in allowing the pieces to come together and cohere, is the physician's love, a love that recognises the patient's total being, and accepts it, with no strings attached' (Ibid., p. 165).

American analyst Thompson (2015), editing a book on Laing's legacy and contemporary relevance, reflects Laing's wide interests. These included not only alternatives to what was then traditional treatment, and attempts at more humane treatment, but also his existentialism and his interest in mysticism and literature. Maureen Patton (2015), writing in the *Independent* newspaper and prefiguring a play and a film about Laing's legacy, catches the wide-ranging opinions of Laing in part of her title: 'Was the counterculture's favourite psychiatrist a dangerous renegade or a true visionary?' Was he a 'discoverer of profound truths about the human psyche' or simply a 'clever showman with good PR'? Patton quotes Laing's own reflections of his possible legacy, broadcast in a television documentary in the year that Laing died. Referring to the view of his psychiatric colleagues, Laing stated, 'I feel I'm regarded as a brilliant man who's pretty disturbed'. Yet Patton recognises Laing's 'grounding sense of humour' and sees him as 'a creature of his time'. Part of his legacy is considered to be 'the more compassionate way we treat mental-health problems these days'.

Modern anti-psychiatry messages

PAUSE FOR REFLECTION: SCIENTOLOGY

Search the Internet for the video 'Anderson Cooper Interviews Scientology CCHR's Bruce Wiseman' (www.youtube.com/watch?v=5kIDLG-hjK8).

Anderson Cooper says, 'Let's get away from bumper-sticker slogans'. Are there examples in what Bruce Wiseman says that you would characterise in this way?

Among anti-psychiatry views, easily available ones are the videos produced by the organisation the Citizens Commission on Human Rights (CCHR, www.cchr.org), founded by the Church of Scientology and Thomas Szasz. Among the videos are *Psychiatric Industry of Death* and *History of Psychiatry*, as well as *The Making of Madness: Are We All Insane?*

Here, we look at one example, *The Marketing of Madness: The Truth About Psychotropic Drugs*, a nearly three-hour-long video presenting information about the perceived wrongs of psychiatry.[1] At the opening of the video, the narrator mentions 'psychological and emotional problems' and 'severe mental distress'. Asking 'What causes mental distress?' the video then looks at examples of early misguided ideas. It is stated that 'early psychiatrists thought that it was an imbalance of humours that could only be cured by bleeding patients with knives or leeches'. We are told that 'today's psychiatrists tell us that the way to fix unwanted behaviour is by balancing brain chemistry with a pill. Did they get it right this time?'

A speaker then explains that, although it may be claimed that mental disorder can be brought about by a brain chemical imbalance of 'serotonin or dopamine', 'there's never been a study to ever prove that – ever'. After showing several people saying that the drugs that they were prescribed made them feel worse, the narrator states, 'In spite of the crippling effect of these drugs, psychiatrists and drug companies have used them to create a huge and lucrative market worth billions'. This has been done by 'naming more and more of life's problems as mental disorders'. Examples are provided. 'Shyness becomes social anxiety disorder; loss of a loved one, major depressive disorder; homesickness, separation anxiety; suspicion, paranoid personality disorder; having ups and downs, bipolar disorder; distractibility, ADHD'.

The video makes some valid points. Some good examples are given of historical examples of misguided psychiatric interventions. It raises legitimate questions about mass drug marketing. Speaking of sales drives, the narrator states, 'Drug companies also attack prescribing physicians on another flank using armies of drug company sales representatives'. A sales representative then says, 'We always did a full-frontal assault'. The narrator later states,

> One way to get people onto psychotropic drugs is through free samples. These are not provided by psychotropic drug companies out of a sense of charity. They are intended to get the patient on a drug regimen he cannot get off of.

In an interview on the *No Drug Show*, the host Larry Byrnes interviews the president of CHRR in Florida, Dave Figaroa, who he says has been investigating terrorism. Figaroa states that

> psychiatrists employ drugs and conditioning techniques in order to change people from what they normally would be into killing machines, and the terrorist factions that we hear about on TV, behind those individual acts of mayhem, you find psychiatrists, psychologists and their drugs.
>
> *(Byrnes, 2013)*

Having now looked at the contributions of Thomas Szasz, Ronald David Laing and Erving Goffman and at modern-day anti-psychiatric messages, we are now able to consider the language used by these sources.

Evaluation of anti-psychiatry views and language

Goffman

Erving Goffman (1961) drew attention to some of the limitations of asylums and encapsulated in his elaboration of the term 'institutionalisation' some of the functions and negative consequences of these 'total institutions'. Not only did this encourage the option of community provision, but in institutions themselves, it led to those responsible becoming more critical of unnecessary ritual and routine. Mac Suibhne (2011), considering 'Erving Goffman's Asylums 50 Years On', recognises that the book is often seen simply as a 'paradigm of anti-psychiatry' but considers that the work is much more than this. More important was the efforts to humanise patients and examine the 'patterns of interaction that de-humanised them' (Ibid., p. 1).

Goffman's language reveals that he was hardly an impartial observer. As he mentions, he 'came to the hospital with no great respect for the discipline of psychiatry' (Ibid., p. 8). The opportunity of 'relief from economic and social responsibilities', which some might see as beneficial in the short term for some individuals, is 'touted' as therapy (Ibid., p. 57). An inpatient is 'anyone, however robust in temperament, who somehow gets caught up in the heavy machinery of mental-hospital servicing' (Ibid., p. 120). Nursing students touring a ward are like sheep, and only go around in a fleeting sort of way, so we are told that a patient might withdraw when 'a flock of nursing students makes a passing tour of the ward' (Ibid., p. 137).

Therapies are looked down on. They 'were conducted in a relatively indulgent atmosphere and tended to recruit the kinds of patients who were interested in contact with the opposite sex' (p. 201). Goffman speaks of 'group psychotherapists who found it necessary to rail at patients for bringing gripes about the institution to the meetings instead of their personal emotional problems' (p. 202). Assumptions are made about staff in general. For example, Goffman refers to a patient who did typing as a job and was therefore in regular contact with staff. Goffman states that 'the only price' the patient had to pay for this 'was to have to overhear the way the staff talked about patients out of their presence' (Ibid., p. 203). Activities such as art classes seemed to attract many patients but this, says Goffman, was only because they wanted to get away from the wards, so 'the various hospital audiences were ones that freely marched into captivity' (p. 202).

Mental disorders are depicted as initiated by relatives or others getting a trouble-maker placed in a 'mental hospital' where his or her alienation is exacerbated and mistaken for 'psychosis'. For example, 'mental patients' are seen as 'persons who caused the kind of trouble on the outside that led someone physically, if not socially, to take psychiatric action against them'. Often 'this trouble was associated with the "pre-patient" having indulged in situational improprieties of some kind' (p. 268). For Goffman, 'stigmatisation as mentally ill and involuntary hospitalisation are the means by which we answer these offences against propriety' (p. 268). The patient might vent frustration by 'banging a chair against the floor', and 'the more inade-quate this equipment is to convey rejection of the hospital, the more the act appears as psychotic symptoms'. In turn, the more likely it is 'that management feels justified in assigning the patient to a bad ward' (p. 269). Despite the psychiatric doctrine, the hospital as an institution runs on the assumption that patients will respond to rewards and punishments, hence the possibility of secondary adjustments (p. 270, paraphrased).

Szasz

Szasz ([1960]/2010), as we have seen, regarded mental disorder not as an illness but as a 'metaphor' (Ibid., p. 267). Psychiatric diagnoses are phrased in a way to resemble medical diagnoses but are only labels, 'applied to persons whose behaviour annoys or offends others'. Psychiatric language fundamentally disguises imperative sentences as indicative ones so that it looks as though the collusion between a wife and a doc-tor to get a husband 'confined to a hospital' is simply a statement of a characteristic of the husband (he is 'psychotic') (Ibid., pp. 120–121). Such arguments seem less convincing today than perhaps they did decades ago, although some people still find merit in the idea that a psychosis label is an aid to managing unwanted behaviour.

Perhaps today Szasz's rhetoric is more noticeable and does not carry readers on the tide of his message as powerfully as it might once have done. The terms 'quacks' and 'peddle' and 'fake' are nicely balanced in the phrasing comparing the 'old quacks' with the 'new quacks'. The rhetorical balance of 'theocracy' and 'pharmacracy' is witty. But it is less likely to be accepted today that all pharmacy is 'chemical pacification' and that all treatment is 'medical coercion' (Ibid., p. 300). Treatment as 'psychiatric slavery' (Ibid., p. 278) has a fine rhetorical ring to it, but where individuals and their relatives have experience of the positive effects of psychiatric treatment, including using medication, it seems overstated. Instead of considering the question of public safety set against concerns about 'involuntary psychiatric interventions', Szasz can see only one side of the issues and simply labels such interventions as 'crimes against humanity' (Ibid., p. 268).

Laing

Laing ([1960]/1965 and 1969) is of interest to anyone concerned with language and psychosis because he expresses views about the nature of communication of an individual experiencing schizophrenia. Much of this communication, he states, is 'simply nonsense, red-herring speech' and 'prolonged filibustering'. It is directed at 'dangerous people' whom it is intended to throw 'off the scent'. This seems to include physicians because we are told that a schizophrenic is 'often making a fool of himself and the doctor'. He is 'playing at being mad' so as not to be held responsible 'for a single coherent idea or intention'. Directed at other people, the language of the schizophrenic is intended to 'create boredom and futility' (Ibid., p. 164, emphasis in original). In other words, an individual with schizophrenia is often in control of the way she or he uses language and manipulates the effect that it has on others. Schizophrenia ceases to exist once the individual meets someone 'by whom he feels understood'. The bizarre manifestations then 'simply evaporates' (Ibid., p. 165).

The evidence for these claims has not been substantial enough for them to be considered an accurate account of the communication of individuals with schizophrenia. Laing makes a stronger point perhaps when he recognises the importance of acceptance by a physician of the patient, saying, 'The main agent in uniting the patient, in allowing the pieces to come together and cohere, is the physician's love, a love that recognises the patient's total being, and accepts it, with no strings attached' (Ibid., p. 165).

Anti-psychiatry videos

Contemporary video presentations taking an anti-psychiatry view seem to have their own language and conventions. In *The Marketing of Madness: The Truth About Psychotropic Drugs*, one section begins talking about 'severe mental distress' but this later becomes 'unwanted behaviour', as if they were one and the same thing, without any explanation as to why. There is also the implication that if 'early psychiatrists' got their ideas of the causes of mental disorder wrong, modern psychiatrists may be unlikely to do any better.

Later, when the video mentions apparent equated terms, it can be seen that they are not equal. Anyone who has experienced bipolar disorder will be unlikely to say it was just one of life's 'ups and downs'. Again, there is a difference between having a suspicion about something and behaving in a way that suggests 'paranoid personality disorder'. A further point to notice about the commentary is the comment, 'In spite of the crippling effect of these drugs, psychiatrists and drug companies have used them to create a huge and lucrative market worth billions'. If there were adverse ('crippling') effects on some people, it is not mentioned that some people have no side effects or only mild ones. It is not made clear whether 'psychiatrists' means all psychiatrists, some, or a few. Did any psychiatrists take care to note whether patients developed unpleasant side effects and act to mitigate these? None of the issues are raised because they are covered by generalisations.

More broadly, it is worthwhile taking almost any segment of the video and analysing the techniques that are used in presenting the information. These techniques include:

- subtly eliding terms so that they change without the viewer always noticing and allowing statements to be made that could otherwise be challenged but that are missed (e.g. 'severe mental distress' becomes 'unwanted behaviour');
- equating mental disorders with everyday experiences (e.g. paranoia with being a bit suspicious);
- non sequiturs, such as past poor interventions imply that recent interventions are equally invalid (e.g. leeches were useless so modern drugs would be too);
- generalisations that may not be justified;
- emotive language (e.g. 'crippled').

Broadcaster Anderson Cooper interviews Scientologist Bruce Wiseman, then president of CCHR, and challenges some CCHR claims.[2]

Under the headline 'The Scientology Hate Group CCHR Protests Psychiatry' is a video that includes an interview by John Gever of *MedPage Today*.[3] It took place at the American Psychiatric Association meeting in San Francisco. Outside the meeting were protesters for Scientology and others protesting against Scientology. The interview was with Dr. Nada Stotland, who expressed concern about the effect of anti-psychiatry demonstrations on the well-being of patients. She points out that the public increasingly are aware that 'diseases are real and they don't think that if you're depressed it's not just because you're lazy or didn't pray enough or something. They understand that it's a disease and it's treatable'. Their approach has been 'to counter allegation with fact'. She states that 'we have noticed that the media are getting less and less interested in listening to the allegations of Scientology, many of which are patently ridiculous'.

Conclusion

Anti-psychiatry is seen by some as the resistance to psychiatric ideas that began with the emergence of psychiatry itself. Others regard it as a movement crystallising in the 1960s and 1970s and associated with Goffman, Szasz, Laing and others. Again, some commentators regard anti-psychiatry as a waning influence, while others perceive it in different forms in the present day. In considering anti-psychiatry, this chapter has examined the views and language of people associated with its development, as well as contemporary anti-psychiatry messages, offering an overview of some issues raised and the language that is used to express them.

Goffman (1961) drew attention to some of the limitations of asylums, discussing 'institutionalisation' and some of the functions and negative consequences of these total institutions. This encouraged the option of community provision, and led staff in institutions to be more critical of unnecessary ritual and routine. More important was the efforts to humanise patients and examine de-humanising patterns of interaction. Goffman's language indicates his often-low opinion of psychiatry, therapy and hospitals and their staff.

For Szasz ([1960]/2010), mental disorder was not as an illness but a metaphor. Psychiatric diagnoses are phrased in a way to resemble medical diagnoses but are merely labels for individuals whose behaviour annoys or offends others. Psychiatric language fundamentally disguises imperative sentences as indicative ones so that, for example, a desire to have someone confined to a hospital can be disguised as a statement of a characteristic of the offending person. Szasz's rhetoric (pharmacy as chemical pacification, treatments as psychiatric slavery, involuntary interventions as crimes against humanity) may not today convince readers as powerfully as it might once have done.

Laing ([1960]/1965 and 1969), discussing the nature of communication of an individual experiencing schizophrenia, sees much of it as nonsensical, filibustering, purposely evasive and 'playing' at being mad. Directed at other people, the language of the schizophrenic is intended to create boredom. An individual with schizophrenia is often in control of the way he or she uses language, manipulating the effect it has on others. Schizophrenia ceases to exist once the individual meets someone, whom he or she feels understands. Claims about the purpose of the language associated with schizophrenia have not been substantiated, although the power of acceptance is a stronger point.

Contemporary video presentations taking an anti-psychiatry view seem to have their own language and conventions. Techniques include subtly eliding terms so that they change without the viewer always noticing and allowing statements to be made that could otherwise be challenged but that are missed; equating mental disorders with everyday experiences; non sequiturs, such as past poor interventions implying that recent interventions are equally invalid; unjustified generalisations; and emotive language.

Thinking points

Readers may wish to consider:

- the trend of anti-psychiatry from the early 1960s to the present day and the continuity or lack of continuity of its development;
- the extent to which there might be a particular style of language techniques that typify anti-psychiatry.

Notes

1 This can be found by searching for the title and adding 'video' and is available on YouTube, for example.
2 www.youtube.com/watch?v=5kIDLG-hjK8, uploaded 2011.
3 www.youtube.com/watch?v=P00D6J8sh6A

Key texts

Goffman, E. (1961) *Asylums: Essays on the Social Situation of Mental Patients and Other Inmates* New York, Anchor Books Doubleday.

   While aspects of the book are dated, its influence is undeniable and it still reads powerfully today.

Laing, R. D. ([1960]/1965 and 1969) *The Divided Self: An Existential Study in Sanity and Madness* London, Penguin Books.

   This effort to try and make madness comprehensible can now also be seen in retrospect as a product of the 1960s counterculture.

Szasz, T. ([1960] 2010) *The Myth of Mental Illness: Foundations of a Theory of Personal Conduct* New York and London, Harper-Perennial.

   This fiftieth-anniversary edition includes a preface by Szasz written half a century after the original publication of the book.

Whitaker, R. (2010) *Anatomy of An Epidemic: Magic Bullets, Psychiatric Drugs, and the Astonishing Rise of Mental Illness in America* New York, Crown.

   In this book, science journalist Robert Whitaker draws attention to the extensive use of drugs and the spread of diagnoses.

8

SLANG AND HUMOUR

Introduction

Slang expressions about mental disorders are widespread, and jokes about such disorders are commonplace. Both share features such as a casual irreverence allowing them to be considered together. But what is slang, who uses it and why? Slang is used with reference to psychiatrists and psychotherapists. It is employed to refer to mental disorder in instances where there are, for example, historical derivations, certain analogies and implications or incorrect ideas. The causes of madness also have slang terms. Jokes as an example of humour tend to have particular purposes and work in identifiable ways. Jokes about madness concern psychosis, schizophrenia, delusions, hallucinations and psychiatry and psychoanalysis. Certainly, the content of jokes reveals something of public views of psychosis and the way jokes 'work' is various, for example through word play. Slang and humour about madness endure, seemingly immune to any distaste expressed by people who dislike them.

The nature of slang

In current definitions, slang is associated with similar terms such as 'argot', 'patois', 'cant' and 'colloquialisms' (Waite, 2008). *Encyclopedia Britannica* defines slang in terms of being 'unconventional'.[1] It is 'flippant, irreverent, indecorous' and may be 'indecent or obscene' (Ibid., accessed October 2016).

An older but still interesting view of slang is that of Dumas and Lighter (1978), who suggest that slang exhibits at least two of four criteria.

- It deflates the 'dignity' of formal speech or writing.
- It implies that the user is familiar with what is referenced (or with those who are familiar with it and use the terms).

- It is taboo in ordinary communication with those of higher social status.
- It replaces a conventional synonym mainly to avoid discomfort caused by the accepted alternative.

Reflecting the point about deflating dignity of formal expressions, slang is usually regarded as a very informal type of spoken language. It may comprise individual words, such as 'jugs' for 'ears', or consist of phrases or longer expressions, for example 'old Dutch' for 'wife'.

In line with the user being familiar with what is referenced, slang may be associated with particular groups of people. Examples are Cockney rhyming slang ('apples and pears' for 'stairs' or rhymes at one remove as in 'titfer' meaning 'hat' with the intermediary step of 'tit for tat') or prison slang ('porridge' or 'stir' drawing on dietary allusions to refer to 'a prison sentence'). Its currency in particular groups means that slang may be unintelligible if heard more widely. A particular view of the world or of other people that is conveyed by such slang may be found offensive by others outside of members of the groups that use it.

To the extent that slang is taboo with others of higher status, this implies that it has certain qualities that aid the group cohesiveness of those that do use it. Where slang supplies a word or phrase that helps the user to avoid discomfort, it may be seen as euphemistic.

Specified groups and taboo areas

Slang is used by clearly specified groups towards other specified groups, including minorities. Hence there are many slang terms for lesbians and for homosexual men. Similarly, there is no shortage of slang words for minority ethnic or cultural groups in certain societies.

Slang tends to be used in particular settings. Regarding its context, slang seems to thrive in areas of life and language which are (or were previously) taboo. This may arise because of lack of knowledge, fear or embarrassment. In sexual matters, for example, there are numerous words for the male and the female genitals, as well as for sexual intercourse. Death is another area where slang abounds. It appears that slang is likely to be extensive where:

- there are perceived group differences between those using the slang and those to whom it is applied;
- the topic in question is or was taboo, perhaps associated with lack of knowledge, fear or embarrassment.

This suggests that among the functions of slang is to reinforce group differences and create group solidarity for those using it. Another function may be to deal with taboo areas by alleviating ignorance, fear and embarrassment by using informal, vivid and potentially offensive terms.

If there is something in this suggestion, then the area of mental disorder might be expected to produce many examples. This is indeed the case. If one tries asking acquaintances how many slang terms they have heard for 'madness', it is likely that the proffered list will be long. I consider some examples in this chapter which many people will recognise and may have either used themselves or have heard used.

Slang relating to psychiatrists or psychotherapists

Slang relating to psychiatrists impinges on people with mental disorders to the extent that it can depict patients in a diminished role. The word 'shrink' for a psychiatrist (or other psychotherapist) is the shortened version of 'headshrinker', which appeared in reports about Amazonian Jivaro people who were headhunters and shrunk the heads of captured enemies. In the late 1940s and into the 1950s, 'headshrinker' appears to have been Hollywood slang for a psychotherapist. Scenes in the 1959 movie *Rebel Without a Cause* included characters mentioning going to see a 'headshrinker'. Thomas Pynchon, in his 1960 novel *The Crying of Lot 49*, refers to a psychotherapist character as a 'shrink'.

Reasons for making such a link between a psychotherapist and a headhunter physically shrinking heads are unclear and therefore debated. One possibility is to make a derogatory link to reflect hostility towards psychiatrists. Another explanation is that it might convey the work of psychotherapists reducing the inflated egos of some of their arrogant clients, possibly originally ones working in Hollywood. More generally, it might be taken to imply that the patient had to have his head treated, perhaps with the added notion that the 'head' will be less well functioning and therefore diminished when the process is finished.

Slang for mental disorder

Historical derivations

It is less common to hear the expression 'doolally' today than it was even forty years ago. It comes from the place Deolali in the Maharashtra area of India (northwest of present-day Mumbai) wherein the days of the raj, a transit camp for British troops was situated. Owing to the unpleasant setting and accompanying boredom, the camp was associated with the psychological problems of the soldiers passing through. 'Going doolally' came to mean becoming mentally disordered.

To be in a state of 'bedlam' means to be riotous and dysfunctional. It comes from the Hospital of St. Mary of Bethlehem, founded in 1247 as a priory in London. Gradually, the institution came to be known for taking in mentally disordered people, and when the monasteries were dissolved in the 1500s it became a 'state lunatic asylum'. 'Bethlehem' was eventually contracted to 'Bethlem' and then to 'Bedlam'.

Animal and plant analogies

Occasionally, a belfry may be a separate low-level structure near its accompanying church, as in St. Mary's Church situated in Pembridge, Herefordshire, England. But usually the belfry is on top of the church where the clarion sound can carry to the community. To have 'bats in the belfry' is to have disordered ideas. The analogy is between the bell tower in the upper part of a church and a person's head, and between the supposed erratic flight of bats in an enclosed church space and irrationality or the erratic flight of ideas and thoughts. Derivations appear to be 'bats' or 'batty'. A variation of this theme is the expression 'guests in the attic'. An Australian adaptation is to 'have a kangaroo loose in the top paddock' or, even more colloquially, to 'have a roo loose in the top paddock'. An idea of elevation consistent with the terms 'attic' and 'top' secure the connection with the person's head.

'Barking' or 'barking mad' refers to the uncontrollable madness of a rabid dog. To be 'funny' can mean to be odd or strange, a meaning carried into 1960s' slang of 'funny farm' for psychiatric hospital, which carries notions of people with mental disorder being like animals herded together. 'Snake pit' is a further animal-related expression. It can refer to any institution such as a prison or hospital in which the ethos is inhumane or where people are hostile (like snakes). Working in a psychiatric hospital in Northern England in the 1960s, I was aware that the longer-serving nurses (former asylum attendants) would refer to a ward for patients with severe mental disorders as 'the zoo'.

Many similes referring to 'madness' compare people having mental disorders with animals. 'Mad as a box of frogs', 'mad as a March hare', 'mad as a cut snake', 'mad as a badger', 'mad as a hornet' and 'mad as a wet hen' are just a few examples. Many of these expressions add a quality or a situation to the animal reference that would be expected to make the creature erratic and unpredictable – hence, frogs confined in a box, hares berserk with seasonal lust, a snake that is injured and a saturated hen. In some usages, the 'mad' reference is to uncontrollable anger rather than mental disorder.

Where the slang for head is 'nut', the origins are likely to refer to the skull being a casing to protect the brain, just as the hard nutshell protects the soft kernel. From this connection, a person with a mental disorder (associated with the head) becomes a 'nutcase'. This refers not to a casing for the head but a case or instance of someone requiring treatment for the head. Derivations are that someone is a 'nutter', 'nutty' or 'nuts'. 'Nutty as a fruitcake' is a variation with a further removed derivative being 'fruitcake' or 'fruity'. A psychiatric hospital becomes a 'nuthouse' or a 'nuthatch' or (evolving from 'nutty as a fruitcake') a 'fruitcake factory'.

Terms relating to mental disorder associated with animals or plants such as 'bats', 'barking', 'funny farm', or 'nuts' reflect no human element, thus identifying the phenomena of mental illness as a nonhuman state.

Oddness or incapableness

'Loopy' as slang for 'crazy' can be traced back to the 1920s and implies being misshapen and overcomplicated and full of loops. An earlier Scottish usage suggested being crafty or sly. To go 'haywire' means to become deranged and may derive from the mechanical bailing of hay using wire, which can become tangled and therefore uncontrollable. Similarly, 'going bananas' implies an item out of shape which thus suggests that the individual person is the wrong shape or odd. 'Round the bend' or, a more recent usage, 'round the twist' may be intended to convey similar misshapenness.

It is still quite common to hear the use of 'cuckoo' to refer to mental disorder. This may refer to the repetitive and unvarying call of the bird, suggesting that a person is limited in their repertoire. Accordingly, the Ken Kesey ([1962]/2002) novel and subsequent Miloš Forman movie *One Flew Over the Cuckoo's Nest* refers to a psychiatric hospital as a home for 'cuckoos'. More speculative is the possibility that the cuckoo is born in another bird's nest and the expression suggests an interloper who should not be there – in other words, a misfit.

Although the derivation of 'bonkers' as British naval slang for being drunk is unknown, its adaptation from drunkenness to apply to mental disorder may relate to the idea of being incapable. When a drink was full of balm, it was frothy and excitable. 'Balmy' (or 'barmy') came to mean overexcited and, in some usages, mentally disordered. A 'balm pot' can refer to a disordered person, although it is sometimes used affectionately for someone who is being silly.

'Gaga' derives from the French, meaning 'foolish', and may originate in imitation of the sound of meaningless babble. 'Loco' in American English comes from the Spanish '*loco*' meaning insane, perhaps from an Arabic word '*lauqa*' with a similar meaning. 'Whacky' may derive from the idea of being whacked on the head too many times, leaving one incapable.

Incapableness is suggested by the expression 'the lunatics are in charge of the asylum', which is sometimes used with variations such as 'the monkeys are in charge of the circus', to indicate that the world is turned upside-down, and those who should, it is believed, be minor players because they are not competent are ruling the place.

Loss, incompleteness or dysfunction

To 'lose your marbles' probably derives from the idea of a child losing his marbles (the glass spherical playthings) and being bereft. It extended to mean losing something important and then crystallised into meaning losing sanity. More direct is the expression 'lose your mind', suggesting a complete loss of cognitive faculties.

Incompleteness is indicated by the phrases 'not all there' and 'out to lunch'. It is suggested by several food-related phrases: 'a sausage short of a fry-up/barbeque', 'a few sandwiches short of a picnic', 'a beer (or 'tinny' in Australia) short of a six-pack', 'a few fries short of a Happy Meal' and 'an olive short of a pizza'. Similar phrases of lacking something using monetary terms are 'a quarter short of a dollar' and 'ten pence short of a pound'. Other variations are 'a few clowns short of a circus', 'a few bricks short of a load', 'a scout short of a posse' and 'one put short of a par'. Others are 'not dealing off a full deck' and, more archaically referring to predecimal currency, in England 'not quite the full shilling'.

To 'have a tile loose' suggests that, like the roof of a building with a missing tile, the person has something missing from his or her 'roof' that is from his or her head. In this respect, the expression is similar to 'bats in the belfry' and related phrases.

Dysfunction is implied by the mechanical analogies of 'a screw loose' (or 'screwy') and 'unhinged'. 'Cracked', 'crack-brained' and 'crackpot' convey a sense of damage and unsoundness. ('Potty' may derive from this thread of meaning.) 'Crackers' may have developed its meaning from 'cracked'. 'Crazy' originally meant full of cracks or flaws (a meaning still attaching to crazy paving). Associated words are 'crazed'. A 'cracker box' by extension is slang for a psychiatric hospital. In a similar vein, being 'unglued' conveys a sense of falling apart.

A 'rocker' is part of a mechanism one use of which was to control brush positions in a dynamo. For someone to go 'off his rocker' may suggest he is not functioning properly. Another possibility combines an explanation of 'off his rocker' and 'off his trolley', as both appear to originate from the working of 'trolley' buses and trams. On the top of these vehicles were long, metal, spring-loaded poles which were connected to overhead electric cables for power and were held in place by a metal strip called a 'rocker'. When the rocker came off, the trolley effectively came off power and the driver had to use a long pole to reattach the rocker and regain normal functioning.

'Dotty' appears to derive from 'dote' meaning feebleminded from old age. The expression 'in one's dotage' comes from this source. 'Meshuga' comes from the Hebrew '*meshugga*', part of which means 'to go astray'.

Incorrect ideas of causation or misidentification

It is well known that the idea that mental disorder was related to the phases of the moon led to the term 'moonstruck' or derived from the French '*la lune*', which gave us the word 'lunatic'. This led to the slang terms 'loony' and 'loony tune' (from the 1930s Warner Brothers cartoons of that name). A possible further contribution to the word 'loony' is the loon bird, which is noted for its strange cry. A psychiatric hospital from this line of derivation becomes a 'loony bin' with implications that 'looneys' are no longer of use and are dumped there like rubbish.

'Wacky' and 'wacko', meaning 'fool', probably derive from the idea of being hit on the head repeatedly ('wacked'). 'Mad as a hatter' appears to refer to the effects of the former use of mercury in making hats. Mercury was used in England from the 1700s for producing felt, which was used in hat making. The substance can affect the nervous system, leading to bodily tremors and odd behaviour, leading to the expression being used in relation to 'madness'.

Shortened terms and diminished importance

Where slang uses shortened terms, this may convey disregard or contempt as if the shortened word suggests diminishing the importance of the persons or thing to which one refers. Thus 'psychotic' may become 'psycho', schizophrenic may become 'schizo' and 'lunatic' is replaced by 'loony' or 'loon'.

Causation of madness

Some casual uses of the terms 'mad' and 'madness' appear to suggest an external cause rather than a more nebulous first appearance. Expressions such as 'You are driving me mad' and 'It's driving me mad' suggest an interpersonal or otherwise external precipitate of madness. This is in contrast to expressions that suggest a passive scenario of being visited by madness as in the comment of John Perceval ([1838 and 1840]/1961, p. 3) that 'In the year 1830, I was unfortunately deprived of the use of reason'.

Slang and derogatory language for mental disorders

Earlier I suggested that slang for mental disorders and related matters might reinforce group differences and create group solidarity for those using the slang, and deal with taboo areas by alleviating ignorance, fear and embarrassment. Looking at examples of such slang, it emerged that some terms do not necessarily imply derogatory attitudes. For example, the term 'doolally' has its origins among soldiers who experienced mental disorder associated with a particular place, time and set of events. Similarly, 'bedlam' derives from a particular historical place.

Yet, looking at other examples, it can be seen that the terms reflect a view of mental disorder that is pejorative. Animals and plant analogies such as 'bats', 'barking', 'funny farm' 'cuckoo' or 'nuts' distance themselves from the humanity of mental illness. Oddness or incapableness is conveyed by 'going bananas', 'round the twist', 'round the bend', 'cuckoo', 'bonkers', 'barmy', 'balm pot', 'gaga' and 'loco'. Loss, incompleteness or dysfunction is suggested by 'lost your marbles', 'a sausage short of a fry-up', 'not dealing off a full deck', having 'a screw loose' (or 'screwy'), 'unhinged', 'cracked', 'crack-brained', 'crackpot', 'crackers', 'crazy', 'crazed', 'off his rocker', 'off his trolley', 'dotty' and 'meshuga'. Incorrect ideas of causation or misidentification are indicated by 'moonstruck', 'lunatic', 'loony', 'loony tune', 'loony bin', 'wacky', 'wacko' and 'mad as a hatter'. Shortened terms like 'psycho' and 'schizo' may suggest diminished importance of those who are being spoken about.

Fear and embarrassment may be the source of language that distances itself from the humanity of mental illness and conveys a diminished importance of those being discussed. This corresponds to Dumas and Lighter's (1978) suggestion that discomfort about more formal alternatives is a factor. Lack of knowledge and ignorance may be behind language that conveys the notion of oddness or incapableness, incompleteness or dysfunction, or is based on incorrect ideas of causation or misidentification. More broadly, the ongoing development of new slang that takes into account novel developments in the wider world suggests that it has a continued role.

Humour and jokes

Having considered slang, we now turn to another form of talking about madness, which like slang tends to be informal and irreverent: that of humour in general and jokes in particular.

The nature of humour and its variety

The origins of the word 'humour' lie in the old medical usage of humours (black bile, yellow bile, phlegm and blood) that to varying degrees were thought to affect health and well-being. Humour in the present context refers to something which is funny, comic or amusing. It may be a situation or something that is spoken, written or represented pictorially. It may take the form of cartoons, jokes or comments. Humour is expected to provoke enjoyment and pleasure, often laughter or at least a smile. Someone is said to have a sense of humour if they are quick to express or to recognise the funny side of things. Generally, it is considered a positive thing to have a sense of humour, although there are of course differences of opinion about what is or ought to be funny.

Humour may be associated with a particular environment or a group of people as with 'office humour' or 'locker room humour'. It varies from culture to culture, so that one can speak of an American sense of humour or an Australian sense of humour, although it is difficult to pin down some of the differences. Children may find things amusing and humorous that adults may not. Humour may change over time so that in the same culture, something that was considered funny at one time may not be seen as amusing at a later period.

Although humour can vary from culture to culture and from time to time, attempts have been made to find what precipitates it. Humour may arise from absurdity, incongruity or unexpectedness. It is commonly accepted that having a sense of humour can in some situations be socially beneficial, as when deflating a tense situation with humour or raising a smile in a friend who is feeling low.

More specifically, McGraw, Warren, Williams and Leonard (2012) suggest two influential factors in perceptions of humour. The first is the extent to which the source of the humour is a violation (either severe, as in a tragedy, or mild, as in a mishap). The second feature is one's perceived distance from the violation, whether near or close (spatially, temporally, socially, hypothetically, psychologically). In the view of McGraw and colleagues, tragedies are more humorous when spatially, temporally, socially or hypothetically distant. Mishaps are more humorous when psychologically close. It appears that humour occurs when a violation simultaneously seems benign. Accordingly, distance facilitates humour about tragedies by reducing threat. Closeness aids humour in the case of mishaps by maintaining a sense of threat.

Where humour is irreverent or potentially hostile, it may share some features with slang. Humour, like slang, may reinforce group differences and create group solidarity for those using it. One of its functions may be to alleviate fear and embarrassment about taboo topics. Where slang uses informal, vivid and potentially offensive terms, humour may also use material that is derogatory to some people.

In one perspective then, humour relating to mental disorders and their treatment would tend to be used to reinforce group solidarity and ease fear and embarrassment about mental disorder and psychiatry, in a way that others might find offensive.

PAUSE FOR REFLECTION: JOKES ABOUT MADNESS

Search the Internet for the video 'I'm a Schizophrenic and So Am I' (www. youtube.com/watch?v=2gbgmOnrE7s).

Do you find the jokes made by 'Bob' amusing? To what extent does the context of the movie and the situation within the movie contribute to your opinion?

Jokes and their qualities

Jokes may be taken as examples of humour. They have the advantage, as far as attempts at analysis are concerned, that they are formal and repeatable. By contrast, a witty repost in the flow of conversation often requires the context to be explained in order to be fully appreciated (e.g. in the common saying 'You had to be there'). Jokes are complete in that they provide sufficient context to be comprehensible.

Freud ([1905]/2001), in his essay *Jokes and Their Relation to the Unconscious*, examines examples in French, Italian and English, as well as German. He suggests that an essential feature of a joke is that it provokes 'an explosive laugh' (Ibid., p. 82), while part of its general character is a 'tendency towards economy' (Ibid., p. 44). In their technique, Freud considers jokes which depend on 'condensation', on 'multiple use of the same material' and on 'double meaning' (Ibid., pp. 41–42 for a summary). Further possible groupings are puns, absurd jokes, jokes that show faulty reasoning, overstatement and others (Ibid., pp. 47–89). The purpose of a joke may be 'innocent', as when it has 'an aim in itself', or 'tendentious' (Ibid., p. 96). Tendentious jokes may be exposing or obscene, aggressive (hostile), cynical (critical, blasphemous) or sceptical (Ibid., p. 115).

In considering the relationships between pleasure and the genesis of jokes, Freud ([1905]/2001) suggests how tendentious jokes operate. They serve purposes so that, 'by using the pleasure from jokes as a fore-pleasure', they 'produce new pleasure by lifting suppressions and repressions' (Ibid., p. 137). In other words, jokes are connected with freeing people from feelings or views that they are suppressing or repressing. The joke acts as a preliminary pleasure which then gives further pleasure by lifting that which is held back. Freud gives an example of someone having an urge to insult someone else. But propriety or 'aesthetic culture' opposes this so that the insult does not take place. It is then supposed that a joke derived from the idea of the insult is constructed and delivered. The pleasure in the joke is released from other sources not connected with the inhibition. But the joke which has allowed the insult effectively to take place is accompanied by the pleasure of delivering the insult (Ibid., p. 136).

One of the motives for telling jokes, Freud ([1905]/2001) suggests, is to arouse one's own laughter by making someone else laugh. Although the novelty of the joke cannot be recaptured once one has heard it, the teller can at least enjoy and participate in the amusement freshly experienced by the new hearer (Ibid., pp. 155–156). (In the present day, where jokes are distributed on Internet sites, one may assume that the distributer derives pleasure from imagining the laughter that the joke might provoke in new 'hearers', although the infectiveness of the laughter of the recipient of the joke will be denied to the 'teller'.)

Freud also seeks to relate 'joke-work' to the 'dream-work' that he had discussed in his earlier book, *The Interpretation of Dreams* (Freud, [1900]/2001; Freud, [1900 and 1901]/2001). He argues that dream-work features such as 'condensation', 'displacement' and 'indirect representation' are also identifiable in 'joke-work'. He hypothesises that in the person creating the joke, a 'preconscious thought' is momentarily 'given over' to 'unconscious revision', the outcome of which is immediately grasped by 'conscious perception' (Ibid., p. 166).

Finally, Freud broadens his discussion to the comic more generally, identifying types of comic expression such as the 'naïve' (Ibid., pp. 182–184). Comic 'methods' include 'parody' and 'unmasking' (p. 189). Distinguishing jokes and the comic according to their 'psychical localization', Freud suggests that the joke is 'the contribution made to the comic from the realm of the unconscious' (p. 208).

Jokes relating to madness

Jokes relating to madness can be about psychosis, schizophrenia, delusions, hallucinations and psychiatrics and psychoanalysts. Hundreds, perhaps thousands, of examples are found in various Internet sources, a glimpse of which is given in the following sections.

Jokes about psychosis

A psychiatric hospital director heard that one of the patients had saved another from suicide by pulling him out of a bathtub. Interviewing the patient later, the director said, 'Your records and your heroic behaviour indicate that you are ready to go home. I am only sorry that the man you saved later killed himself with a rope round his neck'. 'Oh, he didn't kill himself', replied the patient. 'I hung him up to dry'.

(www.ahajokes.com/p018.html) (abbreviated)

A psychotic rapist escaped from a mental institution. He ran into a laundromat and finding two women in there, forced them to have sex with him and then ran out of the back door. The next day a newspaper headline read, 'NUT SCREWS WASHERS AND BOLTS'.

(www.sickapedia.net)

What's the most manic and psychotic animal in the world? A bipolar bear.

(www.sickapedia.net)

Contrary to popular belief, most clowns aren't psychotic maniacs, hell-bent on splitting your skull open with an axe. But it's probably best to shoot them on sight to be on the safe side.

(www.sickapedia.net)

A psychotic thinks that $2 + 2 = 5$. A neurotic knows that the answer is 4, but it worries him.

(www.healthquestions.medhelp.org/psychotc-jokes)

Jokes about schizophrenia

Did you know that every two in one people are schizophrenic?

(www.hahas.co.uk/schizophrenic/)

Roses are red, violets are blue . . . I'm schizophrenic and so am I.

(www.esmartass.com/schizophenia-jokes)

I used to be schizophrenic but we're all right now.

(www.esmartass.com/schizophenia-jokes)

Student: Sometimes I think I have schizophrenia.
Teacher: Well, stop acting up in class or I'll throw both of you out!

(www.esmartass.com/schizophenia-jokes)

Schizophrenia beats being alone.

(www.esmartass.com/schizophenia-jokes)

I may be schizophrenic but at least I have each other!

(www.esmartass.com/schizophenia-jokes)

What do you call a schizophrenic Buddhist? Someone who is at two with the universe.

(www.jokebuddha.com/Schizophrenic)

A schizophrenic bumped into me on the tube today. Who the hell does he think he is!

(www.hahas.co.uk/schizophrenic/)

My doctor told me I was schizophrenic and I told him he was talking to the wrong person.

(www.esmartass.com/j/schizophrenia-jokes)

Jokes about delusions

Patient: Doctor, I keep thinking I'm a pair of curtains.
Doctor: Well pull yourself together.

(www.rubble.heppell.net/jollyology/doctor)

Patient: Doctor, I think I'm a dog.
Doctor: Well just sit on the couch.
Patient: I'm not allowed.

(www.rubble.heppell.net/jollyology/doctor)

Patient: I think I'm turning gold.
Doctor: Don't worry. It's just a gilt complex.

(www.euphoria.force9.co.uk/realhumour/jokes/)

Patient: I keep thinking I'm a bell.
Doctor: Take these pills and if they don't work give me a ring.

(www.euphoria.force9.co.uk/realhumour/jokes/)

Patient: I think I'm a deck of cards.
Doctor: I'll deal with you later.

(www.euphoria.force9.co.uk/realhumour/jokes/)

'Doctor', said the receptionist over the phone, 'there's a patient here who thinks he's invisible'.

'Well, tell him I can't see him right now'.

(www.psychologytoday.com)

When a new patient was settled on the psychiatrist's couch, the doctor said, 'I'm not aware of your problem so perhaps you had better start at the very beginning'. 'OK', the patient replied, 'In the beginning I created the heavens and the earth'.

(www.juliantrubin.com/psycholgyjokes)

Jokes about hallucinations

Every now and then my boxer shorts have strange hallucinations and talk haphazardly. My doctor says it's a brief psychotic disorder.

(www.sickapedia.net)

I used to think I had schizophrenia, then I realized that is just what the voices want me to think!

(www.esmartass.com/j/schizophrenia-jokes)

Two schizophrenics are on the roof of a building in a town in a middle of the night with an electric torch. The other points the light beam to the roof of another building and says, 'Could you now walk on the light beam to the other building?' The other says, 'Of course I could . . . but I am afraid you turn the light off when I am in the middle!'

(www.bouldertherapist.com/html/humor/MentalHealthHumor/schizos)

Jokes about psychiatry and psychoanalysis

A well-known quip about psychiatry and psychiatrists was attributed to the movie mogul Sam Goldwyn who is supposed to have said, 'Anyone who goes to see a psychiatrist ought to have his head examined'.

Neurotics build castles in the sky. Psychotics live in them. Psychiatrists collect the rent.

(www.juliantrubin.com/psycholgyjokes)

What happens if you tell a psychiatrist you are schizophrenic? He charges you double.

(www.juliantrubin.com/psycholgyjokes)

Question: What do you call a mental patient whose insurance has run out?
Answer: Cured.

(www.healthyplace.com/blogs/funnyinthehead/)

Many more mental health jokes can be found at www.guy-sports.com/humor/pictures/picture_mental_health.htm.

Madness jokes

The content and purpose of madness jokes

In considering the content of jokes about madness, it is worth remembering the psychiatric definition of psychosis which referred to delusions, hallucinations, disorganised speech, grossly disorganised or catatonic behaviour and negative symptoms (American Psychiatric Association, 2013, p. 99).

Of these aspects of psychosis, delusions and hallucinations have carried through into jokes but not the other features. So, what might be the reasons? Perhaps disorganised speech is difficult to isolate for the purpose of jokes because it can arise in many other situations, such as drunkenness. Therefore, a joke that hinged on remembering that madness may be associated with it would tend not to work. Highly disorganised or catatonic behaviour may not be a widely known aspect of psychosis and so would not lend itself to humour which often depends on a shared understanding of what it being joked about. Negative symptoms such as self-neglect, like disordered speech, can be associated with too many other circumstances, such as dementia, to be closely associated with psychosis and may not be widely known as a feature of psychosis anyway.

Some of the content of the jokes about *psychosis* convey the possible dangerousness of psychotic patients who might even after doing something heroic ruin it by their lack of understanding and kill someone in hanging them 'up to dry'. A 'psychotic rapist' is the subject of the laundromat tale. Most clowns may not be 'psychotic maniacs' but you might want to shoot them.

The content of many jokes about *schizophrenia* play with the idea (indeed the misconception) that it refers to a mind split into two equal parts (probably based on the casually used term 'split personality'). Plays on singular and plural, one and two, 'I' and 'we' are staples of such jokes. The Buddhist variation plays with the idea of being 'one with the universe' to subvert it along the schizophrenia 'double' lines. Some schizophrenia jokes use the notion of confused personal identity, as with 'who the hell does he think he is?' and the doctor 'talking to the wrong person'.

A number of jokes about *delusions* were formulaic doctor-patient exchanges conveying the ridiculousness of the beliefs carried to their extreme. Thinking you are a dog implies that you cannot sit on the couch. Starting at the beginning, if you are God means talking about the creation of heaven and earth. Other jokes give doctor's reposts to patients' beliefs that play with words or phrases: 'pull yourself together', 'gilt complex', 'give me a ring', 'deal with you later' and 'can't see him now', which are all typical phrases given a new double meaning by the context of the delusion.

Turning to jokes about *hallucinations*, the content reflects the double bind of not knowing what to believe. You might have thought that you had schizophrenia but the voices that are the very signs of it wanted you to think that. You might believe that you can walk on a light beam, but your fears still have a strange and distorted relation to reality as you perceive it – what if the beam is switched off?

Jokes about *psychiatry and psychoanalysis* reflect views about the perceived rapaciousness of these professionals. You need your head examined if you go to see one. They 'collect the rent' or 'charge you double' or say you are cured if you have no more cash. By implication, psychotics in these scenarios are duped into handing over their money and are better off staying away.

The mechanics of madness jokes

In looking at the various jokes about madness, I have grouped them according to their content: 'jokes about psychosis', 'jokes about schizophrenia', 'jokes about delusions', 'jokes about hallucinations' and 'jokes about psychiatry and psychoanalysis'. There are certain devices that can be identified in the structure of the language that allow the jokes to work for those who find them amusing. Playing with words and meaning is one device. Thinking you are a pair of curtains leads to the response that has an unexpected double meaning 'well pull yourself together'. Similarly, someone thinking they are a deck of cards is used to set up the response with the double meaning of 'I will deal with you later'.

Perhaps relatedly another technique is challenging how certain words are used, for example 'suffer' as with the quip, 'I don't suffer from insanity. I love every minute'. The rather overstretched set up in the laundry allows the final line to play on several meanings in announcing, 'NUT SCREWS WASHERS AND BOLTS'.

Another device is using the shock of literalness when one is not expecting it. The literalness of following up what a patient is saying is brought home with a jolt when someone thinks they are a dog, and of course they are not allowed to sit on a couch. Similarly, if someone thinks they are God, starting at the beginning has to involve creating the heavens and the earth. An echo of this is found in the already-mentioned story of the psychiatric hospital director and the life-saving patient who ruined his heroic behaviour through the literal way in which he dried out the person that he had saved.

PAUSE FOR REFLECTION: WHAT'S SO FUNNY?

Search the Internet for the video 'What's So Funny about Mental Illness?' (www.youtube.com/watch?v=mbbMLOZjUYI).

Where the audience laughs, what is the source of the humour?

The enduring use of slang and humour associated with mental disorder

Distaste of slang and humour

Wahl (1995) clearly expresses the distaste for slang and humour about 'mental illness', stating that they 'fail to recognise the painful seriousness of psychiatric disorders and to respect the sensitivities of those with mental illness who may be in their audience'. Furthermore, he maintains,

> Such references put forward a view of mental illness as a trivial matter, worthy of laughter rather than empathy. They communicate that mental illness makes one less worthy of respect. And they display and encourage insensitivity in their failure to see people with mental illnesses as individuals who could be hurt or offended by being so often the butt of jokes.
>
> *(Ibid., p. 35)*

Persistence of slang

Despite such protestations, going back many years, slang continues unabated. It is expressed in everyday life, as well as in the media. For example, during the 2016 US presidential campaign, there were examples of mental disorder slang. A March 2016 upload of the 'Jimmy Dore Show', for example, was headlined, 'Chuck Todd Makes Bernie Sanders Answer Trump's Insane Attacks'. Another was headed, 'Chris Matthews Goes Full Batsh★t Bonkers on Chris Christie'. So why does slang continue to be used? Does it serve any other purpose than to be abusive?

Where slang is an indication of exclusion, it tends to be perceived as abusive by those excluded. Another feature of slang is that at the same time as it is exclusive of one group, it is inclusive of the group that uses the slang. The bonding nature of slang is perhaps not sufficiently considered in seeking reasons why slang persists. Efforts to persuade people to avoid slang are unlikely to reach them in the first place as the persuaders and the users are likely to be in different groups.

Continuation of humour

It seems that just as people will continue to use slang so will they persist in using humour about mental disorder and related matters. In 2009 a popular Monty Python sketch 'Spot the Loony' from the 1970s was uploaded onto YouTube, attracting over 166,000 hits by 2016 and eliciting enthusiastic comments of those who enjoyed the sketch. With Spanish subtitles, the sketch had attracted over 117,000 hits by 2016 and more appreciative comments, such as 'Truly some of the best comedy ever done'. The script is also available online. The sketch is of a game show in which the panel, who are 'all looneys', have to 'spot the looney' in various settings shown on film clips. The 'looneys' all behave very oddly; for example, one of the panel, 'a Swedish mammal abuser and part-time radiator', is seen 'standing on his head on the desk with his legs crossed in a yoga position. He wears a loin cloth and high heeled shoes. He talks through a megaphone which is strapped to his head'.

For Wahl (1995), people who joke about mental disorder 'fail' to recognise its seriousness and are insensitive in depicting mental disorder as 'trivial', 'less worthy of respect' and unworthy of empathy. However, such views do not explain the persistence of jokes about madness in different cultures and across time. If the answer was simply that people are ignoring others' sensitivities, trivialising them and treating them with no respect, why is this not simply expressed directly? In other words, why are jokes used as the vehicle if the content or the intention is simply downright nastiness?

It has already been suggested that humour may reinforce group solidarity of those who do not experience mental disorder and ease fear and embarrassment about mental disorder and psychiatry, in a way that others might find offensive. If it is correct that a joke may be 'innocent' as when it has 'an aim in itself' (Freud ([1905]/2001, p. 96) then some jokes perhaps motivated by embarrassment or fear may be a way to shape language to create laughter from that situation. In other words, the structure of what makes people laugh is used as a vehicle for content which some might consider offensive in order to provoke laughter. Other jokes about mental health may fit Freud's category of being 'hostile' (indicating aggression) and this in turn may relate to feelings of fear and embarrassment.

Conclusion

Slang expressions and jokes about mental disorders are widespread, both sharing features such as a casual irreverence. Slang is used with reference to psychiatrists and psychotherapists. It is used to refer to mental disorder where there are historical derivations; uses relating to plants and animal analogies; examples conveying oddness or incapableness; loss, incompleteness or dysfunction; and incorrect ideas of causation or misidentification. Shortened slang terms are employed suggesting diminished importance. The causes of madness also attract slang terms.

Humour generally is nebulous and diverse. Jokes as an example of humour appear to have particular purposes and to work in identifiable ways. Jokes about madness may concern psychosis, schizophrenia, delusions, hallucinations and psychiatry and psychoanalysis. The content of jokes reveals something of public views of psychosis. The mechanics of jokes about madness can involve playing on words or revealing the literalness of a joke character's response when it is unexpected. The enduring nature of slang and humour concerning madness seems unresponsive to distaste expressed by people who dislike such usage.

Thinking points

Readers may wish to consider:

- the range of reasons for the continuing use of slang and humour about mental disorders and whether greater knowledge would be likely to reduce it;
- any ways in which the nature of slang and humour about mental disorders might have changed over time and the possible reasons.

Note

1 www.britannica.com/topic/slang

Key text

Wahl, O. F. (1995) Media Madness: *Public Images of Mental Illness* New Brunswick, New Jersey, Rutgers University Press
    This book is still a good aid to understanding the influence of media on views about mental health.

Internet resources

The following include jokes about psychosis, schizophrenia, delusions, hallucinations, psychiatry and psychoanalysis:

www.ahajokes.com/p018.html
www.sickapedia.net
www.healthquestions.medhelp.org/psychotc-jokes
www.hahas.co.uk/schizophrenic/
www.esmartass.com/schizophenia-jokes
www.jokebuddha.com/Schizophrenic
www.hahas.co.uk/schizophrenic/
www.rubble.heppell.net/jollyology/doctor
www.rubble.heppell.net/jollyology/doctor
www.euphoria.force9.co.uk/realhumour/jokes/
www.psychologytoday.com
www.juliantrubin.com/psycholgyjokes
www.sickapedia.net
www.esmartass.com/j/schizophrenia-jokes
www.bouldertherapist.com/html/humor/MentalHealthHumor/schizos
www.juliantrubin.com/psycholgyjokes
www.healthyplace.com/blogs/funnyinthehead/
www.guy-sports.com/humor/pictures/picture_mental_health.htm

9

MEDIA COVERAGE

Introduction

Intersections between the media, society and individuals, and mental disorder have been broadly discussed in various texts over the years. After outlining a broad view of media, this chapter focuses on a negative aspect that has been the subject of interest for some years: that of the representation of 'psycho killers' in the media and the public appetite for such representations. We look at television drama and at movies before discussing the themes that occur in these depictions and at the possible effect of such representations. Next, we turn to news stories giving accounts of psychotic killers and discuss some issues arising. More broadly, the chapter considers reasons that negative depictions might predominate. Finally, we look at ideas that have been put forward that might increase understanding of mental disorders and suggestions that have been made for promoting some positive images of mental disorders.

Media and mental health

In an early contribution to 'public images of mental illness', Wahl (1995) aimed to 'examine the *extent, nature, accuracy, and potential impact* of public images of mental illness' (Ibid., p. xii). One point that the book made was that media presentations of 'mentally ill people' tended to show them as 'fundamentally different from others' and as *'violent, criminal and dangerous'* (Ibid., p. xiii). Morris (2006, p. 2, fig. 1.1) suggests a 'tri-partite relationship' between the media (including mass media and social media), individual/society and mental health issues. In discussing these matters, he covers key topics such as stigma and labelling in the context of mental health issues, as well as the promotion of positive health. Harper (2009) questions the notion of mental 'illness', seeing it as a psychiatric construction of mental distress. Indeed, he states that madness is best understood 'in relation to its social, political and economic contexts' (Ibid., p. 1). While regarding some contemporary media depictions as positive and sympathetic (Ibid., p. 151), Harper suggests that they can reinforce unequal relationships relating to gender, race and social class. Rubin (2012) and colleagues look at representations of mental illness in popular culture, including cartoons, advertising, marketing, movies, theatre and literature. The various essays suggest broadly that the relationship between mental illness, mental health and popular culture is complex and conflicted and can be related to discourses on other aspects of identity, including race and gender, and to economic issues, including globalisation.

Breadth of media coverage

What is meant by media? Often it is taken to signify daily press and news coverage, but a wider view may be taken. This would include newspapers, magazines and periodicals; literature such as novels, plays, short stories and essays; television and radio drama, documentary, news and discussions; and movies. Published illustrations, photographs, cartoons, comic strips and advertisements are further examples. Popular songs and poems, published copies of paintings and sculptures and recordings of dance and mime are also part of media output. Internet sources including social media are increasingly consulted.

Psycho-killer interest

As Torrey (2013, pp. 336–344) notes, there are accurate and serious depictions of schizophrenia in the movies and have been for many years. An early example is Ingmar Bergman's 1961 movie *Through a Glass Darkly*. In this, the central character Karin returns from hospital in remission from schizophrenia and finds her symptoms gradually returning, including auditory hallucinations. Her family struggles, unable to help, and she eventually returns to hospital.

Yet in addition to these more serious depictions, commentators, for example Hinshaw (2007), have drawn attention to the plethora of negative media depictions, particularly of 'psychotic killers' and 'dangerous maniacs', perhaps highlighting the stigma that can be attached to mental disorders and calling for change. Nevertheless, depictions of psychotic killers, whether in movies, television shows or stories, continue unabated. This chapter will focus on examples from television drama and movies, showing that this form of representation has continued appeal to the present day. I also look at newspaper reports illustrating a similar continued interest.

Television drama

Police drama

Charlie's Angels was a crime drama about a group of women who, having graduated from Los Angeles Police Academy, were recruited by the mysterious Charlie who gave them assignments and referred to them as his 'angels'. Series 2, episode 21, 'Little Angels of the Night' (1978) sees the protagonists go undercover to find out how three prostitutes have been murdered. One of the characters, Kris, finds herself trapped with a 'psychotic killer'.[1] *Hawaii Five-O*, a police procedural series, covered the actions of a small state police task force around Honolulu (Hawaii being the fiftieth state explains the 'Five-0' of the title). Season 4, episode 6, '. . . And I Want Some Candy and a Gun That Shoots' (1971), involves a 'psychotic sniper' who fires at cars on a highway from a hillside bunker.[2] *Kojak* was a popular American crime drama series depicting the various cases of a New York City Police Department detective. In series 4, episode 4, 'Out of the Shadows' (1976), a 'psychotic killer' terrorises Manhattan with knife murders apparently of people who have duped him financially.[3]

In other plots, characters come across psychotic criminals. In *The A-Team*, a group of Vietnam veterans get together from time to time for special assignments. Series 1, episode 9, 'Holiday in the Hills' (1983), has the team in a plane which crash-lands in the backwoods, bringing them into contact with 'crazed mountain men'.[4] *The Hitchhiker* series concerned a wanderer who in each episode finds himself in unusual situations. Season 6, episode 17, 'A Whole New You' (1983), has to do with a 'psychotic criminal' protected by the police who demands facial surgery to acquire a new identity.[5] *Baywatch* was a series about Los Angeles County lifeguards. Season 3, episode 17, 'The Tower' (1993), has an 'escaped psychopath' taking two women hostage in a lifeguard watchtower. With the structure primed with explosives, a rescue attempt is made before the 'maniac' has a chance to escape or harm his hostages.[6]

Similar representations include *The Following*, an American television drama (2013–2015) involving a 'brilliant and charismatic, yet psychotic' serial killer. He communicates with other killers, forming a cult of members who obey his orders.[7] For example, in the first season (2013), a former FBI agent tries to capture the killer Joe Carroll after his prison escape. It emerges that Carroll has gathered around him a group of similarly minded people, some of whom he met in prison and formed a close-knit band of killers.

Other examples

Wonderland was a medical television drama series that aired in 2000 depicting daily life in the psychiatric and emergency room units of a New York City hospital. In the opening episode, a man with schizophrenia goes on a shooting spree in Times Square, hitting bystanders and two police officers.[8]

Many films and television adaptations have grown out of the 1960s book *Psycho* and the Hitchcock movie of the same name. A recent example is the US television series *Bates Motel* (2013–2016), which reveals a backstory to the killer Norman Bates, in which his mother is also homicidal.

Movies

From the earliest days of cinema, movies such as *The Cabinet of Dr. Caligari* (1920) have depicted mad and evil doctors. The horror movie *Repulsion* directed by Roman Polanski tells of a young woman slipping into schizophrenia until hallucinations take over, leading to murder. Across the years, many well-remembered movies feature psychosis as an unsettling threat. Examples are taken from the 1970s to the present.

In *Halloween* (1978) having, as a 6-year-old child, stabbed to death his teenage sister on the night of Halloween, Michael Myers is sent to an institution under psychiatric care. Fifteen years later he escapes and returns to his home neighbourhood of Haddonfield, Illinois, the day prior to Halloween. As his psychiatrist Dr. Loomis and the local sheriff search for him, Myers goes on a killing spree. The movie led to several popular sequels.

Clownhouse (1989) is an American horror film involving three young brothers. Left at home alone in an isolated farmhouse when their mother visits relatives, they are attacked by three mental patients who have escaped from the local state asylum and who are disguised as clowns.

Criminal Law (1988) involves a psychotic killer who is successfully defended by his defence lawyer before the attorney discovers that he is in fact guilty. Because the killer cannot be tried again for his crimes, the lawyer tries to get the offender to incriminate himself.

In *Five Corners* (1987), a psychotic man released from prison returns to his neighbourhood where he seeks out the woman (played by Jodie Foster) who he previously attempted to rape and the man who protected her.

I Saw What You Did (1988) depicts two teenage girls making prank calls on the telephone who inadvertently call a psychotic killer who has just killed someone. When the girls say, 'I saw what you did', the killer thinks they saw the killing that he perpetrated and begins to stalk them.

In *Misery* (1990), a psychological horror film based on Stephen King's 1987 novel, a psychotic fan Annie Wilkes holds an author hostage, forcing him to write stories for her.

Out for Justice (1991) involves a drug-addicted psychotic man, Richie Madano, killing a police detective Bobby Lupo and the subsequent manhunt involving the officer's partner, Gino Felino.

The Silence of the Lambs (1992) tells the story of a psychiatrist who was also a killer. On the back cover of Thomas Harris's *Silence of the Lambs* is the blurb, 'On the loose is a psychotic killer. Locked away is a psychotic madman. To catch one, the FBI needs the other' (cited in Wahl, 1995, p. 61).

Directed by Martin Scorsese, *Shutter Island* (2010) depicts US Marshall Teddy Daniels (Leonardo DiCaprio) apparently investigating the disappearance of a woman murderer who escaped from a hospital for the criminally insane on the island. Teddy has been traumatised by his World War II experiences and has unpleasant flashbacks involving his wife and children. The truth gradually emerges about the real situation and about Teddy's past. (See, e.g., *Screen Rant* for a discussion.)

In *Psychotic* (2012), publicised as 'delusional, deranged, depraved', the resident psychologist in an 'insane asylum' wakes tied up in a morgue along with 'insane patients' who have escaped from their prison cells. In an attempt to secure her safety, she sides with a 'dangerous patient' (Brain Damage Films).

Themes in movie and television depictions

When we look at the way that psychosis is often negatively depicted in television drama and movies, certain features become noticeable.

Psychotic-killer character

Police dramas find frequent use for killers who are 'psychotic'. They do not as often depict other characters in the story as psychotic, for example a victim or a witness. Characters are a 'psychotic killer', a 'psychotic sniper', 'crazed mountain men', a 'psychotic criminal' and a 'brilliant and charismatic, yet psychotic' serial killer. In one movie description, 'psychopath' and 'maniac' are incorrectly used synonymously. The term 'psychopath' is sometimes confused by the media with 'psychotic'. In fact, today, psychiatrists tend not to use the expression 'psychopath' and the alternative term 'personality disorder' is preferred.

A whole industry seems to have grown out of *Psycho*, with sequels and prequels developing the story of the psychotic killer (and his mother). Perpetrators might be a mad and evil doctor (*The Cabinet of Dr. Caligari*), or a killer who is a child (*Halloween*). To create even more bizarre experiences, mental patients from a local 'state asylum' might be disguised as clowns. Also highlighting the bizarre is *Misery*, in which a psychotic fan forces a hostage author to write stories for her.

Psychotic killer in cat-and-mouse plots

A psychotic killer is used as a stock character in cat-and-mouse plots. Returning to the old neighbourhood is one theme used in *Halloween*, where Mike Myers is released and returns to his former haunts. In *Five Corners* too, release from prison leads to a similar setup. A backfiring prank sets up the tension in *I Saw What You Did* so that a psychotic killer pursues teenage girls. A twist to the theme occurs in *Criminal Law*, where the psychotic killer becomes the mouse and the defence lawyer the cat.

Psychotic killer as suspense device

Unpredictability and psychosis are linked in plot lines where the 'psychotic killer' is somehow brought into close proximity with a potential victim. In *The Silence of the Lambs*, the irony of course is that the tension is brought about by a strange conflict. FBI agent Clarice Starling's vulnerability in pursuing a psychotic killer is one part of the equation. The other is that she has to reveal aspects of her past to another killer (a psychiatrist) who can help quid pro quo. Similarly, in *Psychotic*, the resident psychologist in an 'insane asylum' tries to secure her safety by siding with a 'dangerous patient'. The idea of 'how do you know who is sane and who you can trust?' is threaded throughout *Shutter Island* (2010), leading the viewer to reassess everything by the end. In the *Baywatch* episode 'The Tower' (1993), the 'maniac' holds two women hostage in a lifeguard tower primed with explosives, setting up a situation that combines so many kinds of danger that it is hard to know where to start.

The effect of representations in movies and television drama

Wahl (1995) argues that, regarding mental disorders in general, 'television and film portrayals feature actors with unusual appearances' (Ibid., pp. 54–55). Also, 'inaccurate and unfavourable images of people with mental illnesses lead to misconceptions and stigma'. Such images add to 'confusion and misunderstanding' of mental disorders which then influence how those experiencing them are treated. Media's 'persistent and pervasive inaccurate stereotypes' perpetuate negative attitudes toward people with mental disorders, helping maintain 'stigma, rejection and discrimination'. Mass media's 'demeaning portrayals' of those with psychiatric disorders 'undermine the self-esteem and recovery' of those encountering such representations of themselves (Ibid., pp. 108–109).

A chicken-and-egg argument continues. Does the making of movies and television series about psychotic killers create the public appetite for them that would otherwise not exist? If not for perverse movie producers and directors, would members of the public show no interest in these characters? Or are members of the public generally keen to see fiction in which psychotic characters appear predominantly? The more convincing view it seems is the latter. If this is true, then it leads to a further question: why do so many people enjoy such movies, shows and stories?

We considered in an earlier chapter how the widespread use of slang and humour about mental disorder including psychosis may relate to fear of mental illness and of psychosis. Lack of knowledge about psychosis may sustain such communication. But even where people stop to think that psychosis does not often equate with dangerous behaviour, the residual fear and discomfort, I suggest, would persist because the possibility exists. Some people fear crime in general out of all proportion to its existence in their locality. Lack of proportion and fear is not the preserve of worries about mental disorder.

If this transfers to attitudes towards movies and television drama, the fear and a wish to feed it for pleasure or to temporarily abate it through the dramatic playing out of that fear will remain strong. Those holding such attitudes and feelings are likely to resist well-meaning suggestions that they should not see such drama. Occasional efforts to depict mental disorder including psychosis 'sympathetically' in drama continue of course but seem to have no effect on the kick that so many people get from a 'good' psycho slasher movie. Some commentators no doubt believe that the behaviour of others of whom they disapprove can be changed by exhorting them not to see such movies or television dramas. They may hold the view that filmmakers ought to be more careful and respectful.

Maybe the positions of fans and critics of psycho-killer dramas are not inevitably in conflict. Perhaps someone can go and see such a movie and then quite compatibly visit and enjoy the company of a relative or friend who has psychosis and barely connect the two. Psychosis is one of many factors in dangerous behaviour and like the other factors is rare. Other drivers include intense jealousy and greed that can both be a motive for murder. Yet no one it seems thinks that inevitably a jealous or greedy person that they know will be likely to kill someone. It is at the extreme and therefore such a thing rarely happens. Similarly, with psychosis, some people seem to be able to recognise that the 'psycho' in a movie is not the same as their friend who is receiving treatment for psychosis. In other words, perhaps negative depictions of psychosis in drama are quite separable from people's real-life experiences. Such works enable people to experience the fear of mental disorder which is genuine and then return to the real life where they know very well that mental disorder does not generally equate with murder and mayhem.

PAUSE FOR REFLECTION: NEGATIVE AND POSITIVE DEPICTIONS

Select one or several of the television shows or movies discussed or ones that you know of in which psychosis is depicted. What are the potentially negative and positive aspects of the depictions? Why do they have this effect?

Having looked at some of the negative depictions of psychosis associated with violence in movies and in television series, we turn now to news stories.

News stories

The range of sources of news

News may be depicted in television, radio, newspapers, magazines, Internet news sites and other sources. Increasingly, news and pseudonews (and fake news) is passed around by users of social media, and items that are trending are then sometimes reported in turn by mainstream media.

1,200 killed by mental patients

A UK newspaper, the *Sun*, reported in 7 October 2013 the headline, '1,200 Killed by Mental Patients: Shock 10-year Toll Exposes Care Crisis'. This piece criticised the lack of communication between agencies, as well as serious failings of community care.[9] Cited was the story of 16-year-old Christina Edkins who on her way to school on a bus was 'knifed to death by paranoid schizophrenic Phillip Simelane'.

In another example, 13-year-old schoolgirl Casey Kearney was stabbed to death in a park in Doncaster, Yorkshire, in 2012 by 'killer Hannah Bonser, 26'. She had a 'history of mental illness and had warned her care staff a month earlier that she should not be around other people because she wanted to kill them'. A further incident occurred in March 2012, when father of two Gino Nelmes from Bristol, England, was stabbed seventeen times with a samurai sword by Marc Carter, 'a "dangerous" paranoid schizophrenic who was on trial release from a secure mental hospital'. In Swindon, Wiltshire, England, 21-year-old Carl James was stabbed to death on the doorstep of his home by 'his schizophrenic lifelong pal Michael Harris'. Harris had 'developed schizophrenia due to his drug habit, which started in his early teens'. He had admitted urges to 'kill others', but his 'mental health workers – who were aware of this – did not intervene'. In Newcastle, England, in 2006, mental health worker Ashleigh Ewing, aged 22 years, died after being stabbed thirty-nine times by 'paranoid schizophrenic' Ronald Dixon after taking a letter to him about money that he owed. Maureen Tyler, aged 79 years, was killed by her son Mark at her house in Basildon, Essex, England. He shot her 'in the face' using a sawed-off shotgun as she sat on the sofa in the family home. Four days later, he shot himself in the bathroom. Mark Tyler had a 'history of drug use' and months before the killing had been for a 'psychiatric consultancy' and had been told that 'he was "dangerous" and "psychotic" – but no diagnosis was made'. In one section, the article quotes Paul Farmer of MIND, a mental health charity, who points out that 'mental health is far too often spoken of in terms of aggression and violence'. He adds that 'we must remember that there are 1.2 million people in touch with mental health services – and the overwhelming majority are not hurting others'. But MIND is 'campaigning for better crisis care'.

Website comments on the article included: 'Find out who let these people loose in the community and charge them with manslaughter'; 'If you are a danger to society, you should be locked away from that society'; and 'Care in the community kills'.

The real Norman Bates psycho killer

As mentioned earlier, the Hitchcock movie *Psycho* (itself based on a fictional book of the same name derived from a true story) has generated many movie and television series spin-offs. *Psycho* is still used to frame news stories many decades after the movie was made.

In a *Daily Mail Online* article by Stephanie Linning dated 19 June 2015, the story was headed, 'The Real Norman Bates'. The subheading states, '"Psycho" killer who stabbed his mother to death then dressed up in a pink track suit to make neighbours think she was still alive is jailed for life'. Top-of-the-story information added, 'Emmanuel Kalejaiye stabbed his mother Tolu Kalejaiye more than 40 times'; 'He dressed up in women's clothing to make neighbours think she was alive'; 'case echoed 1960 Hitchcock film in which killer impersonated dead mother'. The report continues, 'A cross-dressing Psycho-style killer who killed his mother in a frenzied attack has been jailed for life'. The case had 'strong echoes of the 1960 Alfred Hitchcock film – in which killer Norman Bates impersonated his dead mother'. A real-life story originally led to a fiction book, which was made into a hit movie, which is then referred to in order to illustrate another real-life killing. Interaction between real life and fiction could hardly be more apparent.

Psychiatrist slain, sad debate deepens

An essay in the *New York Times* of 19 September 2006 written by Benedict Carey is headed, 'A Psychiatrist Slain, and a Sad Debate Deepens'. It tells of the September 2006 killing of 53-year-old Dr. Wayne Fenton, 'a prominent schizophrenia specialist'. In his district, Dr. Fenton was 'the therapist of last resort, the one who could settle down and get through to the most severely psychotic, resistant patients, seemingly by sheer force of sympathy and good will'. On the afternoon of his death, Dr. Fenton had arranged to see Vitali Davidov of North Potomac, a 'nineteen-year-old patient suffering from severe psychosis'. Montgomery County Police found the psychiatrist 'dead in his small office, a few minutes' drive from his house'. The patient he had seen was soon tracked down and 'admitted he had beaten the doctor with his fists', according to the charge documents.

Naturally, the killing had 'deeply shaken mental health workers around the country'. Many had wondered 'about their own safety and about the dangers of allowing patients with severe psychosis to go without medication'. Experts said that Dr. Fenton's death could become a touchstone for the debate about 'whether people suffering from psychosis should be compelled to accept treatment to reduce the risk of violent outbursts'. Several states, including New York and California, 'have tightened their treatment laws to compel some mental health patients to accept treatment, even if they have not committed a crime'. Following Dr. Fenton's killing, 'some patient advocates cautioned against exploiting the tragedy to promote forced treatment'. A 'mental health advocate' stated that 'the main concern is that we do not let fear and stereotypes based on this case drive public policy' in support of forced commitment and drug treatment.

A schizophrenic, a slain worker, troubling questions

On a similar theme several years after the 'psychiatrist slain' report, a *New York Times* story of 16 June 2011 written by Deborah Sontag carried the heading 'A Schizophrenic, a Slain Worker, Troubling Questions'. This report tells of the killing in Boston of Stephanie Moulton, a 'petite, street-smart 25-year-old' by 27-year-old Deshawn James Chappell, 'a schizophrenic with a violent criminal record'. Stephanie Moulton was a health worker in the group home where Deshawn Chappell was based. Prosecutors stated that Chappell 'beat her, stabbed her repeatedly and then dumped her partially nude body in a church parking lot'.

In some detail, the report discusses possible factors in the killing, including reductions in health spending. It states that

> many people wondered aloud whether the system had failed both the suspect and the victim. How had Ms Moulton ended up alone with a psychotic man who had a history of violence and was off his medication? How had Mr. Chappell been allowed to deteriorate without setting off alarms? Should he have still been living in a group home, or did he need tighter supervision in hospital?

What a tragic waste

On 17 June 2016, the *Daily Mail* (Greenwood, Brooke and Dolan, 2016, p. 1) reported the death the day before of Jo Cox, a member of Parliament in the United Kingdom who was 'allegedly murdered by a troubled loner'. She was 'shot three times with a sawn-off shotgun and stabbed repeatedly with a foot long hunting knife in frenzied attack'. The killer 'kicked, stabbed and then shot' the MP 'at almost point blank range'. The subheading above the headline stated that Jo Cox was 'brutally murdered by a loner with a history of mental illness'.

Killer nanny who beheaded a 4-year-old girl 'kept her schizophrenia secret'

In March 2016, the *Mail Online* (accessed August 2016) reported that a 'killer nanny' Gyulchekhra Bobokulova, aged 38, beheaded a 4-year-old girl. She had 'kept her schizophrenia a secret'. Bobokulova told police that 'she had been haunted by "voices"'. She had 'been registered at a psychiatric clinic in her homeland Uzbekistan'. Her condition 'had been deteriorating in recent months'. The 'hijab-wearing nanny' walked the Moscow streets, 'brandishing the head of the child Nastya Meshcheryakova'. A source said, 'There is an explanation: she had schizophrenia', adding that the killer was 'registered in the local psychiatric clinic for a long time'. It appeared that 'her parents watched her and tried to send her to the psychiatric clinic'. However, 'her condition was gradually deteriorating' (*Mail Online* published 1 March 2016).

News depictions of psychotic killers

Selection

Let us reconsider the news stories that have been described earlier in relation to why they might have been selected by the newspaper. They all draw on people's interest in crime accounts, especially those of killing. They focus attention on an example of killing that creates extra anxiety among readers because it is related to people who are considered at least temporarily to be out of touch with 'reality' as others see it.

Therefore, the actions of these people, the reader will expect, are likely to be both dangerous and unpredictable.

Often, the perpetrators are briefly identified in terms of being killers and psychotic. There is a 'paranoid schizophrenic'. Another is 'killer Hannah Bonser'. Further, there is 'a dangerous paranoid schizophrenic . . . on trial release from a secure mental hospital'. We are presented with a 'cross-dressing Psycho-style killer'. Another perpetrator was 'a schizophrenic with a violent criminal record'. There was also 'a loner with a history of mental illness'. Bringing out the unpredictability of attacks, showing the danger even of friends, is a victim being killed by 'his schizophrenic lifelong pal'. Similarly, a figure that you might expect to be safe and trustworthy, a nanny, is not but is instead (in the apparent view of the press reporter) dangerous, sinister and duplicitous – a 'killer nanny' or 'hijab-wearing nanny' who 'kept her schizophrenia a secret'.

Victims are described in terms with which reader will readily identify and sympathise. Youth is mentioned where appropriate, sometimes linked to the fact that victims were still of school age or even younger, as with a '16 year old . . . on her way to school on a bus'; a '13-year-old school girl' and a '4-year-old girl'. Professionals who were trying to help are identified as with 'mental health worker Ashleigh Ewing aged 22 years' and 'a prominent schizophrenia specialist' who helped patients by 'sheer force of sympathy and good will'. The notion of someone dying and leaving innocent dependents is conveyed when parents are killed, such as a 'father of two'. While the vulnerability of age is flagged up with the reference to a 'mother . . . aged 79 years', the vulnerability of diminutive size is indicated by 'petite, street-smart 25-year-old'.

Details of attacks are conveyed vividly. Stabbings are linked with places that readers might consider safe. One victim was 'stabbed to death in a park' and another was 'stabbed to death on the doorstep of his home'. Repeated stabbing is regularly mentioned and where it is, the expression 'frenzied' may underline the ferocity of the attack. The type of knife is mentioned where it adds to the depictions, for example a hunting knife or a sword. Accordingly, a victim was 'stabbed 17 times with a samurai sword', another 'died after being stabbed 39 times' and a mother was stabbed 'more than 40 times' in a 'frenzied attack'. A further victim was 'shot three times with a sawn-off shotgun and stabbed repeatedly with a foot long hunting knife in a frenzied attack'. Of one victim, it is stated that the attacker 'beat her, stabbed her repeatedly and then dumped her partially nude body in a church parking lot'. A mother was shot 'in the face'. The nanny killer who had beheaded a 4-year-old girl walked the streets 'brandishing the head of the child'.

In sketching a picture for the reader, the journalist has to use simple outlines to draw the killer as nothing more than a killer and the victim as someone with whom the reader can identify while conveying the horror of the attack in vivid colours. This is not of course to diminish the impact of such killings on relatives of the deceased or the local communities. It is to try to show that reports are crafted to show the events in a particular way following certain conventions and stock phrases.

Balance

It is sometimes suggested that where an individual is killed, for example, by someone with schizophrenia that the story explains that such incidents are rare. Several of the stories that we examined tried to do this. But it is sometimes overlooked that when someone reads in newspapers or hears on television of a 'maniac' murdering an innocent passer-by, it does not matter to him or her that this is rare. The fact that it happens at all is enough.

It might be further suggested that it is not always necessary to mention that an attack involved a perpetrator who experienced a mental disorder. This needs to be considered if it is unclear what influence any mental disorder might have had in the attack. But newspaper editors cannot be expected to airbrush out the mention of mental disorder where there is reason to believe that it is a factor.

Killings discussed as examples in policy debate

Accounts are sometimes brought together to argue for a particular approach to mental health with which the readers of the newspaper or magazine article are likely to agree. The *Sun* report, for example, criticises the lack of communication between agencies, as well as failings of community care. One perpetrator had been for a 'psychiatric consultancy' and had been told that 'he was "dangerous" and "psychotic" – but no diagnosis was made'. Some accounts try to present different views about the best response. The killing of psychiatrist Dr. Fenton leads the journalist to mention mental health workers' concerns 'about their own safety and about the dangers of allowing patients with severe psychosis to go without medication'.

Mention is made of debate about 'whether people suffering from psychosis should be compelled to accept treatment to reduce the risk of violent outbursts'. Several states 'have tightened their treatment laws to compel some mental health patients to accept treatment, even if they have not committed a crime'. Some 'patient advocates cautioned against exploiting the tragedy to promote forced treatment'. A 'mental health advocate' was concerned that 'we do not let fear and stereotypes based on this case drive public policy' for forced commitment and drug treatment. Another report discusses possible factors in a killing, including reductions in health spending. Questions were posed about how a health worker had 'ended up alone with a psychotic man who had a history of violence and was off his medication' and whether he should have still been 'living in a group home' or needed 'tighter supervision in hospital'

Reasons for negative depictions

Reasons for negative depictions of mental disorder can include profit, ignorance, history, socialisation, psychological reassurance and lack of consumer feedback (Wahl, 1995, pp. 110–131). To make a *profit*, the mass media has to present what the public will buy, offering mental disorder as a 'dramatic and puzzling' topic for a public seeking arousal, excitement, fear and titillation. Homicides involving mental illness tend to be 'even more terrifying', making them 'more likely to sell newspapers'. In movies, 'mentally ill killers are equally profitable' (Ibid., pp. 110–111). Turning to *ignorance*, media professionals depicting people with mental disorders as 'different and dangerous' are often unaware of the inaccuracy (p. 113). Of course, 'those with mental illness sometimes do kill', but individual media depictions accumulate to 'create an inaccurate stereotype' (p. 114). In *history*, mental disorder has been associated with evil and 'possession', while physical features like 'dishevelled hair' have been associated with depictions of madness (p. 117). Also influential is *socialisation* through stories such as Greek myths portraying mental illness as a punishment of the gods (p. 121).

Presenting 'mentally ill characters as different and dangerous' may provide *psychological reassurance*. Mental illnesses threaten crucial faculties, so considering their impact is 'discomforting'. Recognising that advantages such as education and wealth may not preclude mental illness is 'threatening', leading to people taking refuge in believing it only affects others 'fundamentally different' from them. Media depictions reflecting this are 'reassuring'. Relating violence to mental disorder avoids considering social factors contributing to both (pp. 124–128). Finally, *lack of consumer feedback* might contribute to media misrepresentations when mental health professionals, individuals with mental disorders and their relatives and friends do not sufficiently challenge or complain about media misrepresentations (pp. 128–131).

Strategies for increasing understanding of mental disorders

Among strategies for increasing public understanding of mental disorders is public education through various sources including booklets, Internet information, posters, videos, days or weeks highlighting mental health matters and so on. This may take the form of providing clear, factual information about different conditions. Also important is public education about the way that some media outlets depict distorted representations of mental disorder. This might be conveyed in the context of a wider awareness of media representations and misrepresentations.

Another approach is to provide guidance to the media on the use of terminology, including suggestions about words which some may find offensive. Public figures speaking out about their experience of mental disorder, either from personal experience or in connection with relatives or friends, are further contributions to a fuller understanding.

Promoting more positive images

More positive images could be (and are) promoted in different ways. Mental Health America (www.mentalhealthamerica.net) is a community-based nonprofit organisation aiming to help 'all Americans achieve wellness by living mentally healthier lives'. It seeks to 'promote mental health as a critical part of overall wellness'. The organisation believes that mental health conditions should be treated long before they reach the most critical points 'in the disease process' (website accessed March 2016). Their website provides factual information on psychosis and schizophrenia, including in children and youth. Periodically, the organisation produces research papers and reports that concern mental health policy and advocacy.

The American Mental Health Foundation (www.americanmentalhealthfoundation.org) is a research organisation aiming to advocate for and to advance 'mental health and well-being in society'. It carries out research, organises educational seminars and 'webinars' and publishes books.

The National Institute of Mental Health (www.nimh.nih.gov) is a federal agency for research on mental disorders. It is one of the twenty-seven institutes and centres that constitute the National Institutes of Health, America's health research agency. It aims to 'transform the understanding and treatment of mental illness through basic and clinical research, paving the way for prevention, recovery, and cure'. The National Institute of Mental Health is part of the US Department of Health and Human Services (website accessed March 2016).

The National Alliance on Mental Illness (www.nami.org) is a 'grassroots mental health organisation dedicated to building better lives for the millions of Americans affected by mental illness'. It is associated with many local affiliates, state organisations and community volunteers who seek 'to raise awareness and provide support and education that was not previously available to those in need'. The alliance aims to educate, advocate, listen and lead (website accessed March 2016).

Factual information from such sources, it is believed, can counteract information such as that from newspapers that might, for example, give a negative impression of community care by emphasising when it goes wrong.

Consumer complaints can help to change advertising that is deemed offensive to advocacy groups. A well-known example is Georgia peanuts being advertised as 'Certifiably Nuts', with a sack of peanuts wrapped in a straightjacket with commitment papers and a string-pull that produced maniacal laughter. The then National Alliance for the Mentally Ill asked members and affiliates to write to the creators and distributors of the product and to contact the organisers of the advertising industry award who had given an award to 'Certifiably Nuts' as a campaign. Stores selling the nuts were also contacted. All this led to the advertising being withdrawn.

In addition to providing information for the public, organisations may work with media sources directly, providing guidelines for editors and writers in various media outlets. They might raise issues which contribute to stigmatising individuals with mental disorders. Media watch campaigners look out for potentially misleading and offensive material and draw the attention of the sources to their concerns.

Mental illness awareness weeks or days may be organised. A good example in the United Kingdom is the Epsom Mental Health Week, a thriving concern which runs many talks and events bringing together those with mental disorders, mental health professionals and others.

In addition to organisations that challenge negative portrayals of mental disorders, efforts are also made to promote more accurate, positive images and references. This includes the use of media of all types, including clips posted on the Internet.

Conclusion

Intersections between the media, society and individuals, and mental disorder often recognise the broad range of media. An example attracting persistent interest is the media representation of 'psycho killers'. Television drama, movies and news accounts represent and report on 'psycho killers' with continuing vigour because of the public appetite for such stories. Examples from television police dramas include episodes from the shows *Charlie's Angels, Hawaii Five-O, Kojak, The A-Team, The Hitchhiker, Baywatch* and *The Following*. Other examples are *Wonderland* and *Bates Motel*. In movies, examples linking psychosis or schizophrenia include *The Cabinet of Dr. Caligari, Repulsion, Halloween, Clownhouse, Criminal Law, Five Corners, I Saw What You Did, Misery, Out for Justice, The Silence of the Lambs, Shutter Island* and *Psychotic*. In such representations, the psychotic killer character is a device used in cat-and-mouse plots and as a suspense aid generally, drawing on the audience's ideas of the unpredictability of such characters. It has been suggested that depictions like these perpetuate notions that are inaccurate and stereotyped and can lead to misconceptions, stigma and rejection of people with mental disorders. The attraction of frightening depictions of mental disorder may arise from a wish for titillation or to temporarily assuage fear. The castigation of these shows and movies by some commentators seems to have had no impact on the appetite of audiences for them.

Turning to news reports relating psychosis and violence, they can be summarised by banner headlines such as '1,200 Killed by Mental Patients', 'The Real Norman Bates Psycho Killer', Psychiatrist Slain, Sad Debate Deepens', A Schizophrenic, a Slain Worker, Troubling Questions', 'What a Tragic Waste' and 'Killer Nanny Who Beheaded a Four Year Old Girl Kept Her Schizophrenia Secret'. In these stories, the perpetrators are briefly identified as being killers and psychotic, while victims are described in terms with which reader will readily identify and sympathise. Details of attacks are conveyed dramatically. Reports are shaped to depict events in a particular way following certain conventions. Collections of such accounts are sometimes used to illustrate the effect of policy towards people with mental disorders.

It has been maintained that reasons for negative depictions of mental disorder include profit, ignorance, history, socialisation, psychological reassurance and lack of consumer feedback. Among strategies for increasing public understanding of mental disorders is public education through various sources; providing the media with information and guidance on terminology; and encouraging public figures to speak about their experience of mental disorder. More positive images are promoted by organisations such as charities, foundations and institutes who may also provide clear, factual information about mental health. Consumer complaints can sometimes help to change advertising that is deemed offensive. Mental illness awareness weeks or days may be organised. Some people at least seem to be able to separate television and movie drama and news 'hype' from real knowledge and understanding of those that they know who have mental disorders.

Thinking points

Readers may wish to consider:

*   further reasons for the continued popularity of psycho-killer dramas;
*   other techniques used in constructing news accounts involving violence and psychosis;
*   strategies for promoting better understanding of mental health including psychosis and how they might be made more effective;
*   whether, as suggested, there is a 'disconnect' between individuals viewing psychosis in drama and that same person's likely response to psychosis in real life (i.e. the extent to which people distinguish between media representations and their own experiences).

Notes

1 https://en.wikiquote.org/wiki/Charlie%27s_Angels_(TV_series)#Little_Angels_of_the_Night.27_.5B2.23.5D
2 *Hawaii Five-O* '. . . And I Want Some Candy and a Gun that Shoots' (1971), USA, http://www.imdb.com/title/tt0598005/
3 www.tvguide.com/tvshows/kojak/episode-4-season-4/out-of-the-shadows/100246/
4 www.radiotimes.com/tv-programme/e/cys4y/the-a-team--s1-e9-holiday-in-the-hills/
5 *The Hitchhiker* 'A Whole New You' (1991), www.imdb.com/title/tt0602136/combined
6 www.imdb.com/title/tt0394353/
7 www.imdb.com/title/tt2071645/?ref_=fn_al_tt_1
8 www.ovguide.com/wonderland-9202a8c04000641f8000000005c0b2f6
9 www.thesun.co.uk/sol/homepage/news/5183994/1200-killed-by-mental-patients-in-shock-10-year-toll.html

Key texts

Harper, S. (2009) *Madness, Power and the Media: Class, Gender and Race in Popular Representations of Mental Disorder* London, Palgrave Macmillan.
     This book questions the medical picture of mental 'illness' as a psychiatric construction of mental distress. It suggests that contemporary media images can reproduce inequalities associated with gender, race and social class.
Morris, G. (2006) *Mental Health Issues and the Media: An Introduction for Health Professionals* London and New York, Routledge.
     Chapters discuss labelling and stigma, as well as positive descriptions of mental health. Media is taken to include news, literature, movies, television and the Internet.
Rubin, L. C. (Ed.) (2012) *Mental Illness in Popular Media: Essays on the Representation of Disorders* Jefferson, NC, McFarland.
     A wide-ranging collection of essays on media and disorders.

10
CONCLUSION

Introduction

Here, we take an overview of the areas discussed in the book, such as personal accounts of psychosis, psychiatry, advocacy and media coverage. We then look at whether language styles can reflect the motives of people who adopt those styles and, if it can, what might be the consequences. I consider attempts to change the words used to discuss 'psychosis' and possible implications.

Overview

Changes in terms over time

When suggesting a chronology of developments relating to mental disorders and to psychiatry, one must select what constitute important events and decide their sequence. Regarding history, further judgements are made about how to interpret events and their likely causes. In shaping a history of madness and psychiatry, views are sometimes polarised, as in the persistency/recency debate about schizophrenia. Historical changes as indicated by alterations in terminology reflect the development of understandings of psychosis and schizophrenia. Expressions such as 'mad', 'insane', 'lunatic' and 'maniac' demonstrate this, where, for example, 'lunatic' fell into disuse as a formal term as it became known that madness is not effected by moon cycles.

In broader historic contexts, the influence of the early French School and the work of German-speaking psychiatrists in central Europe involved debates about the meaning and scope of expressions such as psychosis and schizophrenia. Efforts are sometimes made to change words that are used to refer to mental disorders when they are perceived in some quarters to harbour negative connotations. This occurred comparatively recently with 'psychosis' and 'schizophrenia' as they became extensively used.

Personal accounts

Personal accounts possess authority based on experience, but it is questioned how far it is possible to convey madness from the 'inside'. Also, accounts are shaped, making elements of artifice unavoidable. A further difficulty faced by individuals trying to describe psychotic episodes is that at the time of the episode the individual is not in touch with everyday reality, making the translation of the experiences after psychotic periods difficult. Yet from personal testimony emerges common features that aid our understanding of psychosis and schizophrenia. Accounts may arise from questioning by others about what was happening. An individual who has gone through a psychotic episode will likely want to try and understand what he or she experienced and perhaps what other people later reported that he or she said or did.

Language used to describe experiences of psychosis may be illustrative, comparing the experience with something else with which the listener might be familiar. Or relatedly, it may be fashioned to make what happened more understandable to the person who experienced the episode. Such use of language (and observations of behaviour) can have some use in helping understanding, including the diagnosis of psychosis for professionals.

Psychiatry

Contemporary psychiatry sees mental disorders as influenced by biological, environmental and other factors. It is not assumed that administering medication is the inevitable response to mental disorders. There is no presumption that schizophrenia is static over time or that symptoms will remain. *DSM-5* does not describe psychoses as 'diseases' nor does it mention the conditions being 'cured' or being 'incurable'. It categorises psychotic disorders according to features such as delusions and hallucinations. Diagnostic criteria exist for several psychotic disorders grouped as 'schizophrenia spectrum and other psychotic disorders' (which include schizophrenia itself). Other disorders can also be associated with psychotic episodes. Definitions of mental disorders, the notions of diagnosis, causal factors, prevalence and incidence and treatment all reflect a scientific stance. Expressions relating to psychosis may be in everyday language or in medical-type terminology where there is no exact plain-language equivalent. Greek and Latin medical terms for psychosis can give an exaggerated impression of exactitude and scientific rigour. Neo-Kraepelian categories imply a boundary between wellness and illness, that there are several discrete mental disorders and that research helps to improve the validity and reliability of diagnoses and classification. Suitable 'best-fit' classifications can help communication between individuals affected by mental disorder, and health professionals, while identifying conditions has implications for provision and outcomes.

Despite the apparent precision of some terms, there are still challenges, as with notions of prevalence.

For those taking a categorical view of psychosis and other disorders, the question is whether distinctions are possible and justifiable (even if there is a continuum from wellness through to mental disorder), for example in terms of severity of symptoms and their impact. A relativist view of psychosis may take insufficient account of evidence from observation or research in accepting that no one person's view is better than another's. Critics of the scientific leanings of psychiatry see it as a 'medical model' which overemphasises individual 'within person' factors and which is biological and simplistic. By contrast, a 'social model' focuses more on environmental factors. Certainly, the terminology of classification, aetiology, diagnosis, prognosis and so on can appear overly distant. But physicians and therapists can recognise the scientific aspect of their work while maintaining human warmth and understanding.

Psychoanalysis and beyond

Among key aspects of Freud's theories are the id, ego and super ego and the oral, sadistic–anal and phallic (Oedipal) phases of sexual development. Psychoanalysis allows clients to express uncensored self-observations enabling the analyst to deduce and reveal repressed unconscious material. Freud proposes that psychosis results from a disturbance in the relationships between the ego and the external world. He further suggests that psychosis first moves ego away from reality, then attempts to create a new reality which avoids the objections of the old one. Freud's interpretations have been criticised for appearing in scientific mode yet rarely being amenable to scientific testing, while his language and tone has been likened to religious exegesis rather than scientific exposition. Klein pioneered the insights from work with children to adult psychotic patients, seeing the withdrawal and bizarre behaviour of psychotic adults as desperate attempts to ward off the terrors she believed that she had seen in children's play. For her, the mind was a succession of primitive, phantasmagoric images, fantasies and terrors expressed in terms of the 'paranoid-schizoid position' and the 'depressive position'. Kleinian language faces considerable challenges in attempting to explore and refer to preverbal infancy and in trying to convey adult views about it. Relatedly, Bion's writings are often obscure. But the language conveying findings from observations of mother-child interaction, for example, and other explorations is always likely to be complex and difficult. Sometimes commentators can clarify original work, perhaps by setting it in a historical and cultural context.

In *Écrits*, Lacan reconsiders Freudian theories and their possible relationships with language. For Lacan, with a person experiencing psychosis, the 'name of the father' (as a primordial signifier) is 'foreclosed' and not integrated into the symbolic order. This is brought about when some signifier which the individual cannot assimilate is triggered, leaving a 'hole' in the symbolic order. When the foreclosed 'name of the father' appears in the 'real', the subject is unable to assimilate it, precipitating the onset of psychosis. The realm of the symbolic, being insufficiently bound to the realm of the imaginary, leads to failures in meaning. Lacan's language has been censured for being obscure, pretentious and vacuous in its misuse of scientific and mathematical vocabulary. Regarding Deleuze and Guattari, their *Anti-Oedipus* brought together threads of Freudian thinking and Marxist theory. Deleuze and Guattari's work uses the image of schizophrenia as creating thought in a personal and political sense. Their clinical understanding of schizophrenia as a creative state seems romanticised. The notion that the revolutionary learns from the psychotic how to evade Oedipal constraint and the influence of power in order to form a radical politics appears far-fetched. Their language includes scientific analogies that confuse rather than explain.

Advocacy

Advocacy groups may be motivated by a desire to represent individuals who have experienced or who are experiencing mental disorders. Naturally, not all such individuals have the same perspectives, although some of these groups have particular views that they wish to promote. For example, there is the notion that if one changes language, one changes thought and belief. This is reflected in the wish to discourage certain phrases such as 'mental illness' and 'psychotic' and substitute other words like 'survivor' and 'human being'.

Underlying such views seems to be the fear and perhaps the direct experience of negative labelling and subsequent stigmatisation and discrimination. If it is social views that change language and not the other way around, such efforts to shape the use of language are unlikely to be successful. A more effective strategy might be, for example, to challenge unfair discrimination through providing examples and information.

Anti-psychiatry

Anti-psychiatry views associated with Szasz, Laing, Goffman and others persist to the present day in different degrees. For Szasz, mental disorder was a metaphor. Psychiatric diagnoses are phrased to resemble medical diagnoses but are merely labels for an individual whose behaviour annoys or offends others. Psychiatric language disguises imperative sentences as indicative ones so that a desire to have someone confined to a hospital can be presented as a statement of a characteristic of the offending person. Szasz's rhetoric (pharmacy as chemical pacification, treatments as psychiatric slavery, involuntary interventions as crimes against humanity) may not today convince readers. Laing, discussing the nature of communication of an individual experiencing schizophrenia, sees much of it as nonsensical, filibustering, purposely evasive and 'playing' at being mad. Directed at other people, the language of the schizophrenic is intended to create boredom. An individual with schizophrenia is often in control of the way they use language, manipulating the effect it has on others. Schizophrenia ceases to exist once the individual meets someone by whom he or she feels understood. Never the less, evidence for such claims is lacking.

Goffman highlighted limitations of asylums in discussing 'institutionalisation' and pointed to some of the functions and negative consequences of these total institutions. This encouraged the option of community provision, and led staff in institutions to be more critical of unnecessary ritual and routine. More important was the efforts to humanise patients and examine de-humanising patterns of interaction. Goffman's language reveals his low opinion of psychiatry and therapy and of hospitals and their staff. Contemporary anti-psychiatry videos have their own language and conventions. Techniques include subtly eliding terms so that they change without the viewer always noticing and allowing statements to be made that could otherwise be challenged; equating mental disorders with everyday experiences; non sequiturs such as that past poor interventions imply that recent interventions are equally invalid; unjustified generalisations; and emotive language.

Slang and humour

Slang expressions and jokes about mental disorders are widespread, both sharing features such as a casual irreverence. Slang may refer to psychiatrists and psychotherapists. It is used regarding mental disorder where there are historical derivations; plant and animal analogies; examples conveying oddness or incapableness; loss, incompleteness or dysfunction; and incorrect ideas of causation or misidentification. Shortened slang suggests the diminished importance of what is being referenced. Causes of madness also attract slang terms. Humour generally is nebulous and diverse. Jokes, however, appear to have particular purposes and to work in identifiable ways. Jokes about madness may concern psychosis, schizophrenia, delusions, hallucinations, psychiatry and psychoanalysis. Their content reveals something of public views of psychosis, while their mechanics may involve word play or can reveal the unexpected literalness of a joke character's response.

Slang and humour concerning madness endures, seemingly unresponsive to distaste expressed by people who dislike it. If the motivation for slang and humour is some underlying fear of psychosis and other mental disorders, coupled with lack of knowledge, then challenging such usage would need to address these motivations. Otherwise, trying to discourage the slang and the jokes is like throwing buckets of water at the garden shed while the house is on fire – it seems the right thing to do but is directed in the wrong place.

Mass media

Interactions take place between the media, society and individuals, and mental disorder. An example attracting persistent interest is the representation of 'psycho killers'. Television drama, movies and news accounts represent and report on 'psycho killers' with continuing vigour because of the public appetite for such stories. These representations may show negative depictions, and there may be faults in the people who absorb them. Nevertheless, they remain popular plot devices in fiction, drama and news accounts. One response to such depictions is to increase understanding of mental disorders and promote competing positive images. Perhaps many people are capable of putting television and movie drama and news 'hype' in separate compartments from real understanding of people whom they know and that have mental disorders.

Mass media language tends to reflect everyday use. Where slang and jokes about mental disorder exist, the media is likely to reflect this. There are, of course, occasional 'successes' as they are perceived by those wanting to ban certain words and phrases, but 'distasteful' mass media coverage evident thirty and more years ago persists. Anyone checking Internet sites where mental disorders are discussed (other than advocacy or professional sites) will witness the extensive use of slang and jokes. Perhaps this is more apparent today because the Internet and social media gives a voice as much to those who are 'offensive' as to those who are 'sensitive'.

Can style reflect motives?

To what extent can style reflect motives? The answer it appears is 'to some extent'. *Historical terminology* reflects motives and understandings of the time. This can help present-day writers and others thinking about mental disorders to be more aware of how contemporary language can obscure, as well as reveal. *Personal accounts* of mental disorder in their use of analogies and descriptions of feelings can help the individual who experienced the disorder and others gain some grasp of what was happening. The motive here appears to be one of trying to understand. In *psychiatry*, highly prescriptive language can suggest a striving to make phenomena more exact than they perhaps are and may sometimes hide a lack of conviction in the exactness of what one is saying.

Within *psychoanalysis*, Freudian terminology and concepts relating to psychosis are considered by some to be limited in their sourcing and application. Klein and her followers grapple with the problems of trying to understand and describe in adult language the prelanguage experiences of infants and the implications for understanding psychosis. In subsequent postmodern paths, the associated language tends to be obscurantist and overblown. The adoption of apparent Freudian terms can be deceptive here, concealing a motive to liberate others, including those experiencing mental disorder, from what is perceived to be the political and social oppressiveness of 'society'. *Advocacy* for example where it is euphemistic may represent a desire or motive to protect or to change the way others speak of mental disorder regarding negative labelling, consequent stigma and resulting oppression. *Anti-psychiatry* in its rhetoric and use of the techniques of propaganda seems to be harnessing passionately felt feelings of oppression and misuse of those with mental disorders by psychiatrists and others. Instead of tackling any such individual abuse as it arises (through the protection of others) the response is to generalise instances of abuse to all psychiatrists and all of psychiatry. This motive of demeaning all psychiatry and all psychiatrists makes the points raised impossible to deal with because all psychiatry is presented as culpable, not the particular psychiatrist or other health professional that is accused of perpetrating the abuse originally.

Slang and humour, in diminishing mental disorder, may be motivated by fear and lack of knowledge. Or it may be that people can switch from this kind of language because it is nonserious to them (whatever others think of it) and so can be dropped with no feelings of incongruity when real people with real mental disorders are encountered. *Mass media* may reflect (like slang and humour) the everyday way of talking about mental disorder for many people. The motivation is likely to include selling information in newspapers of other outlets by using language that readers understand because they use language in that same manner themselves. Identifying in this way with readers is likely to boost sales. Again, recipients of mass media depictions may be quite capable of distinguishing media types from any real-life contact they may have with someone who experiences mental disorder.

If style reflects motives, what are the consequences?

If language style does sometimes reflect motivations, this suggests that examining style and considering what those motives are will be revealing. One response to language that people disapprove of has for decades been to try to ban words or make people use other words. That this approach lacks impact is evident in the continued use of 'disapproved' terms.

If we examine motives in parallel with language, the response might be different. In this scenario, people with different views about mental disorder might recognise the very different motives of others and try to understand them. This could legitimately lead to an expectation that others will try to comprehend one's own motives and at the same time try to understand one's own use of language. Motives and views can be challenged in the context of the language that is being used. This is more likely to lead to discussions between parties who now do not communicate because they are caught up in language wars, such as political correctness versus plain speaking.

Will this lead people to change their views? In some cases, it will; in other cases, not. In real-life exchanges, what difference might this make? In the challenging language scenario, someone using slang and telling jokes about mental disorders would meet an advocate for a mental disorder group. Naturally, the advocate would point out how offensive the language was, and the slang user would have no appreciation of what the advocate was talking about. Of course, the slang user would correct the advocate for using euphemism and (to them) silly terms like 'citizen' instead of 'psychotic', and the advocate would be equally unaffected.

If motives or possible motives were discussed to a similar extent to which attempts are made to police language, it might emerge that the slang user was fearful of mental disorder and knew little about it. It might become apparent that the advocate was anxious about the impact of other people stigmatising those with mental disorders.

This might be a more productive arena for exchanging views and ideas than solely focusing on language in an attempt to change it.

To take another example, the approach to addressing terms used in mass media would not be what often sounds like 'Could you stop using these words because some of us find them offensive'. An obvious reply to this is what it has been tacitly for decades: 'Never mind. Some of us do not'. The exchange would be more about tackling the profit motives that drive the stories speaking in the language of their readers. This in turn leads back to the motivations of those readers and viewers using slang and humour that is considered inappropriate.

Attempting to change words relating to 'psychosis' and implications

A recurring theme as we examine different ways of discussing psychosis and other mental disorders is that certain words can and should be discouraged and others encouraged. Often the aim is to avoid offending someone, or to encourage more equal treatment.

Historical terms have changed for different reasons. People tend not to speak of 'lunatics', except in slang because evidence contradicts the once-popular idea that the moon influences episodes of mental disorder. The word 'mania' continues in current use as a suffix to the focus of excessive and excitable attachment, as in 'kleptomania' and 'pyromania'. However, to speak of someone being a 'maniac' has fallen into disuse except in slang and in some mass media outlets, perhaps because mania is recognised as part of a broader disorder. To speak of someone who is psychotic as 'mad' is also avoided in more formal language because, as well as being offensive for some, it is inaccurate. In fact, psychosis can be characterised by excessively withdrawn behaviour, as well as highly active conduct. Consequently, the term 'mad', which conveys frenzied excitement, does not fit well with the nature of psychosis in general.

Where words are not used or are less used because they are deemed offensive, substitutions have been encouraged. Rather than 'mad' or 'maniac', terms such as 'mental disorder' tend to be preferred. It is as if 'mad' and 'maniac' have become tainted, and new words are needed, carrying greater neutrality and less offence. Yet, attempts to ban words or avoid them in other quarters have tended not to work.

The implications for psychosis, and to some extent other mental disorders, is not to assume that changing words changes views or behaviour. (For a parallel discussion in relation to disabilities and disorders including intellectual disabilities, please also see Farrell, 2012.) If 'schizophrenia' has negative connotations, changing the word for another one does not tackle supposed negative associations. What tackles negative views is to address the concerns and the realities behind them. This might mean accepting that some negative connotations are true, as well as putting forward positive aspects.

For example, if schizophrenia is a negative word to some people because they have heard it associated with violence in movies or in news stories, this is because the condition can be so associated. To deny this or to immediately sweep it under the carpet with claims that it is rare does not do justice to genuine worries. Neither does it do justice to the people who have been harmed or have harmed themselves. Among the questions that need considering are, what is being done to reduce the risk of harm? How effective are such precautions? What is the right balance between keeping people safe and restricting the liberty of persons with schizophrenia who may hurt others or themselves?

If these points are not faced or are swept aside in rhetorical statements, they cannot be resolved. Recall Szasz's ([1960]/2010) comments that 'if there is no mental illness, there can be no hospitalization, treatments, or cure for it' (Ibid., p. 267); that treatment is seen as 'psychiatric slavery' (Ibid., p. 278); and that 'there is no medical, moral, or legal justification for involuntary psychiatric interventions' which are considered 'crimes against humanity' (Ibid., p. 268). If that sort of rhetoric is the end of the discussion, then how can anyone expect worries about schizophrenia and violence to be put into context?

If a relative, a friend or a community is reeling from a loved one being killed by someone with schizophrenia, they are unlikely to be immediately interested in the fact that individuals with psychosis are more likely to be victims of violence than perpetrators. One has to discuss the real concerns and what is being done (or not done) about them. Then discussion might move on to contextual issues such as the rarity of violence by people with schizophrenia against others. The approach is to recognise genuine concerns and try to do something about them before attempting to challenge incorrect or misinformed beliefs with information and alternative views.

Better understanding and responses to the challenges of psychosis is not generally achieved by telling people that they cannot use certain words. Consequently, the persuasive power of advocacy groups is more limited than it might otherwise be. Implying (e.g. as on the MindFreedom International website) that someone should not use the word 'mentally ill' but should instead use words like 'citizen' does not address the issues at all. It evades the issues and merely reinforces the views of those who already think that there is no place for 'schizophrenia', only 'citizenship'.

A final few words

I hope that for the reader, the examination of the language associated with psychosis has held intrinsic interest. Also, looking at such language I trust can open doors to different ways of debating old perspectives such as political correctness versus plain speaking, euphemism versus slang and humour, psychiatry versus anti-psychiatry, and similar positions that have too often become fruitlessly polarised.

REFERENCES

Legislation and related regulations

Handicapped Pupils and School Health Service Regulations of 1945.
Mental Deficiency Act 1913.

Books and articles

Acocella, J. (2000) 'Introduction' in Nijinsky, V. (Ed.) ([1919]/2000) (Unexpurgated Edition) *The Diary of Vaclav Nijinsky* (Edited by J. Acocella and Translated from the Russian by K. Fitzlyon) New York, Farrar, Straus and Giroux (pp. vii–xlvi).

American Psychiatric Association (2013) *Diagnostic and Statistical Manual of Mental Disorders Fifth Edition (DSM5)* Washington, DC, APA.

Ashok, A. H., Baugh, J. and Yeragani, V. K. (2012) 'Paul Eugen Bleuler and the origin of the term schizophrenia (Schizopreniegruppe)' *Indian Journal of Psychiatry* 54, 1, 96 January–March.

Barham, P. and Hayward, R. (1995) *Re-Locating Madness: From the Mental Patient to the Person* London, Free Association Books.

Barnes, C. (1998) 'The social model of disability: A sociological phenomenon ignored by sociologists?' in Shakespeare, T. (Ed.) *The Disability Reader: Social Science Perspectives* London, Cassell (pp. 65–78).

Bateson, G. (Ed.) (1961) 'Introduction' in Perceval, J. (Ed.) ([1838 and 1840]/1961) *Perceval's Narrative: A Patient's Account of His Psychosis 1830–1832* Stanford, Stanford University Press (pp. v–xxii).

Becker, H. (1963) *Outsiders* New York, Free Press, https://archive.org/stream/percevalsnarrati 007726mbp#page/n7/mode/2up

Beer, M. (1995) 'Psychosis: From mental disorder to disease concept' *Hist Psychiatry* 6, 177–200.

Bentall, R. P. (2003) *Madness Explained: Psychosis and Human Nature* London and New York, Penguin.

Bion, W. R. (1955) 'Group dynamics: A re-view' in Klein, M., Heiman, P. and Money-Kyrle, R. E. (Eds.) *New Directions in Psychoanalysis* London, Maresfield Reprints (pp. 440–477).

Bion, W. R. ([1967]/1988) 'Notes on memory and desire' in Bott-Spillius, E. (Ed.) *Melanie Klein Today* London, Routledge (Volume 2, pp. 17–21).

Bleuler, E. ([1911]/1950) *Dementia Praecox or the Group of Schizophrenias* New York, International Universities Press (Translated from the German by J. Zinkin).

Blumer, H. (1986) *Symbolic Interactionism: Perspective and Method* Berkeley, University of California Press.

Borch-Jacobsen, M. and Shamdasani, S. (2011) *The Freud Files: An Inquiry into the History of Psychoanalysis* Cambridge, Cambridge University Press.

Boyles, D. C. (2004) *My Punished Mind: A Memoir of Psychosis* Lincoln, NE, iUniverse.

Bromet, E., Drew, M. and Eaton, W. (2002) 'Epidemiology of psychosis with special reference to schizophrenia' in Tsuang, M. T. and Tohen, M. (Eds.) *Textbook of Psychiatric Epidemiology* New York and London, Wiley (pp. 363–387).

Buchanan, I. (2008) *Deleuze and Guattari's Anti Oedipus: A Reader's Guide (Continuum Reader's Guides)* London and New York, Continuum.

Buchanan-Parker, P. and Barker, P. (2009) 'The convenient myth of Thomas Szasz' *Journal of Psychiatric and Mental Health Nursing* 16, 87–95, www.mentalhealth.freeuk.com/ Convenientmyth.pdf

Burgy, M. (2008) 'The concept of psychosis: Historical and phenomenological aspects' *Schizophrenia Bulletin* 34, 6, 1200–1210.

Campbell, P. (2010) 'Surviving the system' in Basset, T. and Stickley, T. (Eds.) *Voices of Experience: Narratives of Mental Health Survivors* Chichester, Wiley-Blackwell (p. 22).

Canstatt, C. F. (1841) *Handbuch der Medizinischen Klinik* Stuttgart, Germany, Enke.

Chamberlin, J. (1977) *On Our Own: Patient-Controlled Alternatives to the Mental Health System* Lawrence, MA, National Empowerment Center, Inc.

Conroy, F. ([1968]/1970) 'Foreword' in Séchehaye, M. (Ed.) ([1951]/1970) *Reality Lost and Regained: Autobiography of a Schizophrenic Girl* (with analytic interpretation by Marguerite Séchehaye) New York, Signet/New American Library (pp. ix–xiii) (Translated from the French by G. Rubin-Rabson).

Cooke, A. (Ed.) (2014) *Understanding Psychosis and Schizophrenia: Why People Sometimes Hear Voices, Believe Things That Others Find Strange, or Appear Out of Touch with Reality, and What Can Help* Canterbury, British Psychological Society Division of Clinical Psychology/ Canterbury Christchurch University.

Cooley, C. H. ([1902]/1983) *Human Nature and Social Order* (Social Science Classics Series) Piscataway, NJ, Transaction Publishers.

Cooper, D. G. (1967) *Psychiatry and Antipsychiatry* London, Tavistock Publications.

Cooper, D. G. (1980) *The Language of Madness* London, Pelican Books.

Corker, M. and Shakespeare, T. (2002) 'Mapping the terrain' in Corker, M. and Shakespeare, T. (Eds.) *Disability/Postmodernity: Embodying Disability Theory* London and New York, Continuum (pp. 1–17).

Dain, N. (1971) *Disordered Minds: The First Century of Eastern State Hospital in Williamsburg, Virginia, 1766–1866* Charlottesville, University Press of Virginia.

Dawkins, R. (1998) 'Postmodernism disrobed' *Nature* 394, 141–143 July.

Deegan, P. E. (1993) 'Recovering our sense of value after being labeled mentally ill' *Journal of Psychosocial Nursing and Mental Health Services* 31, 4, 7–11, www.ncbi.nlm.nih.gov/ pubmed/8487230

Deleuze, G. and Guattari, F. ([1972]/1983) *Anti-Oedipus: Capitalism and Schizophrenia* Minneapolis, University of Minnesota Press (Translated from the French by R. Hurley, M. Seem and H. R. Lane).

Department of Education and Skills (2005) (2nd. Edition) *Data Collection by Special Educational Need* London, DfES.

Derrida, J. ([1967]/1997) *Of Grammatology* Baltimore, Johns Hopkins University Press (Translated from the French by C. Spivak, corrected edition).

Derrida, J. ([various dates and 1967]/1968) 'Cogito and the history of madness' in *Writing and Difference* London and New York, Routledge (Translated from the French by A. Bass).

Dinnage, R. (2000) 'Introduction' in Schreber, D. P. (Ed.) ([1903]/2000) *Memoirs of My Nervous Illness* New York, New York Review of Books (pp. xi–xxiv) (Edited and Translated from the German by I. Macalpine and R. A. Hunter).

Dix, D. (1843) *On Behalf of the Insane Poor: Report to the Legislature of Massachusetts of January 1843* New York, Arno Press (reprint).

Dryden, J. (1693) 'Contributions to the satires of Decimus Junius Juvenalis together with satires of Aulus Persius Flaccus' in Dearing, V. A., Chambers, A. B. and Frost, W. (Eds.) *The Works of John Dryden, Vol 1: Poems 1693–1696* Oakland, University of California Press.

Dumas, B. K. and Lighter, J. (1978) 'Is slang a word for linguists?' *American Speech* 53, 5, 14–15.

Elliott, A. (2002) *Psychoanalytic Theory: An Introduction* New York, Palgrave Encyclopedia Britannica, www.britannica.com/topic/slang

Esquirol, E. ([1838]/1845) *Mental Maladies: A Treatise on Insanity* Philadelphia, Lea and Blanchard (Translated from the French by E. K. Hunt).

Falk, K. (2010) *Understanding Bipolar Disorder: Why Some People Experience Extreme Mood States and What Can Help* Leicester, UK, British Psychological Society.

Falret, J. P. (1854) 'Memoire sur la folie circulaire' *Bulletin de l'Academie de Medicine* 19, 382–415.

Farrell, M. (2010) *Debating Special Education* London and New York, Routledge.

Farrell, M. (2012) *New Perspectives in Special Education: Contemporary Philosophical Debates* London and New York, Routledge.

Farrell, M. (2014) *Investigating the Language of Special Education: Listening to Many Voices* Basingstoke, UK and New York, Palgrave Macmillan.

Feuchtersleben, E. von (1845) *Lehrbuch der Ärztlichen Seelenkunde* Wien, Austria, Gerold.

Fielding, H. ([1734]/2004) *The Intriguing Chambermaid* Whitefish, MT, Kessinger Publishing.

Fink, B. (2004) *Lacan to the Letter* Minneapolis, MN, University of Minnesota Press.

Fink, M., Shorter, E. and Taylor, M. A. (2009) 'Catatonia is not schizophrenia: Kraepelin's error and the need to recognize catatonia as an independent syndrome in medical nomenclature' *Schizophrenia Bulletin* 36, 2, 314–320 March.

Flemming, C. F. (1859) *Pathologie und Therapie der Psychosen* Berlin, Germany, Hirschwald.

Foucault, M. ([1961, 1972 and 1994]/2006) *History of Madness* London and New York, Routledge (Translated from the French by J. Murphy and J. Khalfa).

Freud, S. ([1900]/2001) 'The interpretation of dreams: First part' in *The Standard Edition of the Complete Works of Sigmund Freud* London, Vintage Books (Volume 4) (Translated from the German under the general editorship of James Strachey).

Freud, S. ([1900 and 1901]/2001) 'The interpretation of dreams: Second part and on dreams' in *The Standard Edition of the Complete Works of Sigmund Freud* London, Vintage Books (Volume 5) (Translated from the German under the general editorship of James Strachey).

Freud, S. ([1905]/2001) 'Jokes and their relation to the unconscious' in *The Standard Edition of the Complete Works of Sigmund Freud* London, Vintage Books (Volume 8) (Translated from the German under the general editorship of James Strachey).

Freud, S. ([1911]/2001) 'Psychoanalytic notes on an autobiographical account of a case of paranoia (dementia paranoides)' in *The Standard Edition of the Complete Works of Sigmund Freud* London, Vintage Books (Volume 12, pp. 4–79) (Translated from the German by Alix Strachey and James Strachey under the general editorship of James Strachey).

Freud, S. ([1923 and 1924]/2001) 'Neurosis and psychosis' in *The Standard Edition of the Complete Works of Sigmund Freud: The Ego and the Id and Other Work* London, Vintage Books (Volume 19, pp. 147–153) (Translated from the German by J. Riviere under the general editorship of James Strachey).

Freud, S. ([1924]/2001) 'The loss of reality in neurosis and psychosis' in *The Standard Edition of the Complete Works of Sigmund Freud: The Ego and the Id and Other Work* London, Vintage Books (Volume 19, pp. 181–187) (Translated from the German by J. Riviere under the general editorship of James Strachey).

Freud, S. ([1940]/2003) *An Outline of Psychoanalysis* London, Penguin Books (Translated from the German by H. Ragg-Kirkby).

Friedreich, J. B. (1836) *Historisch-Kritische Darstellung der Theorien über das Wesen und den Sitz der Psychischen Krankheiten* Leipzig, Germany, Wigand.

Frith, C. D. and Johnson, E. (2003) *Schizophrenia: A Very Short Introduction* Oxford, Oxford University Press.

Furnham, A. (2015) 'The anti-psychiatry movement' *Psychology Today* 7 May 2015, www.psychologytoday.com/blog/sideways-view/201505/the-anti-psychiatry-movement

Goffman, E. (1961) *Asylums: Essays on the Social Situation of Mental Patients and Other Inmates* New York, Anchor Books Doubleday.

Goldberg, A. (2001) *Sex, Religion and the Making of Modern Madness: The Eberbach Asylum and German Society 1815–1849* Oxford, Oxford University Press.

Goldner, E., Hsu, L. and Waraich, P. (2002) 'Prevalence and incidence studies of schizophrenic disorders: A systematic review of the literature' *Canadian Journal of Psychiatry* 47, 833–843.

Greenwood, C., Brooke, C. and Dolan, A. (2016) 'What a tragic waste' *Daily Mail* June, p. 1.

Häfner, H. (2013) 'Karl Jaspers: 100 years of "allgemeine psychopathologie" (general psychopathology)' *Nerenarzt* 84, 11, 1281–1282 November (Article in German).

Halliday, A. (1828) *General View of the Present State of Lunatics and Lunatic Asylums in Great Britain and Ireland* London, Underwood.

Hare, E. (1988) 'Schizophrenia before 1800? The case of the Revd George Trosse' *Psychological Medicine* 18, 2, 279–285 May.

Harper, S. (2009) *Madness, Power and the Media: Class, Gender and Race in Popular Representations of Mental Disorder* London, Palgrave Macmillan.

Hecker, E. (1871) 'Die hebephrenie' *Archiv für Pathologische Anatomie und Physiologie und für Klinische Medicin* 52, 394–429.

Hinshaw, S. P. (2007) *The Mark of Shame: Stigma of Mental Illness and an Agenda for Change* Oxford and New York, Oxford University Press.

Hurd, H. M. (Ed.) (1916–1917) *The Institutional Care of the Insane in the United States and Canada* (4 Volumes) Baltimore, Johns Hopkins University.

Husserl, E. ([1913]/1980) *Ideas Pertaining to a Pure Phenomenology and to a Phenomenological Philosophy–Third Book: Phenomenology and the Foundations of the Sciences* Dordrecht, Kluwer (Translated from the German by T. E. Klein and W. E. Pohl).

Husserl, E. ([1913]/1982) *Ideas Pertaining to a Pure Phenomenology and to a Phenomenological Philosophy–First Book: General Introduction to a Pure Phenomenology* The Hague, Nijhoff (Translated from the German by F. Kersten).

Husserl, E. ([1913]/1989) *Ideas Pertaining to a Pure Phenomenology and to a Phenomenological Philosophy–Second Book: Studies in the Phenomenology of Constitution* Dordrecht, Kluwer (Translated from the German by R. Rojcewitcz and A. Schuwer).

Janzarik, W. (2003) 'The concept of psychosis and psychotic qualities' *Nervenarzt* 74, 1, 3–11 January (Article in German).

Jaspers, K. ([1913]/1997) *General Psychology* (Volumes 1 and 2) Baltimore, MD, Johns Hopkins University Press (Translated from the German by J. Hoenig and M. W. Hamilton).

Johnstone, E. C., Crow, T. J., Johnson, A. L. and MacMillan, J. F. (1986) 'The Northwick Park study of first episodes of schizophrenia: I. Presentation of the illness and problems relating to admission' *The British Journal of Psychiatry* 148, 2, 115–120 February.

Kales, A., Kales, J. and Vela-Bueno, A. (1990) 'Schizophrenia: Historical perspectives' in Kales, A., Stafanis, C. and Tablott, J. (Eds.) *Recent Advances in Schizophrenia* New York, Springer-Verlag (pp. 3–23).

Kamal, A. and Sarhan, W. (1989) 'Arab and Islamic civilisation contribution to psychiatry' *Arab Federation of Psychiatrists* (1975), 59–63 (In Arabic).

Kasanin, J. (1933) 'The acute schizoaffective psychoses' *American Journal of Psychiatry* 90, 97–126.

Kasper, S. and Papadimitriou, G. N. (Eds.) (2009) (2nd. Edition) *Schizophrenia: Biopsychosocial Approaches and Current Challenges* (Medical Psychiatry Series) New York and London, Informa Healthcare.

Kesey, K. ([1962]/2002) *One Flew over the Cuckoo's Nest* London, Penguin Books.

Klein, M. ([1932 and 1975]/1998) *The Psychoanalysis of Children* London, Karnac Books (Translated from the German by A. Strachey and revised in collaboration with A. Strachey and H. A. Thorner).

Klein, M. ([1935]/1964) 'A contribution to the psychogenesis of manic-depressive states' in *Contributions to Psychoanalysis 1921–1945* New York, McGraw Hill.

Klein, M. ([1940]/1964) 'Mourning and its relation to manic-depressive states' in *Contributions to Psychoanalysis 1921–1945* New York, McGraw Hill.

Klein, M. ([1957]/1975) *Envy and Gratitude and Other Works 1946–1963* New York, Delacorte.

Kleist, K. (1928) 'Über zycloide, paranoide und epileptoid psychosen und über die frage der degenerationspsychosen' *Schweizer Archive für Neurologie und Psychiatrie* 23, 1–35.

Klerman, G. L. (1978) 'The evolution of a scientific nosology' in Shershow, J. C. (Ed.) *Schizophrenia: Science and Practice* Cambridge, MA, Harvard University Press (pp. 99–121).

Kraepelin, E. ([1899]/1991) *Psychiatry: A Textbook for Students and Physicians* (2 Volumes) Canton, Watson Publishing International (Edited by J. M. Quen and Translated from the German by H. Metoui and S. Ayed).

Lacan, J. ([1955–1956]/1997) *The Psychoses 1955–1956: The Seminar of Jacques Lacan Book III* New York and London, W.W. Norton (Edited by J.-A. Miller and Translated from the French by R. Grigg).

Lacan, J. ([1966]/2006) *Écrits* New York and London, W.W. Norton (Translated from the French by B. Fink in collaboration with H. Fink and R. Grigg).

Laing, R. D. ([1960]/1965 and 1969) *The Divided Self: An Existential Study in Sanity and Madness* London, Penguin Books.

Leonhard, K. ([1957]/1979) (5th. Edition) *The Classification of Endogenous Psychoses* New York, Irvington Publishers (Translated from the German by R. Berman).

Letchworth, W. P. (1889) *The Insane in Foreign Countries* New York, Putnam's.

Lewis, A. J. (1967) 'The psychopathology of insight' in *Inquiries in Psychiatry: Clinical and Social Investigations* London, Routledge and Keegan Paul (pp. 16–29).

Lewis, B. (2010) 'A mad fight: Psychiatry and disability activism' in Davis, L. J. (Ed.) (3rd. Edition) *The Disability Studies Reader* London and New York, Routledge (Chapter 12, pp. 160–176).

Lloyd, G. (Ed.) (1983) *Hippocratic Writings* London, Penguin Classics (Translated from the Greek by E. T. Withington, I. M. Lonie and W. N. Mann).

Lothane, Z. (1992) *In Defence of Schreber: Soul Murder and Psychiatry* Hillsdale, NJ and London, The Analytic Press.

Mac Suibhne, S. (2011) 'Erving Goffman's asylums 50 years on' *British Journal of Psychiatry* 198, 1–2, www.bjp.rcpsych.org/content/bjprcpsych/198/1/1.full.pdf

Majeed, A. (2005) 'How Islam changed medicine: Arab physicians and scholars laid the basis for medical practice in Europe' *British Medical Journal* 331, 7531, 1486–1487 24 December.

Marx, K. ([1859]/1981) *A Contribution to the Critique of Political Economy* Moscow, Progress Publishers and London, Lawrence and Wishart (Translated from the German by S. W. Ryazanskaya).

McGraw, A. P., Warren, C., Williams, L. and Leonard, B. (2012) 'Too close for comfort, or too far to care? Finding humour in distant tragedies and close mishaps' *Psychological Science* 23, 10, 1215–1223.

Mead, G. H. ([various dates and 1934]/1967) *Mind, Self and Society from the Standpoint of a Social Behaviourist (Works of George Herbert Mead Volume 1)* Chicago and London, University of Chicago Press (Edited by C. W. Morris).

Mitchell, S. A. and Black, M. J. ([1995]/2016) *Freud and Beyond: A History of Modern Psychoanalytic Thought* Philadelphia and New York, Basic Books/Perseus Books.

Möbius, P. J. (1892) 'Über die Einteilung der Krankheiten. Neurologische Betrachtungen' *Centralbibliothek Nervenheilkd Psychiatr* 15, 289–301.

Muratori, F., Picchi, L., Casella, C., Tancredi, R., Milone, A. and Patarnello, M. G. (2002) 'Efficacy of brief dynamic psychotherapy for children with emotional disorders' *Psychotherapy and Psychosomatics* 71, 2838.

Nasrallah, H. A. (2010) 'The anti-psychiatry movement: Who and why' *Current Psychiatry* 10, 12, 4–53.

Nasser, M. (1995) 'The rise and fall of anti-psychiatry' *Psychiatric Bulletin* 19, 743–746.

Nemeroff, C. B., Weinberger, D., Rutter, M., MacMillan, H. L., Bryant, R. A., Wessely, S., Stein, D. J., Pariante, C. M., Seemüller, F., Berk, M., Malhi, G. S., Preisig, M., Brüne, M. and Lysaker, P. (2013) 'DSM-5: A Collection of psychiatrist views on the changes, controversies and future directions' *BMC Medicine* 11, 202.

Newbigging, K., Ridley, J., McKeown, M., Sadd, J., Machin, K., Cruse, K., De La Haye, S., Able, L. and Poursanidou, K. (2015) *Mental Health Advocacy-the Right to be Heard: Context, Values and Good Practice* London and Philadelphia, Jessica Kingsley Publishers.

Nietzsche, F. ([various dates 1861–1869]/1997) *Selected Letters of Friedrich Nietzsche* Chicago, IL, University of Chicago (Edited and Translated by C. Middleton).

Nijinsky, V. ([1919]/2000) (Unexpurgated Edition) *The Diary of Vaclav Nijinsky* New York, Farrar, Straus and Giroux (Edited by J. Acocella and Translated from the Russian by K. Fitzlyon).

Oaks, D. (2016) 'Let's Find Language More Inclusive Than Mentally Ill' MindFreedom website accessed 2016, www.mindfreedom.com

Oliver, J. (2006) 'The myth of Thomas Szasz' *The New Atlantis* 13, Summer, pp. 68–84.

Oliver, M. (1990) *The Politics of Disablement* Basingstoke, Macmillan.

Oliver, M. (1996) *Understanding Disability: From Theory to Practice* Basingstoke, Macmillan.

Oliver, M. (1999) 'Capitalism, disability and ideology: A materialist critique of the normalisation principle' in Mitchell, D. (Ed.) *Special Educational Needs and Inclusive Education: Major Themes in Education: Volume 1 Systems and Contexts* London and New York, Routledge-Falmer.

Oswald, P. (1991) *Nijinsky: A Leap into Madness* New York, Lyle Stuart.

Patton, M. (2015) 'R. D. Laing: Was the counterculture's favourite psychiatrist a dangerous renegade or a true visionary?' *Independent* Monday, 30 November.

Pembroke, L. R. (2012) *Self Harm Perspectives from Personal Experience* London, Survivors Speak Out, http://kreativeinterventions.com/SelfHarmPerspectivesfromPersonalExperience.pdf

Perceval, J. ([1838 and 1840]/1961) *Perceval's Narrative: A Patient's Account of His Psychosis 1830–1832* Stanford University Press (Edited by G. Bateson), https://archive.org/stream/percevalsnarrati007726mbp#page/n7/mode/2up

Perfect, W. (1787) *Select Cases of the Different Species of Insanity* Rochester, Gillman.

Petersen, D. (Ed.) (1982) 'The writings of George Trosse and John Perceval' in *A Mad People's History of Madness* Pittsburgh PA, University of Pittsburgh Press.

Pinel, P. ([1801 and 1809]/2008) (2nd. Edition) *Medico-Philosophical Treatise on Mental Alienation* London, Wiley Blackwell (Translated from the French by G. Hickish, D. Healy and L. Charland).

Read, J. and Dillon, J. (Eds.) (2013) (2nd. Edition) *Models of Madness: Psychological, Social and Biological Approaches to Psychosis* London and New York, Routledge.

Renfrew, C. (2007) *Prehistory: The Making of the Human Mind* London, Weidenfeld and Nicolson.

Richards, S. B., Brady, M. P. and Taylor, R. L. (2014) (2nd. Edition) *Cognitive and Intellectual Disabilities: Historical Perspectives, Current Practices and Future Directions* New York and London, Routledge.

Rubin-Rabson, G. [1951]/1970) 'Translator's preface' in Séchehaye, M. (Ed.) *Reality Lost and Regained: Autobiography of a Schizophrenic Girl* (with analytic interpretation by M. Séchehaye) New York, Signet/New American Library (pp. v–vi) (Translated from the French by G. Rubin-Rabson).

Saks, E. R. (2008) *The Center Cannot Hold: My Journey Through Madness* New York, Virago.

Scharfetter, C. (1987) 'Psychiatric vulnerability–Canstatt 1841: On the history of the concept of vulnerability, predisposition and psychosis in the first half of the 19th century' *Nervenartz* 58, 8, 527 August (Article in German).

Schatzman, M. (1973) *Soul Murder: Persecution in the Family* London, Allen Lane.

Schiller, L. and Bennet, A. (1996) *The Quiet Room: A Journey Out of the Torment of Madness* New York, Warner Books.

Schneider, K. (1959) *Clinical Psychopathology* New York, Grune and Stratton (Translated from the German by M. W. Hamilton).

Schreber, D. P. ([1903]/1955 and 2000) *Memoirs of My Nervous Illness* New York, NY, Review Books (Edited and Translated by I. Macalpine and R. A. Hunter).

Scruton, R. (1985) *Thinkers of the New Left* Harlow, UK, Longman.

Scull, A. (2011) *Madness: A Very Short Introduction* Oxford, Oxford University Press.

Scull, A., MacKenzie, C. and Hervey, N. (2014) *Masters of Bedlam: The Transformation of the Mad-Doctoring Trade* Princeton, NJ, Princeton University Press.

Séchehaye, M. ([1951]/1970) *Reality Lost and Regained: Autobiography of a Schizophrenic Girl* (with analytic interpretation by M. Séchehaye) New York, Signet/New American Library (Translated from the French by G. Rubin-Rabson).

Shakespeare, T. (2006) *Disability Rights and Wrongs* London, Routledge.

Shorter, E. (1997) *A History of Psychiatry: From the Era of the Asylum to the Age of Prozac* New York and Chichester, John Wiley.

Skelton, J. (circa 1489) 'Upon the Dolorous Death and Much Lamentable Chance of the Most Honourable Earl of Northumberland' (The Poetical Work of John Skelton Ex Classics Project 2015), www.exclassics.com

Sokal, A. and Bricamont, J. ([1997]/1998) *Intellectual Impostures: Postmodern Philosopher's Abuse of Science* London, Profile Books (Translated from the French by the authors).

Stefanis, C. N. and Stefanis, N. C. (2009) 'Schizophrenia: Historical roots and brief review of recent research developments' in Kasper, S. and Papadimitriou, G. N. (Eds.) (2nd. Edition) *Schizophrenia: Biopsychosocial Approaches and Current Challenges* (Medical Psychiatry Series) New York and London, Informa Healthcare (pp. 1–16).

Sullivan, H. S. (1938) 'The data of psychiatry' in *The Fusion of Psychiatry and Social Science* New York, Norton.

Sullivan, H. S. (1940) *Conceptions of Modern Psychiatry* New York, Norton.

Szasz, T. ([1960]/2010) *The Myth of Mental Illness: Foundations of a Theory of Personal Conduct* New York and London, Harper-Perennial.

Thomas, C. and Corker, M. (2002) 'A journey around the social model' in Corker, M. and Shakespeare, T. (Eds.) *Disability/Postmodernity: Embodying Disability Theory* London and New York, Continuum.

Thompson, M. G. (Ed.) (2015) *The Legacy of R. D. Laing: An Appraisal of His Contemporary Relevance* London, Routledge.

Torrey, E. F. (2013) (6th. Edition) *Surviving Schizophrenia: A Family Manual* New York and London, Harper Perennial.

Trosse, G. ([1714]/1974) *The Life of the Reverend Mr. George Trosse Written by Himself and Published Posthumously According to His Order* Montreal and London, McGill-Queen's University Press (Edited by A. W. Brink).

Tsuang, M. T. and Tohen, M. (2002) *Textbook of Psychiatric Epidemiology* New York and London, Wiley.

Wahl, O. F. (1995) *Media Madness: Public Images of Mental Illness* New Brunswick, NJ, Rutgers University Press.

Waite, M. (2008) (3rd. Edition, revised) *Compact Oxford Thesaurus* Oxford and New York, Oxford University Press.

Wancata, J., Freidl, M. and Unger, A. (2009) 'Epidemiology and gender' in Kasper, S. and Papadimitriou, G. N. (Eds.) (2nd. Edition) *Schizophrenia: Biopsychosocial Approaches and Current Challenges* (Medical Psychiatry Series) New York and London, Informa Healthcare (pp. 16–25).

Warner, R. and de Girolamo, G. (1995) *Epidemiology of Mental Disorders and Psychosocial Problems: Schizophrenia* Geneva, World Health Organization.

Webster, R. (2005) *Why Freud Was Wrong: Sin, Science and Psychoanalysis* Oxford, The Isis-Orwell Press.

Weinstein, R. M. (1994) 'Goffman's Asylums and the total institution model of mental hospitals' *Psychiatry* 57, 348–367 November.

White, H. (1995) 'Response to Arthur Marwick' *Journal of Contemporary History* 30, 233–246.

Wolitzky, D. I. (2003) 'The theory and practice of traditional psychoanalytic treatment' in Gurman, A. S. and Messer, S. B. (Eds.) *Essential Psychotherapies: Theory and Practice* New York, Guilford Press (pp. 24–68).

Yadav, D. S. (2010) 'Cycloid psychosis: Perris criteria revisited' *Indian Journal of Psychological Medicine* 32, 1, 54–58.

Television

The A-Team series 1 episode 9 'Holiday in the Hills' (1983), USA.

Bates Motel (2013–2016), USA.

Baywatch season 3 episode 17 'The Tower' (1993), USA.

Charlie's Angels series 2 episode 21 'Little Angels of the Night' (1978), USA.

The Following (2013–2015) season 1 'Pilot' (2013), USA.

Hawaii Five-O season 4 episode 6 '. . . and I Want Some Candy and a Gun That Shoots' (1971), USA.

The Hitchhiker season 6 episode 17 'A Whole New You' (1983), USA.

Kojak series 4 episode 4 'Out of the Shadows' (1976), USA.

Wonderland season 1 episode 1 'Pilot' (2000), USA.

Film

The Cabinet of Dr. Caligari, dir. Robert Wiene (1920), Germany.
Clownhouse, dir. Victor Salva (1989), USA.
Criminal Law, dir. Martin Campbell (1988), USA.
Five Corners, dir. Tony Bill (1987), USA.
Halloween, dir. John Carpenter (1978), USA.
I Saw What You Did, dir. Fred Walton (1988), USA.
Misery, dir. Rob Reiner (1990), USA.
Out for Justice, dir. John Flynn (1991), USA.
Psycho, dir. Alfred Hitchcock (1960), USA.
Psychotic, dir. Johnny Johnson (2012), USA.
Shutter Island, dir. Martin Scorsese (2010), USA.
The Silence of the Lambs, dir. Jonathan Demme (1992), USA.

Newspaper reports

Carey, B. (2006) 'A psychiatrist slain, and a sad debate deepens' *New York Times* 19 September.
Greenwood, C., Brooke, C. and Dolan, A. (2016) 'What a tragic waste' *Daily Mail* 17 June.
Linning, S. (2015) 'The real Norman Bates: "Psycho" killer' *Daily Mail On-line* 19 June.
Mail on Line (2016) 'Killer Nanny who beheaded a four year old girl "kept her schizophrenia secret"' March.
Sontag, D. (2011) 'A schizophrenic, a slain worker, troubling questions' *New York Times* 16 June.
Sun (2013) '1,200 killed by mental patients: Shock 10 year toll exposes care crisis' 7 October, www.thesun.co.uk/sol/homepage/news/5183994/1200-killed-by-mental-patients-in-shock-10-year-toll.html

Online resources

Byrnes, Larry (2013) 'Scientology CCHR madness and deceit' *No Drug Show*, 15 January, www.youtube.com/watch?v=rxkXUbVCOoY
IMDb 'Baywatch (1989–2001), USA', www.imdb.com/title/tt0096542/
IMDb 'The Following (2013–2015), USA', www.imdb.com/title/tt2071645/
PBS NewsHour (2011) 'Young man on being diagnosed with psychosis' 9 February, https://www.youtube.com/watch?v=Rws1niDxqK8
Radio Times, www.radiotimes.com/tv-programme/e/szrf/the-a-team-episode-guide/series-1/3/
Oaks, D. (2016) 'Let's find language more inclusive than mentally ill' MindFreedom, accessed 2016, www.mindfreedom.com
Sussex Partnership (2014) 'Simon says: Psychosis!' Sussex Partnership NHS Foundation Trust 'Early Intervention in Psychosis Service', 10 March, accessed 4 August 2016, https://www.youtube.com/watch?v=GXh9hPzHHi4

INDEX